Knowing the unknown: through science and Sufism

DR GHAYUR AYUB

authorHOUSE®

AuthorHouse™ UK
1663 Liberty Drive
Bloomington, IN 47403 USA
www.authorhouse.co.uk
Phone: 0800.197.4150

Published by AuthorHouse 06/08/2016

ISBN: 978-1-5246-3562-6 (sc)
ISBN: 978-1-5246-3561-9 (e)

Print information available on the last page.

I dedicate this book to

my

Spiritual Guide

Raja Akram (Shaheed)

known also

as

Raja Sahib

of

Bari Imam

CONTENTS

Contents

PREFACE

History tells us that human mind played an essential role in the progress of civilisation. As mind depends on development of the brain, so in turn, the evolved brain took active part in the race of evolution. Thus evolution appeared in;

Development of human brain;

Development of civilisation;

Development in religious beliefs which constituted Faith.

As humans progressed socially in living style through improved customs and cultures, the faith also progressed accordingly. So societal customs and beliefs in faith ran side by side symbiotically for centuries putting human values in practice as the societies advanced. Consequently, the human values changed with passage of time and moulded according to the needs of the prevailing societies as the custom and culture changed. Similarly, faith became the defender of those values and took a unique role progressing not only as a parallel player but becoming a leading partner in advancement of societies.

With passage of time as the human mental acumen advanced, faith took the shape of pristine religion which progressively changed into organised religions. The historic personality who gave a solid shape to organised religion was Abraham around 1900 BC at Ur in Mesopotamia. During shaping of organised religions, conflicting voices appeared in societies but, generally speaking, the religion took a leading role in disciplining human mind at individual and communal level as societies progressed.

Such disciplining of human mind through religion took a beating in recent centuries because of rapid progress in the knowledge of science and the scientific way of evaluating human values. Thus science became a strong rival and major threat to religion. There are three major reasons for this;

- First, science played a pivotal role in making the day-to-day life easy for humans, while religion remained rigid in its stance, following centuries-old norms and making life difficult for ordinary man.
- Second, science kept itself aloof from the standards of morality prescribed by religion.
- Third, religions frequently clashed with each other.

The opponents of religions took advantage of this diversity and proved with statistics that more blood was shed in the name of religions than any other natural calamity. They blame religions for all the ills stressing that religions created hurdles in harmonising humanity and in the progress of societies. Their arguments might carry some weight as recent history tells us that religions did play negative role in creating hate amongst fellow humans.

So how can this anomaly be corrected?

The answer could be hidden in the role of spiritualists especially the Sufis. Sufis, because they belong to a religion which has been targeted by the world media after the 9/11 attacks.

Against this background, I tried to present the true picture of Sufism in this book and tell the readers that it is the real, soft, and the progressive face of Islam which can fit in any society of modern world of science according to the developing human mental acumen. I tried to shed light on the fact that Sufis, because of their advanced knowledge of the Quran, can correlate scientific theories with verses of the Quran; about the beginning of universe; creation of life and its progress up until the present day; and the end of the universe.

I also tried to put the point that it is important for the spiritualists of different faiths to work in unison with the scientists, logicians and parapsychologists and find ways to bring humans together in harmony for long lasting global peace. Otherwise world War III could become imminent with disastrous consequences as it will be a nuclear war. For this purpose, in the last chapter, I proposed creating a podium titled 'Baith-e-Ibrahim' (House of Abraham) in different parts of the world to prove that;

- Religion is not a negative influence on society provided we understand our own religion properly;
- Religion can have a positive impact on society provided we understand the religions of others;
- Different religions can stand together on one platform;
- Science and religions can work together without antagonising each other.

This is not an easy task; in fact, it is a gigantic undertaking. But as they say, the long journey always starts with the first step. Let this be a small but a firm step following the footsteps of those ancestors who left positive imprints on the pages of history and are remembered today as the pioneers who changed societies.

I, for a second, do not pretend to be one of them, but I hope to succeed in sending the message I believe in religiously and follow it socially. In that context, if I were able to convey 20% of the message to the reader, I would consider it as an accomplishment of my humble duty and count myself fortunate.

Dr Ghayur Ayub

CHAPTER ONE

The Beginning

Living in the world of the known, so much is unknown about;

1. The universe and its beginning;
2. The earth, the life on earth and the evolutionary processes it went through;
3. The place of godhead, the spirit and the soul in all the evolutionary processes.

An attempt is made in this chapter to explain the complexities of the above, addressing both the believers and the non-believers.

Science, according to the prevailing theories, talks about the beginning and a possible end of the universe. Using the cosmological time parameter, it divides existence of the universe into three major phases. We should remember that the descriptions of first two phases and early part of the third phase are based on speculations since the scientists are unable to accurately measure and thus evaluate the environments of those phases through existing physical tools.

The three phases are:

1. Singularity
2. Inflation
3. Expansion

1)...Singularity

The best available measurements as of today suggest that Singularity existed about 13.7 billion years ago [1- 2].

Singularity is a type of a black hole which was in an immeasurable state, the time depth of which is theorized to be between10^{-60} to 10^{-100} seconds. The type of energy it contained cannot be assessed by the available tools of measurement so its quantitative and qualitative nature cannot be known. In this state of the unknown, the environment was held in a space-time warp- meaning, singularity was devoid of space and time. So nothing can be calculated and so estimated correctly about Singularity as conditions within it cannot be observed, assessed or experimented by existing physical laws. All one can say is that Singularity was something, where all known laws of physics failed. Thus mentally it cannot be conceptualized because it is beyond our present day mental grasp.

For example, if for a moment, we mentally conceive it as a unit and let an object enter its space-time warp, that object will not come out as it was out before it had entered. In other words, there is no concept of 'in' or 'out' in Singularity having no 'boundaries' or 'sides'. In simple terms it is a non-entity state in which everything is in infinite unity without existence of unity the way unity is defined.

In short, the universe as Singularity was in a state of infinite time, infinite density, infinite space, and infinite existence intertwined all in an indescribable unity following unknown rules of unknown energy. According to Paul Davies [3], "Singularity is not an event. It is a state of infinite density or something like it, where space and time ceases." Thus the universe as Singularity was the ultimate unknowable with no-how, no-where and no-when. As there was no space or time in Singularity there was no light either, because light requires four dimensions to travel. With no light, there was no colour. That is why Singularity is also called the Black Hole to make us understand according to our mental grasp [4-8].

So, Singularity cannot be measured by available scientific tools or conceptualized and understood within the realm of human mind. In other words, science has not reached to a level where it can probe and explore Singularity. Physicists and mathematicians are proposing hypotheses to make us understand about its existence. Scientifically speaking these are just theories which may or may not turn out to be true. We have seen many theories have changed or even deleted. Thus far, we can only guess how the universe existed as Singularity billions years ago.

Those who oppose this theory such as William Lane Craig, an American analytic philosopher, philosophical theologian, and Christian apologist believe the universe started from 'nothing' by the First Cause. [9-10]

Philosophically when we use the term ' nothing' we indirectly point to a 'thing' which is not there. In that sense, we cannot name a single physicist or scientist who calls Singularity as a 'thing' describable in the knowledge framework of physics or science. Yes, they do hypothesize the size of Singularity being less than 10^{-56} meters at the estimated time depth of 10^{-60} to 10^{-100} seconds. This for all practical purposes amounts to nothingness or being a non-entity state. But at the same time, they have been clearly saying that they have not yet reached a knowledgeable mark where they could put a rational theory about the nature of Singularity.

So, in a way, both the scientists and the religious apologists are in agreement on the beginning of Universe or Singularity. Both groups talk about the nothingness of its existence or its non-entity state. But they are looking at it through their own bias filled prisms. The custodians of religions believe that a Super Entity called God acting as the First Cause, made the Universe from nothingness and then made it explode. While the scientists believe that as they have not reached the stage to understand the nature of Singularity they do not see themselves qualified to say as to how Singularity evolved and what made it explode. Logically speaking they seem to be right.

There is a third group which also talks of Singularity in more or less the same language as the scientists do. They link their Singularity with beginning of universe in a language identical to the scientists. They call their Singularity 'Ahdiat'. This group is known as 'Sufis'. 'Ahdiat' is based on the concept of Godhead. In that sense, they describe 'Godhead' in identical manner in which the scientists describe 'Singularity'. Can that open a window of opportunity for thinking minds to ponder as to why such similarities should exist and can those similarities be explored further to bring science and Sufism closer?

We know that Sufism is the tolerant face of Islam. The warring world needs such face to avoid clash of civilizations predicted by its proponents. The concept of Godhead as perceived by the Sufis is extremely close to the notion of Singularity described by the scientists. They describe Godhead in three states; 1), 'Ahdiat' which is the highest state; 2), 'Wahdat' which also called the first epiphany; 3), 'Wahdiat' which is also termed as the second epiphany.

'Ahdiat' is the highest state of Godhead where it is in absolute and infinite unity having no otherness. Being indefinable, it is formless, limitless, and colourless. The exact nature of 'Ahdiat' cannot be conceptualized as it is beyond any mental grasp. Just like Singularity, 'Ahdiat' has no body, shape or contour and is not bound by time or space so its existence cannot be perceived logically or measured scientifically.

According to Sufis when Godhead in this state utters 'Kun' (Be) it becomes 'Faya Kun' (It is) [11A] without lapse of time or measured space. In short, in all its essence describing 'Ahdiat' is like describing 'Singularity'. Their immeasurable existence, incommensurable energy, limitless power and infinite strength make the two as one and the same. In other words, 'Singularity' is ditto copy of 'Ahdiat' and vice versa. This commonality becomes more obvious when Singularity is described by a quantum physicist. His reflection of Singularity seems pretty close to Ahdiat described by a Sufi.

The concept of 'Ahdiat' will be discussed later in appropriate chapter, but at this stage one can say that this unknown, non-graspable entity of godhead wanted to be known and with a 'Kun' (Be) it instantly turned to 'Faya Kun' and changed to the first epiphany of

'Wahdat' paving the way to create the universe as we know it today. Thus the 'Kun' of 'Ahdiat' became the 'Big Bang' of 'Singularity'.

According to the scientists, with 'Big Bang' explosion of 'Singularity' the universe started to evolve by entering the phase of 'Inflation'. According to the Sufis, with utterance of 'Kun' and instant 'Faya Kun', 'Ahdiat' changed to 'Wahdat' paving the way for creation of the universe as described in the notion of 'Hamma Oost' (everything is Him) [11B], or 'Hamma Az Oost' (Everything is from Him). [11C]

The close similarities, between 'Singularity' and 'Ahdiat' and the unexplainable change in their states as a result of 'Big Bang' and 'Kun' (Be) respectively that led to the formation of the universe, cannot be ignored.

2)...Inflation

After the explosion of 'Singularity' and beginning of evolutionary universe, a period of 'Inflation' [12] started. The actual duration of 'Inflation' is unknown but is speculated to have ended at 10^{-32} seconds after the Big Bang. It is an era of accelerating super-cooled expansion with properties similar to the dark energy [13A] when the temperature dropped by a factor of 100,000 or so from 10^{27} K down to 10^{22} K. Scientists say that a period of inflation was necessary otherwise the Singularity acting like a black hole would have swallowed the universe at its birth. The inflation ended when its field decayed into ordinary particles in a process called "reheating" [13B]

It is at this point the ordinary Big Bang expansion began and is usually quoted as a time "after the Big Bang". This refers to the time that would have passed in traditional (non-inflationary) cosmology between the Big Bang Singularity and the universe dropping to the same temperature that was produced by 'reheating'. It also means that the universe before the end of inflation was a near-vacuum with a very low temperature. In simple words, the universe after exploding as Singularity did not expand uniformly and it did not drop temperature uniformly; there must had been inequality according to the simplest inflationary models. In the process it not only lost the meaningful time-line but also dropped its temperature making it necessary to 'reheat' again for future evolution [14]. A few scientists propose that the actual duration was much longer than 10^{-32} second. According to them the universe before the end of inflation was a near-vacuum with a very low temperature of 10^{22} and persisted for much longer than 10^{-32} seconds. They believe it can even be infinite (eternal inflation) [15]

This point should be kept in mind when we talk of time in terms of cosmology. In inflationary cosmology, time prior to the end of inflation, which some scientists calculate roughly 10^{-32} second after the Big Bang, does not follow the traditional big bang time-line.

Although the actual time-line of Inflation is unknown but certain durations linked to it and labelled as 'epochs' are crucial to remember. Most of these 'epochs' passed through one second durations but that one second was the most important time during which the fundamental physical laws were created according to which the future universe including the planet earth are run today. The same laws also helped create life on planet earth.

Having said that, we know that all ideas concerning the very early universe are speculative. No accelerator experiments have yet probed energies of sufficient magnitude to provide any experimental insight into the behaviour of matter at the energy levels that prevailed during that period. That is why we see different scenarios proposed by various scientists on Inflationary period.

It is generally accepted that Singularity lost its originality immediately after the explosion as it came out of the time depth of 10^{-60} seconds and the estimated radius of 10^{-56} meters and entered the phase of 'Inflation'. In doing so, this phase passed through two epochs a)..Plank epoch, b)..Grand unification epoch.

a)....Plank epoch;

The duration of this epoch lasted up to 10^{-43} seconds; although this figure has been questioned by a few physicists who stretch it to 10^{-32} seconds equalizing it with the total phase of 'Inflation'. Little is known about physical laws governing this epoch. Different theories propose different scenarios based on general relativity. It is hoped that quantum physics will eventually lead to a better understanding of this epoch. But so far, generally physicists agree that all forces of nature in this epoch were unified in one fundamental force termed as super common energy or gauge force. Not much is known about this force except that it was a condensed force with temperature beyond 10^{40} K (absolute) holding the future forces within at a time depth of 10^{-46} to 10^{-36} seconds with an approximate mean of 10^{-43} seconds.

This epoch is very close to the concept of 'Wahdat' described by the Sufis. They call it the first epiphany of godhead when god decided to be known thus adding 'Sifaat' (Atributes) to its 'Dhaat' (The Essence) in an indescribable, unified and abstract form when multiples were united in unity with no distinction between time, space and light.

It is interesting to note that such a scenario can be seen in the 'Theory of Everything' (ToE) put forward by physicist John Ellis [16]. He claimed to have introduced the term to the technical literature in an article published in Nature in 1986 [17]. In recent decades this theory was highlighted by Stephen Hawking. The theory points to unification of all fundamental interactions and of all particles of nature.

It is also interesting that this theory fits well into the doctrine of 'Hama Oost' (Everything is Him) presented by the great Sufi Ibn-e-Arabi of Andalusia as part of 'Wahdat-ul-Wujood' in 12th century AD [18A]. The doctrine points at the union of everything we find in the universe today. In this context, there is close similarity between the 'The theory of everything' and 'Hama Oost'.

Paul Davies in his book 'Mind of God' called such a scenario an 'intellectual nirvana'. In a way, he assimilates Singularity before big bang to God. Stephen Hawking wrote about it at some length in his best seller 'The history of Time'. Writing in the book, he said, "If we do discover a theory of everything...it would be the ultimate triumph of human reason—for then we would truly know the mind of God." (18B)

Some Sufis approach this theorem indirectly through a doctrine they call 'Hama Az Oost' (everything is from Him). It was passed on by Shaykh Ahmed Sarhindi as 'Wahdat-us-Shuhood'. According to this doctrine, 'the experience of unity between God and creation is purely subjective and occurs only in the mind of the Sufi who has reached the state of fana fi Allah. (absorption into godhead) [19]. This is the state in which a Sufi gets total absorption into the second epiphany of godhead (Wahdiat). They call it absorption in 'Haq' (Reality or Truth). Such a state is reflected in 'Nirvana' preached by the Buddhists and 'Intellectual Nirvana' mentioned by Paul Davies. This state will be discussed later.

In this epoch there were no particles or sub-particles as they were all integrated in super united energy or gauge force making it part of 'Super Unified Theory' (SUT) [20A].

It was at the end of this epoch of inflationary period that the unified super energy or gauge force gave birth to a new energy we call the gravity paving the way for the grand unification epoch.

It was Alan Guth in 1979 who came up with a theory that during inflation the gravitational waves stretched out in fluctuations making the gravity waves observable. According to the theorem gravitational waves can be made observable because these waves have orientation of light waves which leave a pattern in cosmic microwave background called 'B Mode Polarisation'. But this was just a theory until 2006 when a group of scientists made telescopes to find 'B-Mode Polarisation' hoping to find the gravitational waves. They placed telescopes named BICEP1 and later BICEP2 in south pole to look into the patch of sky called the southern hole through which they could find the gravitational waves with comparative ease. It was in December 2012 when they observed signals which had all the characteristic of gravitational waves with distinctive pattern of 'B-Mode Polarisation'. After two years of further analysis and excluding 'Synchrotron Radiation' and 'Dust Emission', this unique discovery was disclosed through a press conference at Harvard in March 2014 but not before Alan Gut was taken in confidence. After all, it was his 'Inflation Theory' which seemed to be proved right through scientific means.

The work was critically scrutinised by the world community of scientists, especially the European scientists such as Francois Bouchet of Plank Collaboration. He produced the results collected from Plank Satellite and challenged the inflationary gravity waves of BICEP2 calling them the 'Dust Emission'. After detailed collaboration between the two teams they came up with the final results on January 20th 2015 explaining that 75% of signals of BICEP2 were coming from galactic dust. The remaining 25 % might be from inflationary gravitational waves. The proponents of Alan Gut theory were not excited with the results never the less they considered it a major breakthrough and one of the greatest discovery about the earliest life of universe. [20B] The search goes on.

b)...The Grand Unification Epoch;

According to the laws of nature energy carries temperature. The scorching temperature during plank epoch was beyond $10^{40}K$ (absolute). As the temperature dropped to $10^{32}K$ (absolute) at the time depth of 10^{-36} seconds and when the universe was measuring 10^{-35} meters, the grand unified epoch started. This epoch falls in the Grand Unified Theory (GUT) which was proposed by Howard Georgi and Sheldon Glashow in 1974 and was preceded by the Pati–Salam model by Abdus Salam and Jogesh Pati who pioneered the idea of unified gauge interactions. [20C]

This epoch is known for creation of gravity which actually was not a creation per se but its separation from the existing unified super energy or the gauge force. No wonder the gauge force is also called 'Super-gravity' by some. It is interesting to note that the doctrine of 'Hama Oost' of Sufism mentioned earlier also talks of similar separation of 'Ruh' (spirit) from godhead during its changing epiphanies. It states that 'Ruh' (spirit) as separated part of godhead is transmitted in everything in universe-living or non-living. According to Sufis there would have been nothing in existing universe had there been no separation of 'Ruh' (spirit) from godhead at the creation of universe. It is for this reason Sufis link 'Ruh' (spirit) to 'Jamadat' (matter) 'Nabatat, (plants) 'Hawanat' (animal) and 'Insani' (human). The concept of 'Ruh' (spirit) will be discussed later.

According to Sufis godhead after shaping from 'Ahdiat' to 'Wahdat' still needed to be known individualised and perceived as such thus it changed into 'Wahdiat'. The Sufis call such a state as second epiphany and literally can fall into grand unification epic. Such state of godhead will be discussed later.

But for now, coming back to the gauge force not much is known about it as opposed to gravity. For example, we know that gravity is considered as an unusual force that cannot be shielded or absorbed. It is weak individually but because of its accumulative quality it gets stronger as the mass of its matter gets bigger. There is no satisfactory explanation for the experimental observation that the gravitational mass of any given body is equal to its inertial mass. However, new ideas on the origin of gravity indicate that gravity may have inertial origins.

Gravity is considered as a negative force in relation to entropy which is a dead end of all energies. This means that with other energies when entropy increases the corresponding energies decrease. But with the gravitational energy it is just the opposite. In Black Hole, for example, when gravitational force is maximum, entropy is at a peak. Gravitational force holds different particles together through messenger bosons called gravitons.

It is interesting to note that if we listen to a physicist talk about gravity and a Sufi talk about 'Ruh' we find acute resemblance in their talks as if they are talking about one and the same thing. The difference is that gravity is a negative force while 'Ruh' is a positive power. Otherwise as the gravity was separated from 'super unified energy', similarly 'Ruh' was separated from godhead at conversion of first epiphany to second epiphany as god's desire to be known. In that sense one is a scientific force, the other a metaphysical.

As the universe expanded and cooled in inflationary phase it kept on crossing temperatures in its transitional states and at each transition energies kept separating from each other much like condensations, filling the phase with quark–gluon plasma. The scientists call this part of inflation 'opaque', meaning by the happenings in the universe is not understood clearly by the available scientific tools. This makes our understanding based on speculations rather than facts. Once again such opacity brings similarity between the 'gauge forces' and god's 'epiphanies'.

During the epoch of 'grand unification' apparently following changes appeared in the universe;

- Space-time warp unwrapped and space and time appeared for the first time
- Light emerged because it needed space and time as tools to travel
- Colour showed as light and space were essential for its appearance. Though physicists do not believe in colour as entity. They say it is our brain cells which perceive waves as colours otherwise out there, there is no such thing as colour.
- With appearance of space and time, particles and sub-particles were disintegrated from gauge forces and started swirling with the speed of light. There were 12 fermions, 4 bosons, 16 Higgs force particles, 16 super-partner force particles, and 65 matter and force particles, 16 Higgsino matter particles, 64 anti-particles, and 129 mother particles (21),
- The gauge energy most probably gave birth to an important energy called 'electroweak energy'. This has not yet been proven scientifically.

At the depth of 10^{-32} seconds the 'Inflation' phase ended making a way for the phase of expansion of the universe.

Sufis bracket this state as the initiation point of 'Hamma Az Oost' (everything is from Him) as mentioned earlier. It is from here the universe started into whirls of expansion as part of evolution we understand it today and mentioned frequently in Quran.

3)...Expansion

According to physicists the 'expansion' phase started at the birth of electroweak energy near the end of grand unification epoch making part of this phase microscopic and part macroscopic. Following epochs fall in the expansion phase.

A)...The electroweak epoch; [22-25]

This phase extended between 10^{-36} seconds and 10^{-12} seconds after the Big Bang when the temperature of the universe dropped to 10^{28}K. The epoch acted like a bridge between the 'inflation' and the 'expansion' phases of universe as the former is believed to have ended at 10^{-32} seconds. The main power source of this epoch is electroweak energy which was pioneered originally by Sheldon Glashow along with Steven Weinberg and Abdus Salam who found a common source for electromagnetic and weak nuclear energies. They called it electroweak force. The process of separation occurred during this epoch at 10^{-12} seconds. They were awarded the Nobel Prize in Physics in 1979 for this discovery [26].

Prior to this discovery James Clark Maxwell in 1860 discovered that electromagnetic energy was actually the common source of electric and magnetic energies. The theory became known as Maxwellian theory of electromagnetism [27].

The difference between the two discoveries was that back in the 19th century, the physical implications and mathematical structure were qualitatively different than in 20th century. One theory was based on conventional physics and the other on quantum physics. But both had scientific backgrounds and no speculations.

So to recap;

1. In traditional big bang cosmology, the electroweak epoch began at 10^{-36} seconds after the Big Bang.
2. In inflationary cosmology, on the other hand, this epoch began when the inflationary epoch ended at roughly 10^{-32} seconds.
3. During this epoch electroweak energy was separated from strong nuclear energy.
4. The electroweak energy gave birth to weak nuclear energy and electromagnetic energy at 10^{-12} seconds.
5. With the end of the inflationary phase the universe started to expand as we understand it today.
6. At the end of this epoch three new fundamental energies were added to the already existing energy of gravity. Those energies were;

   1. **The strong nuclear energy** is a force which holds the nucleus of an atom together through boson particles called gluons. This is the main building force of an atom, and a million times stronger than the energy which combines the atoms together in chemical combinations. It does not follow the inverse square law and it glues nuclear particles together.
   2. **The weak nuclear energy** is a force which causes radioactivity. Its bosons travel at atomic level. They have no charge of their own but its force causes unstable nuclear particles to decay.
   3. **The electromagnetic energy** is a combination of electrical and magnetic energies which were considered as two independent energies prior to 1860. In that year James Clark Maxwell proved these two to have common origin and called it electromagnetic energy or force.

Dr Ghayur Ayub

B)...Quark epoch; [28-29]

This epoch falls between 10^{-12} seconds and 10^{-6} seconds after the Big Bang. At the end of the electroweak epoch, all the fundamental particles were believed to have acquired mass. The fundamental energies of gravity, strong nuclear, weak nuclear, and electromagnetism had taken their forms which exist till present day. The temperature of the universe was still too high to allow quarks to bind together to form hadrons.

These fundamental particles believed to be over 70 and were divided into three groups:

1. Leptons, which mimicked electrons
2. Quarks, which were going to make up the constituents of future nucleus in combinations of twos and threes
3. Messengers, which passed from particles to particles as photons, gravitons, Ws, Zs, etc.

The first two are grouped together as fermions and the last as bosons. Leptons and quarks have separate subdivisions into three layers, based on charge, weight, velocity and duration of decay. It is said that these sub-particles gain weight by accumulating a sticky, colourless substance called the Higgs field. Immersion of these particles in Higgs field makes the leptons and quarks of the second and third layers very heavy and extremely unstable.

C)...Hadron epoch; [30-31]

This epoch falls between 10^{-6} seconds and 1 (one) second after the Big Bang. The universe started to expand with rapidity making unstable particles and sub-particles move with enormous speed giving them their identities according to their weight and density.

Speaking of 'identities' it is interesting to know that at the second epiphany of 'godhead' when universe was being shaped similar 'identities' appeared which the Sufis call 'similitude', 'attributes' of godhead. They also believe that godhead at this stage separated energy from his 'self' called 'Nafs' which played pivotal role in the development of future human. This will also be discussed in coming chapters.

In science this phase belongs to Hadron family which are quark-based particles such as baryons and mesons. A baryon is a composite particle made up of three quarks while a meson comprises of one quark and one anti-quark. The name Baryon comes from the Greek word heavy because, at the time of their naming, most known elementary particles had lower masses than Baryons. The most familiar Baryons are the protons and neutrons which played crucial role in formation of atom at a later time as we will find. Participating in strong interactions, they make up most of the mass of the visible matter in the universe.

Each Baryon has a corresponding anti-particle (anti-baryon) where quarks are replaced by their corresponding anti-quarks. For example, a proton is made of two up quarks and one down quark; and its corresponding anti-particle, the anti-proton, is made of two up anti-quarks and one down anti-quarks

Again a remarkable similarity appears between the notion of 'anti-particle' and a concept mentioned in Quran and quoted by the Sufis. According to Sufis every matter in universe has its anti-matter which is a ditto copy but non-perceivable. They call it 'Jinn' which covers living as well as non-living. According to them 'Jinns' occupy a parallel world as an alternate reality which intersects with our own. According to Quran 'Jinns' are made of 'smokeless' and 'scorching' fire which fits well in the description of environment prevailed during Hadron epoch. In other places Quran mentions it as 'amazing', 'mind-blowing', and 'guidance of truth' etc having physical property of weight. Its varied description suggest that it went through a process of evolution just like other matter (living as well as non-living) in the universe [32].

At the end of Hadron epoch at around one second after the Big Bang we find that;

- Stability appeared in expanding universe.
- The quark-gluon plasma which kept the universe at high temperature and 'opaque' until then, cooled down below two trillion degrees.
- Neutrinos decoupled and began travelling freely through the expanding space.
- The cosmic neutrino background, which may never be observed in detail, was analogous to the cosmic microwave background radiation that was to be emitted much later.

D)...Lepton epoch; [33-34]

This epoch falls between 1 second and 10 seconds after the Big Bang. The majority of Hadrons and anti-Hadrons annihilated each other at the end of the Hadron epoch, leaving Leptons and anti-Leptons dominating the mass of the universe. Approximately 10 seconds after the Big Bang the temperature of the universe fell to a point when new Lepton/anti-Lepton pairs were no longer created and most Leptons and anti-Leptons were annihilated leaving a small residue of Leptons only.

E)...Photon epoch; [35- 36]

This epoch falls between 10 seconds and 380,000 years after the Big Bang. As most Leptons and anti-Leptons were annihilated at the end of the Lepton epoch, the photons dominated the universe through strong nuclear and electromagnetic forces. They kept interacting with protons and neutrons through strong nuclear forces and with electrons through electromagnetic force for the next 380,000 years.

In the process, between 3 minutes and 20 minutes after the Big Bang [37] the temperature fell to a point where protons and neutrons began to interact to form nuclei through process of nucleosynthesis. The duration of nucleosynthesis lasted only for about seventeen minutes since the temperature and density of the universe had fallen to a point where nuclear fusion could not prevail [38].

The strong nuclear force played essential role in nucleosynthesis. Similarly, the electromagnetic force acted on the adjacent swirling electrons and the protons of newly created nuclei and bound them together to create the first atoms 380,000 years after the Big Bang. The expanding universe, by then, had cooled enough to allow electrons to become part of a neutral atom. Before the formation of neutral atoms, the nuclei and the swirling electrons were in an ionized state at around 377,000 years after the Big Bang [39-40].

This was because in the beginning no electrons were bound to the nuclei which made atoms positively charged due to protons in the nuclei. But as the universe cooled down, the negatively charged electrons were attracted to the positively charged protons and neutral neutrons to form electrically neutral atoms. This process was relatively fast and is known as recombination [41]. At the end of recombination, most of the protons in the universe were bound up in neutral atoms making the photons travel freely. This cosmic event is usually referred to as decoupling. We see the same undisturbed photons in the cosmic microwave background (CMB) radiation after being greatly cooled by the expansion of the universe. Therefore, the CMB which is a picture of the universe and the tiny fluctuations of which was observed during the phase of Inflation as mentioned earlier [42].

Hence, we finally reach to the formation of atoms 380,000 years after the Big Bang. The term atom was coined by Democritus in 450 BCE [43]. It means "uncut-table" or "the smallest indivisible particle of matter". Later it was found that the identical atoms made elements. For example, the element hydrogen is made from atoms containing a single proton and a single electron. In that sense an atom can be termed as the smallest element. In 1789, French nobleman and science researcher Antoine Lavoisier defined an element as a basic substance that could not be broken by any method of chemistry [44]. As of today there are 118 known natural and manmade elements.

In the early years of the 20th century, Lord Rutherford [45-46] postulated that an atom is not an elementary particle but is composed of a nucleus that is one-thousand billionth of a centimetre in size. It is surrounded by a cloud of lighter particles, electrons, which spread out to a distance of one hundred millionth of a centimetre from the nucleus. The nucleus itself is settled in the centre with its two subatomic particles - protons and neutrons. These two subatomic particles are 1836 times heavier than electrons [47].

The nuclear energies, working through photons, transmit messages between protons, protons and electrons, and electrons. The stabilizing forces keep the electrons in their orbits without collapsing into the nucleus. The same forces show up as light, heat, microwaves and radio waves. Although these nuclear forces are very strong but they disappear abruptly at a distance of less than the size of a nucleus. So their effect is limited to adjacent particles. Some of these energies fall in the inverse square law of physics, which states that if separation between proton and electron is doubled, the force between them will fall to one quarter of its value; if it is tripled, the force will be one ninth and so on. All the activities in our planet and the universe are due to these forces.

It is theorized that atoms are generally in 'energized' and 'stabilized' state. Electrons, protons and neutrons play essential role keeping them in that state. For example, as the electrons circle around the nucleus with a tremendous speed of billions times every second at different energy levels, they "jump" between those levels like monkeys jumping from branch to branch. Because of these 'jumps', the electrons gain or lose energies accordingly to keep the atoms 'energized'.

At the same time, two forces play their role to keep the atoms 'stable'. The forces are;

- The electromagnetic force;
- The strong nuclear force. This is also called the 'binding force'.

The electromagnetic force keeps an atom stable by maintaining electrical balance between the negatively charged electrons and positively charged protons. While the strong nuclear force holds the nucleus together by keeping a balance between its constituents and maintaining equal number of protons and neutrons within. It also helps to place the electrically neutral neutrons in between the positively charged protons to keep them apart and thus reduce their electrostatic repulsion strength. In the process, it exerts its force on neutrons and protons to maintain nuclear stability. For this reason, one or more neutrons are necessary for each proton to keep them bound in a nucleus. As the number of protons increases, so does the number of neutrons to ensure a stable nucleus and so a stable atom.

An atom is categorized according to the number of protons and neutrons. The number of protons determines its chemical status and the number of neutrons determines its isotopic status [48].

For example, a change in the number of neutrons in a nucleus results in an 'isotope' of that element. Isotope is a Greek term for "at the same place" and was coined by Margaret Todd in 1912 as a suitable name for different atoms that belong to the same element [49].

Thus isotopes are just different versions of atoms of the same element. Such intra-nuclei change may not have drastic effect on nuclear properties but when strong nuclear force becomes incapable of binding such an isotopic nucleus the resulting atom of such nucleus changes to a 'radioisotope'.

Such unstable atoms are radioactive and emit radiation in the form of particles or electromagnetic waves. The exhaustion of this radioactive emission is also called radioactive decay. Such decay occurs on a regular basis round the clock.

The electromagnetic waves of radiation are characterized by frequency, wavelength and velocity having no charge and mass. These waveforms are part of a family in which some of the relatives are very familiar to us, such as light rays, infra-red heat rays, and radio waves. However, the other family members such as X-rays and gamma rays cannot be seen, felt, or heard as our normal senses cannot detect them. The sub-particles that are responsible for these characteristic are photons travelling in pockets of wave-like pattern and moving at the speed of light. Because they travel at the speed of light we know then, according to the relativity theory, that their rest mass must be zero.

It is this background radiation that has helped scientists track the history of universe as shown by BICEP1 and BICEP2 experiments discussed earlier. Similarly, the discovery of the red, blue and green shifts revealed that the universe is expanding and had an apparent beginning and it may be heading towards an end.

Sufis agree with notion of universe expanding by giving Quranic verses to support their claims [50]. On the subject of light, Quran mentions godhead calling itself light; i.e., that light was integral part of godhead just like other energies at the beginning of evolutionary process of universe. In that respect, godhead links that light with heavens (galaxies) and earth as its part [51]. It goes the same for colour, when Quran challenges human intelligence to ponder over the concept of colour [52]. Sufis give special importance to colours when they talk of spiritual centres in human body.

Coming back to the formation of atom, the process of primordial nucleosynthesis was the first type of nucleus generation which produced lighter atoms such as hydrogen and helium for about 20 minutes after the Big Bang before being stopped by rapid expansion and cooling and not letting the elements heavier than beryllium to form. The subsequent nucleosynthesis of the heavier atoms required heavy stars and supernova explosions which theoretically happened as hydrogen and helium condensed into the first stars 500 million years later.

Although major nucleosynthesis occurred within first three minutes of the Big Bang, the process is still continuing. As a result, the hydrogen and helium constitute over 98% of the mass of the sun. According to Fred Hoyle, hydrogen is continuously created in the universe under vacuum and energy, without need for universal beginning [53-54]. His work explained how the abundance of elements increased throughout the universe. With further expansion and cooling, heavy atoms were also created through the process of nucleosynthesis making them the basic building block of future universe.

Whichever way one looks at it, the atoms became a benchmark to understand micro and macro worlds of our planet drawing a line between the principles of Quantum and Convention physics, respectively. For example, at temperatures close to absolute zero (-273K), atoms can form a Bose–Einstein condensate, at which point quantum mechanical effects, which are normally observed at the atomic scale, become apparent on a macroscopic scale. Einstein demonstrated that cooling bosonic atoms to a very low temperature would cause them to fall (or "condense") into the lowest accessible, resulting in a new form of matter [55].

According to Prof Chew of University of Houston, this may not be true anymore with the recent work on super conductivity. The researchers at the University had been able to achieve the temperature of certain materials such as Yitrium to -263K; only 10 degree K warmer than absolute zero. No traces of new matter were formed. One should keep in mind that condensation could happen within a range, called the glide.

Another fascinating phenomenon was observed when studying electrons in the first quarter of the 20th century, Werner Heisenberg realized he could not find a definite position and a definite motion of a particle instantaneously. If he measured one, he could not measure the other. This became the Heisenberg Uncertainty Principle [56]. It still holds true. It simply means that when a particle is measured for its motion, at that precise moment it loses its 'existence' for position or vice versa. In other words, a particle which exists momentarily may be non-existent too! How is it possible for a thing not to exist while existing at the same time? Quoting Stephen Hawkins's logic on this theory, Kitty Ferguson, a science writer and former musician [57], put it rather plainly that, "what we cannot measure cannot happen". But in bizarre way it was happening.

These rather absurd phenomenons happen because according to quantum physicists, at around ten to the power of twenty times smaller than the atomic nucleus, space loses its meaning. This situation was observed earlier at the junction of Plank and Grand Unification epochs.

This also implies that the subatomic particles which make the building blocks of our planet are not really the blocks as we understand them in rational term. Such blocks are actually empty spaces with subatomic particles buzzing around nuclei with enormous speed turning into particles at times, and waves at others. The Greek philosophers were the first to come up with this notion when Democritus [58], and Leucippus proposed that the universe was composed of indivisible atoms moving through vacuum [59]. Some of them like Heraclitus [60] and Parmenides made radical suggestions that all changes were illusions [61-62]. Aristotle did not believe that it was feasible because air, like water, offered resistance to motion. According to him air would immediately rush in to fill a vacuum especially in the absence of resistance [63]. It is contradictions such as these that created differences of opinions between the philosophers; the scientists and the philosophers; the scientists and religious custodians; and even between conventional and quantum physicists.

Coming back to the expanding universe, by then it had travelled a long way from the first three minutes to millions of years and was passing through changes. During the passage, it relied on three principles; space-time; forms of energy; and the relevant physical laws. As we observed earlier, the space-time and forms of energy changed when they were separated during the GUT epoch. The physical laws, on other hand, were applied in the same manner during the passage of time in the following millenniums till the present day.

They were applied, when the universe was filled only with gases composed primarily of hydrogen, helium and deuterium in a storm of fine dust [64-65]. Thus the universe had been governed by the same physical laws throughout its extent and history.

According to Sufis, Quran not being a book of science but a book of signs gives hints to the people of knowledge about the evolutionary process the universe went through and is still going through whether it was the initial Big Bang (Kun) or later the formation of galaxies.

Before the universe reached its present form, concentrations appeared in gases that led to clouds formation. Later, fragmentation and flocculation appeared in clouds from gravitational pull resulting in formation of knots and clumps which changed later into dark blobs as globules. The globules changed into red pro-stars and nuclear reaction within red pro-stars turned them into true stars. The process went through a hierarchical system in which smaller structures formed before the larger ones. The first smaller structures to form were quasars and population III stars as a result of gravitational collapses re-ionizing the surrounding universe from intense radiation. Before that point most of the universe was composed of plasma corresponding to 'Opaque' era mentioned earlier when linear cosmological perturbation theory was applicable which argues that all structures could be understood as small deviations from a perfect homogeneous universe [66]. The phase is thought to have lasted between 150 million to 800 million years after the Big Bang [67].

The stars thus formed went through life cycles fluctuating in brightness, size and heat each lasting for thousands of years. During the ageing process they kept on shedding outer layers into space, exposing the central carbon core naked for helium to glow, giving them yellowish white tinge. These stars are called the 'White Dwarfs'. When they ran out of fuel, they lost their lustre and slowly withered away and dimmed down turning into 'Black Dwarfs', bringing end to their life cycles. Just before their 'death', they gain enormous size turning into 'Red Giants'.

According to computational models, the formation of the first stars, such as Population III started the process of turning the light elements such as hydrogen, helium and lithium into heavier elements [68]. As evolution of expanding universe continued, series of Population Stars kept on forming. The computational studies tell us that Population II stars were formed early followed by Population I stars. Johannes Schedler's project identified a quasar at 12.7 billion light-years away, when the universe was just 7% of its present age [69].

While the stars were going through ageing process, some of them started to pull each other through gravitational force causing collapse of large volume of matter. This led to formation of galaxies filled with stars, clouds of hydrogen, helium and other elements and dust.

According to Sufis when Quran mentions 'dust' as one of the fore-runners of life (other being air, water, clay etc.) it actually points to evolution [70]. They especially press on the wordings of Quran in which it challenges human thinking by saying that such verses are meant for the people of understanding.

People of understanding in science while talking about evolution tell us that the gravitational forces pulled these galaxies together forming groups, clusters and super-clusters. Since the expansion of the universe appears to be accelerating, super clusters are likely to be the largest structures that will ever form in the universe. The present accelerated expansion prevents any more inflationary structures entering the horizon and prevents new gravitationally bound structures from forming

In support of their understanding they refer to a discovery in October 2010 of UDFy-38135539, the first observed galaxy to have existed during the re-ionization period, which lasted between 150 million to 1 billion years confirming galactic evolution during these times [71- 72].

There was also a report in January 2011 of yet another galaxy that existed 480 million years after the Big Bang. Another Hubble image recently showed an infant galaxy forming, which means this happened very recently on the cosmological time-scale proving the fact that new galaxy formation in the universe is still occurring. That is what the Sufis have been telling us for the last 1400 years.

On July 11, 2007, Richard Ellis of the California Institute of Technology at Pasadena [73] and his team found six star forming galaxies about 13.2 billion light years away when the universe was only 500 million years old [74]. Similarly, the Hubble Ultra Deep Field shows a number of small galaxies merging to form clusters at 13 billion light years, when the universe was only 5% its current age [75].

There are probably more than 100 billion galaxies in the observable universe. They are shaped spiral, elliptical, lenticular and irregular[76A]. Excluding the early small galaxies, typical galaxies range from dwarfs with as few as ten million stars up to giants with one trillion stars, all orbiting the galaxy's centre of mass. Recent studies have shown that such galaxies revolve around black holes [76B]. We should remember that black hole is akin to singularity. A 2010 study by astronomers estimated that the observable universe contains 300 sextillion stars. The diameter of a typical galaxy is 30,000 light-years, and the typical distance between two neighbouring galaxies is 3 million light-years. Based on the emerging science of nucleo-cosmochronology, the galactic thin disk of our galaxy, the Milky Way, is estimated to have been formed 8.8 billion years ago. It is roughly 100,000 light years in diameter [77].

The star of our solar system- the Sun, is a late-generation star, incorporating the debris from several generations of earlier stars, and formed about 4.56 billion years ago. It lies in the spiral arm of Milky Way about 30,000 light years from the centre and takes 225 million years to complete one cycle.

At present, it is passing through middle age and around 5,000 million years from now, it will reach the end of its life and turn into `Red Giant with drastic consequences to earth. It will engulf the planet earth, destroying it completely, melting and then bursting it out from inside annihilating all form of living and non-living. The destruction will be of unimaginable intensity scattering the mountains like moth balls and changing them into dust, gasses and boiling liquid. This stage will last for about 50,000 years until it changes to `White Dwarf' and later to `Black Dwarf' ending the life cycle of the sun, the earth and the life on earth.

Now let us look at the universe the way Sufis understand it through the verses of Quran and see if there are similarities or dissimilarities between the scientific and Sufi's versions. For example, on creation Quran says, *"Do not the unbelievers see that the heavens (galaxies) and earth were joined together (as one unit of creation) before we cloven them asunder"* [78]. According to Big Bang Theory universe which was in singularity clove asunder with big bang. Quran says, *"Moreover He comprehended in his design the universe and it has been (as) smoke"* [79]. Science tells us that in the process of evolution at some stage in early millenniums the universe was filled with gases. This will be discussed further later. Quran says, *"The heavens we built with power verily we are expanding it"*. Science tells us that after the blast universe has been expanding ever since. Science recently told us about the movements and life span of universe, sun, earth and moon. Quran, on other hand, told us 1500 years ago that, *"He created the heavens (galaxies) and the Earth in the true proportions... He subjected the sun and the moon (to His law) each one follows a course for a time appointed"* [80]. It says again, *"He has created Heavens (galaxies) and Earth for just ends"* [81] Regarding the life cycle of stars Quran says *"He created the Sun, the Moon and the stars governed by laws under His command"* [82]. *The Sun and Moon follow courses (exactly) computed"* [83]. *"And the Sun runs its course for a period determined that is the decree of (him) the exalted in Might, the All knowing"* [84].

As noted earlier light and background radiation played important roles in determining the extent of and happenings in the universe. For example, according to some scientists which is disputed by others, universe is expanding faster than the speed of light. Without going into pros and cons of this, it brings the probability that there is more universe than the one observed so far. This probability is accepted by all the scientists. This also means that the universe can be divided into the one which is within the reach of speed of light; we call it the 'observable' universe, and the one which is beyond the reach of speed of light; we call it 'non-observable' universe. And since we cannot observe space beyond the reach of light it raises a question whether the size of the universe is finite or infinite.

This picture does not seem to be at odd with French definition of the universe which was derived from the Latin word 'universum' [85] meaning "something rotated, rolled, changed". It definitely falls in line with the definition of the medieval philosopher and theologian Johannes Scotus Eriugena [86] who called universe as everything that is created and everything that is not created. The 'created' and 'non-created' parts of universe fit well in the 'observable' and the 'non-observable' universe, respectively!

The term 'observable' simply indicates that it is possible in principle for light or other signals from an object in universe to reach an observer on earth. In practice, we can see light only from as far back as the time of photon decoupling in the recombination epoch, which is when particles were first able to emit photons and reach us as cosmic microwave background radiation (CMBR) as noted earlier. We should remember that before that, the universe was filled with plasma which was 'opaque' to photons as discussed earlier. However, it may be possible in future to observe the still older neutrino background, or even more distant events via gravitational waves of earlier universe as discussed in BICEP1 and BICEP2 experiments.

But for now, because of distinctions between the 'observable', the 'non-observable' (the 'visible') universe, it is possible to conceive a universe with units of disconnected space-times, each existing but unable to interact with one another. It is like visualizing a group of separate soap bubbles, in which observers living on one soap bubble cannot interact with those on other soap bubbles. This concept brought up the notion of multi verse. Though speculative but in principle, these unconnected universes may have; different dimensionality and topologies of space-time; different forms of matter and energy; and different physical laws and physical constants. There are various multi verse theories, in which physicists have suggested that our universe might be one among many universes that likewise exist [87].

Sufis believe in theory of multi universe. They base their belief on the verses of the Quran which do not clash with science [88].

The end of Universe

After going through the brief history of universe, it is time to discuss its ultimate fate. As we do not know what exactly happened in the very early universe, similarly it is not possible to know with certainty how it will end. The following theories are put forward to present possible scenarios in which the universe might end.

1) Big Freeze [89]

This is the most likely scenario as it is linked with the most acceptable theory that the universe has been expanding. Such an end will begin after 10^{14} years when the existing stars will burn out, the new stars will not be created any more, and the universe will go dark [90]. The galaxies, one by one, will evaporate as the comprising stellar remnants will escape into space in fashion of grand unified theories, at around 10^{34} years from now. As a result, the interstellar gas and stellar remnants will change into leptons and photons, eventually reaching a high-entropy state consisting of a bath of particles and low-energy radiation. It is not known whether it will achieve thermodynamic equilibrium.

2) Big Crunch [91]

In this scenario, as the universe goes into 'reverse gear' and reach a state of entropy at the time-scale of 10^{34} years as mentioned above, it will keep contracting up to 100+ billion years towards a scorching hot, dense state as in Singularity causing a reformation of the universe starting with another big bang. Some physicists do not consider this as part of oscillatory universe theory. Others suggest that this model is unlikely to be correct and the expansion will continue or even accelerate.

Sufis are inclined towards this theory quoting verse 21:104 of the Quran which states *"That Day We will fold up heaven like folding up the pages of a book. As We originated the first creation so We will regenerate it. It is a promise binding on Us. That is what We will do."* It is important to mention at this stage that godhead uses the word 'We' and 'Us' instead of 'I' or 'Me' for itself. This according to Sufis points to the state or epiphany of 'Wahdat' of godhead which will be discussed later.

In another verse on this subject Quran says, *"They do not measure Allah with His true measure. The whole earth will be a mere handful for Him on the Day of Rising the heavens folded up in His right hand. Glory be to Him!* He is exalted above the partners they ascribe!" (39:6). Here godhead uses the word 'his right hand' and 'Him' which is pointed towards the state of 'Wahdiat' of godhead. This will also be discussed at a later stage.

3) **Big Rip** [92]

This scenario was published in 2003. According to this theory big rip is possible only if the dark energy which helps universe to expand keeps on increasing. In such scenario, the gravitational forces will fail to hold clusters of galaxies and solar systems tearing them apart disintegrating atomic nuclei, and the universe as we know it will end in an unusual kind of singularity with no gravitational force thus reaching a state of an infinite expansion. The whole process will take about 20+ billion years from now.

Thus we see how the universe came into existence from nothingness, went through evolutionary stages and 13.7 billion years later we can say that there is an observable universe as opposed to a non-observable one. We also theorised how atom was formed which became the foundation of universe the way we know it today. During all this process we saw similarities between scientific theories put forward by the scientists and Quranic verses observed by the Sufis about; creation of universe; the evolutionary process it is going through; and its possible end.

With this, I will stop here and go to the next chapter focusing on formation of planet earth and beginning of life on earth as part of continuity of evolutionary process of universe.

REFERENCES

(1)   (Komatsu, E.; Dunkley, J.; Nolta, M. R.; Bennett, C. L.; Gold, B.; Hinshaw, G.; Jarosik, N.; Larson, D. et al. (2009). "Five-Year Wilkinson Microwave Anisotropy Probe Observations: Cosmological Interpretation". Astrophysical Journal Supplement 180 (2): 330. arXiv:0803.0547. Bibcode 2009ApJS..180..330K. doi:10.1088/0067-0049/180/2/330.)

(2)   ("How Old is the Universe?".) {Delio, Ilia (2011). The Emergent Christ: Exploring the Meaning of Catholic in an Evolutionary Universe. Maryknoll NY: Orbis Books. pp. 183. ISBN 978-1570759086}

(3)   PD is a theoretical physicist and professor of natural philosophy at the University of Adelaide.

(4)   2 ^ S. W. Hawking and G. F. R. Ellis (1975). The large scale structure of space-time. Cambridge University Press.

(5)   3^ Thorne, Kip S.; Misner, Charles; Wheeler, John (1973). Gravitation. W. H. Freeman and Company.

(6)   4^ Wald, Robert M. (1984). General Relativity. Chicago: University of Chicago Press.

(7)   5^ J. A. Peacock (1999). Cosmological Physics. Cambridge University Press.

(8)   6^ Dieter Brill, "Black Hole Horizons and How They Begin", Astronomical Review (2012); Online Article, cited Sept.2012.

(9)   [Keathley, Kenneth (2010). Salvation and Sovereignty: A Molinist Approach. B&H Publishing Group. p. 6. ISBN 0-8054-3198-5. http://books.google.com/books?id=uDsKisgT0f0C&pg=PA6]

(10)   [Smith, Quentin (2007). "Kalam Cosmological Arguments for Atheism". In Martin, Michael. The Cambridge companion to atheism. Cambridge University Press. p. 183. ISBN 978-0-521-84270]

(11)   A(Quran, 2:116-118), [(11 B) Wahdat-ul-Wujood | The Force Holocron.) or 'Hamma Az Oost' (Everything is from Him). [(11 C), God as truth | Latest News & Updates at Daily News)]

(12)   ('Vilenkin, Alexander (1983). "The birth of inflationary universes". Phys. Rev. D27 (12): 2848. Bibcode 1983PhRvD..27.2848V. doi:10.1103/PhysRevD.27.2848.)

(13)   A...Dark energy - Wikipedia, the free encyclopedia)....[(13 B).. Guth, Phase transitions in the very early universe, in The Very Early Universe, ISBN 0-521-31677-4 eds Hawking, Gibbon & Siklos)

(14) (Linde, A.D. (August 1986).. Physics Letters B 175 (4): 395 "Eternally Existing Self-Reproducing Chaotic Inflationary Universe"–400. Bibcode 1986PhLB..175..395L Doi:10.1016/0370-2693(86)90611-8. http://www.stanford.edu/~alinde/Eternal86.pdf.)

(15) (Guth, Alan; Eternal inflation and its implications arXiv:hep-th/0702178)

(16) [2Ellis, John (1986). "The Superstring: Theory of Everything, or of Nothing?". Nature 323 (6089): 595–598. 1986Natur.323..595E.].

(17) [Ref 3,] doi:10.1038/323595a0.)

(18) A.......(REF 1)^ a b Attested by many legendary scholars of Shariah such as al-Alusi al-Hanafi in his magnificent Tafsir where he addressed the Sheikh as: The Sheikh ul Akbar (greatest sheikh), Muhayuddin Ibn Arabi Qudus Allah Ta'la Sira [Ruh ul Ma'ani Volume # 7, Page # 741, the arabic of which states: الشيخ الأكبر ^ a b (2) [محي-الدين بن العربي-قدس الله تعالى سره] Al-Suyuti, Tanbih al-Ghabi fi Tanzih Ibn 'Arabi (p. 17-21))....(18B...The Mind of God - Goodreads)

(19) (Ref.. Encyclopaedia Britannica: http://www.britannica.com/EBchecked/topic/10170/Shaykh-Ahmad-Sirhindi)

(20) A, [(REF...[[1] This paper significantly enhances A. A. Colella's, A Proposed Super Unified Theory, http://knol.google.com/k/antonio-colella/a-proposed-super-unified-theory/3h4y5c7nj2xo/6#view.)] [(20 B) BBC 2: Horizon: Aftershock-the hunt)..] [(20 C) Grand Unified Theory - Wikipedia, the free encyclopedia.]

(21) (Ref..http://knol.google.com/k/antonio-colella/-/3h4y5c7nj2xo/6#_edn1

(22) (1.^ Ryden B: "Introduction to Cosmology", pg. 196 Addison-Wesley 2003,

(23) 2^ Allday, Jonathan (2002). Quarks, Leptons and the Big Bang. Taylor & Francis. p. 334. ISBN 978-0-7503-0806-9.,

(24) 3^ Our Universe Part 6: Electroweak Epoch, Scientific Explorer,

(25) 4^ Lecture 13: History of the Very Early Universe, Dr. Balša Terzić, Northern Illinois Center for Accelerator and Detector Development)

(26) (Ref.^ a b c Glashow's autobiography. Nobelprize.org. Retrieved on 2012-07-27.)

(27) (Ref "James Clerk Maxwell". Encyclopædia Britannica. http://www.britannica.com/EBchecked/topic/370621/James-Clerk-Maxwell.

Retrieved 24 February 2010. "Scottish physicist best known for his formulation of electromagnetic theory")

(28) (1)....Allday, Jonathan (2002). Quarks, Leptons and the Big Bang. Second Edition. ISBN 978-0-7503-0806-9.

(29) (2)...Physics 175: Stars and Galazies - The Big Bang, Matter and Energy; Ithaca College, New York)

(30) (1)...Allday, Jonathan (2002). Quarks, Leptons and the Big Bang. Second Edition. ISBN 0-7503-0806-0.

(31) (2)...Physics 175: Stars and Galazies - The Big Bang, Matter and Energy; Ithaca College, New York)

(32) (Ref: Quran 15:27, 72:1-2, 46:30)

(33) (1)...^ The Timescale of Creation.

(34) (2)...Allday, Jonathan (2002). Quarks, Leptons and the Big Bang. Second Edition. ISBN 978-0-7503-0806-9.)

(35) (1)...^ The Timescale of Creation.

(36) (2)...Allday, Jonathan (2002). Quarks, Leptons and the Big Bang. Second Edition. ISBN 978-0-7503-0806-9.)

(37) [Ref...The Timescale of Creation.],

(38) (Detailed timeline of Big Bang nucleosynthesis processes)

(39) ((1) Ref..Hinshaw, G.; et al. (2009). "Five-Year Wilkinson Microwave Anisotropy Probe (WMAP) Observations: Data Processing, Sky Maps, and Basic Results" (PDF). Astrophysical Journal Supplement 180

(40) (2): 225–245. arXiv:0803.0732. Bibcode 2009ApJS..180..225H. doi:10.1088/0067-0049/180/2/225. http://lambda.gsfc.nasa.gov/product/map/dr3/pub_papers/fiveyear/basic_results/wmap5basic.pdf.).

(41) [Mukhanov, V: "Physical foundations of Cosmology", pg. 120, Cambridge 2005]

(42) (Amos, Jonathan (2012-11-13). "Quasars illustrate dark energy's roller coaster ride". BBC News. http://www.bbc.co.uk/news/science-environment-20303592. Retrieved 13 November 2012.)

(43) (Russell, pp.64–65.)

(44) ("He is also considered as the "Father of Modern Nutrition", as being the first to discover the metabolism that occurs inside the human body. Lavoisier, Antoine." Encyclopædia Britannica. 2007. Encyclopædia Britannica Online. 24 July 2007.)

(45) (1)Ref..^ a b Ernest Rutherford (1911). The scattering of alpha and beta particles by matter and the structure of the atom. Taylor & Francis. p. 688. http://www.math.ubc.ca/~cass/rutherford/rutherford688.html.

(46) (2) ^ M. S. Longair (2003). Theoretical concepts in physics: an alternative view of theoretical reasoning in physics. Cambridge University Press. pp. 377–378. ISBN_978-0-521-52878-8. http:// books.google. com/?id= bA9Lp2GH6OEC&pg=PA377&dq= rutherford+positive+charge+concentrated+nucleus&q= rutherford%20positive%20charge%20concentrated%20nucleus.)

(47) Ref..Woan 2000, p. 8.)

(48) (Ref...^ Leigh, G. J., ed. (1990). International Union of Pure and Applied Chemistry, Commission on the Nomenclature of Inorganic Chemistry, Nomenclature of Organic Chemistry – Recommendations 1990. Oxford: Blackwell Scientific Publications. p. 35. ISBN_0-08-022369-9. "An atom is the smallest unit quantity of an element that is capable of existence whether alone or in chemical combination with other atoms of the same or other elements."

(49) (Ref...Nagel, Miriam C. (1982). "Frederick Soddy: From Alchemy to Isotopes". Journal of Chemical Education 59 (9): 739–740. doi:10.1021/ed059p739.)

(50) (Quran,51:47)

(51) (Quran, 24:35)

(52) (Quran, AR Rum:22)

(53) (Ref [1]...Burbidge, G. (2003). "Sir Fred Hoyle. 24 June 1915 - 20 August 2001 Elected FRS 1957". Biographical Memoirs of Fellows of the Royal Society 49: 213. doi:10.1098/rsbm.2003.0013.

(54) [2]...."William A. Fowler - Autobiography". Nobelprize.org. 14 March 1995. http://nobelprize.org/physics/laureates/1983/fowler-autobio.html. Retrieved 15 September 2011)

(55) (Ref....Arora, C. P. (2001). Thermodynamics. Tata McGraw-Hill. p. 43. ISBN_0-07-462014-2. http://books.google.com/books?id=w8GhW3J8RHIC., Table 2.4 page 43)

(56) (Ref...Paraphrase of Heisenberg's uncertainty paper of 1927)

(57) (US Genweb Archives)

(58) (^ a b c Russell, pp.64–65.)

(59) (^ a b c d e f Barnes (1987))

(60) (Heraclitus Quotes (Author of Fragments)

(61) (1:...According to Czech philosopher Milič Čapek "[Parmenides']
    decisive influence on the development of Western thought is probably
    without parallel", The New Aspects of Time, 1991, p. 145. That
    assessment may overstate Parmenides' impact and importance, but it
    is a useful corrective to the tendency to underestimate it.

(62) (2:...Frag. B 8.11)

(63) (Martin Heidegger, The Principle of Reason, trans. Reginald Lilly,
    (Indiana University Press, 1991), 62-63)

(64) (1...Wollack, Edward J. (June 24, 2011), What is the Universe Made
    Of?, NASA, http://map.gsfc.nasa.gov/universe/uni_matter.html,
    retrieved 2011-10-14.

(65) (2..Eckert 2006, p. 5.)

(66) (Frasca, M. (1998). "Duality in Perturbation Theory and the
    Quantum Adiabatic Approximation". Phys. Rev. A 58 (5): 3439.
    arXiv:hep-th/9801069. Bibcode 1998PhRvA..58.3439F. doi:10.1103/
    PhysRevA.58.3439.)

(67) (Wall, Mike (December 12, 2012). "Ancient Galaxy May Be Most
    Distant Ever Seen". Space.com. http://www.space.com/18879-
    hubble-most-distant-galaxy.html. Retrieved December 12, 2012.)

(68) (Ferreting Out The First Stars; physorg.com]

(69) [apod.nasa.gov/apod/ap070906.html]

(70) (Quran, 22:5, 25:54, 37:11)

(71) [(1).."; Dim galaxy is most distant object yet found". New Scientist.
    http://www.newscientist.com/article/dn19603-dim-galaxy-is-most-
    distant-object-yet-found.html. Retrieved 2010-10-21..

(72) (2)....blogs.rmg.co.uk/rog/tag/udfy-38135539/]

(73) (Curriculum Vitae (MS Word)

(74) [New Scientist" 14th July 2007

(75) [APOD: 2004 March 9 – The Hubble Ultra Deep Field.] (apod.nasa.
    gov/apod/ap040309.html)

(76) A, (www.universetoday.com/87341/galaxy-shapes/)] [.(76 B).
    Horizon: BBC4: Swallowed by Black Hole....].

(77) (Eduardo F. del Peloso a1a, Licio da Silva a1, Gustavo F. Porto de
    Mello and Lilia I. Arany-Prado (2005), "The age of the Galactic
    thin disk from Th/Eu nucleocosmochronology: extended sample"
    (Proceedings of the International Astronomical Union (2005), 1:
    485-486 Cambridge University Press)

(78) (Quran, 21:30)

(79) (Quran, 41:9)

(80) (Quran, 39:5)

(81) (Quran, 26:3)

(82) (Quran, 7:54)

(83) (Quran, 55:2)

(84) (Quran, 36:38)

(85) (www.thefreedictionary.com/universe)

(86) (^ "Johannes Scotus Erigena", Notable Names Database, http://www. nndb.com/people/756/000095471/, retrieved Aug. 5, 2007.)

(87) (www.space.com/18811-multiple-universes-5-theories.html)

(88) (,xeniagreekmuslimah.wordpress.com/.../ the-existence-of-multiple-uni)

(89) (www.universetoday.com/36917/big-freeze/)

(90) (^ a b c d A dying universe: the long-term fate and evolution of astrophysical objects, Fred C. Adams and Gregory Laughlin, Reviews of Modern Physics 69, #2 (April 1997), pp. 337–372. Bibcode: 1997RvMP...69..337A. doi:10.1103/RevModPhys.69.337.)

(91) (www.universetoday.com/37018/big-crunch/)

(92) (www.youtube.com/watch?v=JaImVFRpOR8)

CHAPTER TWO

Earth and the life on earth

───── ❖ ─────

Earth came into existence about 4.6 billion years ago. It was like a ball of molten rocks with atmosphere full of turbulent gases primarily composed of hydrogen, helium, carbon dioxide, methane, ammonia, nitrogen and other volatiles. With passage of time, the dust started to solidify due to gravitational pull, thus moulding itself in a primitive shape. At around 4 billion years as it continued to cool down, its crust buckled and volcanoes erupted spewing out gases while forming scorching atmosphere with sizzling temperatures in access of 60,00,0000 Celsius.

Next one billion years saw a gradual drop in temperature as water condensed and clouds started to form resulting in torrential rains, violent storms and lightning full of radiation. Continuous rain washed the atmospheric chemicals and poured them down into newly formed sea where they settled at the bottom and were converted into inorganic and organic compounds with the help of radiation. The compounds, primarily, were formed of carbon, ammonia, nitrogen and hydrogen. As the earth gradually cooled and torrential storms slowed down, the water from sea started to evaporate leaving behind a viscous liquid of organic compounds at the bottom of the sea known as `Primeval Soup'[1]

Constant floods of radiation of organic compounds for the next 3 billion years resulted in formation of chains of nucleic and amino acids. These chains slowly settled down on the rich sticky clayish surface of the 'Primeval Soup'[2-3]

One billion years later, the earth further cooled down bringing the temperature to around 100 Celsius. Scientists tell us that in the process, the intense radiation acted on the adjacent two types of mineralized fluids composed primarily of fat and phosphorus respectively in the 'Primeval Soup' and formed a double layered membrane [4-5]

Sufis also talk of such phenomenon when they mention Quranic verses stating about similar membrane and calling it a 'barrier' at the bottom of sea when it says, *"He has let free the two bodies of flowing water meeting together between them is a Barrier, which they do not transgress"* [6]

Looking at the two bodies of water mentioned in Quran and the two bodies of mineralised fluids mentioned in science books, one finds acute similarity between the two. Both term it a 'barrier'. It was the non-transgression quality of the membrane which Quran is focusing at and which became the fundamental block of a cell agreed up on by the scientists. In another verse, Quran goes one step further and is more specific when it says, *"It is He who has let free the two bodies of flowing water, one palpable and sweet and other salt and bitter. Yet has He made a barrier between them. A partition that is forbidden to be passed"* [7]. In this verse Quran has symbolized the mineralized fluid composed of fat as sweet and palatable and the other as salty and bitter. Also, it gave a classification to the passage across the barrier by calling it 'forbidden'.

We know that the life of a cell depends on impermeability of its wall for certain ionic substances and that impermeability is governed under strict laws of nature. So the nature which commands or forbids the permeation of certain substances across the cell wall, the divine power does the same thing as mentioned in Quran. In that sense the nature described by the scientists and divinity mentioned by the Sufis are pretty close in working and description if not identical.

Lastly, referring to creation of life from sticky clay at the bottom of 'Primeval Soup', Quran says, *"Thou have we created out of sticky clay"* [8]. It is interesting to find similarity in describing the beginning of life perceived by science and described by Quran in an identical manner but in different vocabulary. Having said that, not for a single second, I am hinting that Quran is the book of science. All I am saying is that it is a book of 'signs' which hinted at certain realities of life that were unknown to the world 1400 years ago.

Science tells us the membrane in the primeval soup interacted with nearby nucleic and amino acids to form the first cell thus introducing life on earth. According to the British Naturalist, Sir David F. Attenborough, if we consider the duration of the earth as one year, the life appeared in the middle of August in the sea. Towards the end of November, the first animal left the water and colonized the land. Soon the pace quickened and the backbone animals invaded the land by the beginning of December. In the middle of December one group could generate heat in their bodies and transformed their scales into feathers. The first furry warm creature appeared around the same time. On 25th of December dinosaurs disappeared and were replaced by mammals. The mammals started transmitting information and instruction carried by the sex cell to their offspring. Thus the experience developed by one generation need not to die with them as it was inherited to youngsters. At the same time the young mammal started to depend on their mother for milk and was protected in their early age. In this way, animal communities were developed transmitting traditions and cultures from one generation to another. In early morning of December 31st apes and ape-man appeared. And Human arrived about two minutes before the end of the last day of December [9].

According to him life appeared after the earth had crossed half of its age. Though he did not specify the way life emerged but other researchers talk about how the membrane became the cardinal step in the eventual process of interdependent system of nucleic acids and proteins of cell life in future. With further evolution, such interdependency paved the way for formation of the pivotal tool of life-the ribonucleic acid (RNA). Carl Woese, Francis Crick and Leslie Orgel were the first scientists to propose that RNA was the first to come and it could self-replicate and possibly serve as enzymes for protein synthesis [10].

In 1983 Thomas Cech and Sidney Altman discovered ribozymes and the ability of RNA to catalyse its own modifications without the use of protein enzymes. They received the Nobel Prize for their work. Eventually the RNA was replaced by DNA (deoxyribonucleic acid) and protein enzymes taking over information storage and enzymatic functions, respectively. The first cell can be compared with the present-day virus structurally and functionally in which the cell membrane acted like gastro intestinal track, lungs and kidneys of evolved organisms.

Quran, in the verse 18:56, not just mentions the word DNA and RNA in its unique style of 'signs' filled with mathematical surprises but also points to the year 1856 in which genetic laws were drawn by Mendel. Sufis argue that it cannot be just a coincidence [11-12].

Before going further, it is pertinent to talk about the two important views about the creation of life;

1. First, the Naturalist view, which believes in the beginning of life as logical event rather than chance occurrence [13].
2. Second, Panspermia hypothesis, which suggests that primitive life could have been planted on earth deliberately or accidentally through a higher intelligent power. It's proponents like Dr. Kenneth W. Minton of the Uniformed Services University of Health Sciences in Bethesda, Maryland, said, "Deinococcus radiodurans, a bacterium highly resistant to radiation, would be a good vector for panspermia. While drifting through interstellar space for many thousands of years, it might acquire a shell of interstellar crud that could protect it from the intense heat generated during entrance into planet's atmosphere" [14].

Despite having these two theories we have seen the life started as membrane in the bottom of the sea at 'Primordial Soup'. Its evolution in the coming centuries resulted in formation of primitive cells known as the Prokaryotes, around 3.5 billion years ago; about 1 billion years after the formation of the earth's crust during Archean period [15].

The Prokaryotes were (still are) the self-maintaining simplest cells which did not have nuclei and lived (still live) independently. On average, they are 1 µm to 10 µm in size, but some reach up to 200 um. As nucleus harbours DNA and with no nucleus, the DNA in Prokaryotes usually floated (still floats) in the cell matrix [16][17][18]. Also, the Prokaryotes lacked any of the intracellular organelles such as mitochondria, chloroplasts, and the Golgi bodies- the essential apparatuses for maintaining life. These functions were taken over by the Prokaryotic plasma membrane [19]. The membrane also took living processes such as oxidative phosphorylation and photosynthesis [20]. To sustain life, the Prokaryotes had three architectural regions:

- Protein appendages called flagella attached to the cell surface;
- A cell envelope consisting of; a capsule; a cell wall; and a plasma membrane;
- A cytoplasm region that contained the cell genome (DNA) and Ribosomes.

Continuous evolution did not change the unicellular status of Prokeryotes and they did not develop or differentiate into multicellular forms. Some of them grew as filaments, or masses of cells, but each cell in the colony remained identical and capable of independent existence. They remained enclosed in a common sheath or slime secreted by the cells without having continuity or communication between individual cells. The 'slime' is called 'biofilms' [21][22][23]. Recent studies mention that the communities in these 'biofilms' often show distinct patterns of gene expression (phenotypic differentiation) in time and space meaning; these changes in expression are the result of cell-to-cell signalling. A phenomenon called 'quorum sensing' [24].

In this way the cells display coordinated group behaviour regulated by quorum-sensing systems that detect the density of other bacteria around them [25]. This strange phenomenon has led some to speculate that this may constitute a circulatory system [26]'. As a result of this phenomenon, many researchers have started calling Prokaryotic communities multi-cellular [27].

This phenomenon of sensing (also labelled as 'vibe') is recently been observed in plants, animals and humans. [27A.] Sufis have been talking about it for the last 1400 years. They call it messaging through means not explainable by logic. Similar non-perceivable link is described by Hunaism-the oldest spirituality in Australasia. The channel is called 'Aka' akin to 'Higgs field' in Quantum physics.

Logically speaking, expression by different cells as one unit, collective behaviour, and uniform signalling, all seem to point out as if they are not individual cells but are part of a multi-cellular organism. The major difference is that these colonies are seldom if ever formed by a single founder as opposed to animals and plants which are formed by single cells.

Moreover, the metabolism of Prokaryotes is far more varied than that of plants and animals. For example, in addition to using photosynthesis from organic compounds for energy, Prokaryotes obtain energy from inorganic compounds such as hydrogen sulphide. This enables them to live in harsh environments as cold as the snow surface of Antarctica or as hot as undersea hydrothermal vents or on the land-based hot springs. Also, they reproduce through asexual reproduction by binary fission or budding, and exchange DNA between two cells through horizontal transfer rather than replication.

The ongoing evolution affected the Prokaryotes and as a result more advanced cells emerged called the Eukaryotes. The oldest known fossilized Prokaryotes were laid down approximately 3.5 billion years ago. While the oldest known fossil Eukaryotes are about 1.7 billion years old proving they were evolved later in the history of life [28]. However, some genetic evidence suggests Eukaryotes might have appeared as early as 3 billion years ago [29]. Other authors argue that the Prokaryotes may have evolved from more complex Eukaryotic ancestors through a process of simplification [30][31][32]. They argue that the three domains of life, Archaea, Bacteria and Eukryotes arose simultaneously from a set of varied cells that formed a single gene pool [33].

Confusions such as these give a chance to the Sufis to raise objections while defending their unbending middle of the road stance on an unknown power regulating the evolution. Supporting their argument and quoting Quran they say that the harmonious change from a simple life of Prokryotes to a complex life of Eukeryotes could not have come on its own accord. They object to the views of natural selection, the foundation of theory of evolution that credits accidental mutation for the survival of life and its progress from simplicity to complexity. They challenge its basic principle as to how it fails to explain the way life was created and how accidents can guide the life towards complexity.

As opposed to this theory they propose evolutionary steps mentioned in Quranic verses which state that God creates in stages. According to them, Quran being the book of signs and not science might not give the details of those stages but it does offer principles that tend to point toward organized evolution [34]. For example, on evolution of life, Quran states that life advanced step by step from dust, water, clay and also from fermenting blackish mud, which subsequently turned into dry, ringing clay [35].

Then on evolution of human which is Eukeryote [36], Sufis quoting Quran point towards four major stages;

1. In the first stage, humans were lifeless material.
2. In the second stage, humans were physically human-like but mentally they were still on the level of animals. They lacked language, articulation and logic.
3. In the third stage, humans developed thinking skills.
4. In the fourth stage, (Homo Sapiens sapiens) humans learned to exist as a society.

So, according to Sufis, Quran does talk about human evolution from lifeless matter to a living mind in stages. This evolution from one stage to another, however, occurred under divine guidance [37].

Whatever the confusion, one thing is obvious from evolutionists' and creationists' point of view that the structural and functional changes point to a gradual evolutionary process from Prokaryotes to

Eukaryotes. Such changes brought the following differences between the two;

1. Generally, Prokaryotes are unicellular while Eukaryotes are unicellular as well as multi-cellular [38].
2. Prokaryotes usually have different cytoskeleton system than Eukaryotes, meaning the former generally have rigid cell walls and the latter are variable [39].
3. Prokaryotes are thought to have no organelles while Eukaryotes have membrane-covered organelles 40][41].
4. Prokaryotes have no nucleus while Eukaryotes have established nucleus [42].
5. The organelles and nucleus of Eukaryotes, unlike Prokaryotes, enable the cells to create parts [43].
6. DNA in Prokaryotes usually floats in cytoplasm while it is encapsulated in nucleus of Eukaryotes [44].
7. Prokaryotes reproduce asexually while Eukaryotes reproduce through a sexual process [45].
8. Prokaryotes feed through phagocytosis and expel through exocytosis while Eukaryotes have complicated mechanism for feeding and excretion [46].
9. No cell can live inside Prokaryotes but other cells can live in Eukaryotes [47].
10. Lastly, Eukaryotic cells are generally a couple hundred times the size of Prokaryotic cells [48].

It took 1.1 to 2 billion years for Prokaryotes to evolve into Eukaryotes most probably in the following manner;

1. The Eukaryotes changed the rigid cell wall of Prokaryotes to the one that could shape easily according to the variable surroundings. This meant that Eukaryotes needed some other way of supporting and strengthening the cell surface. So, they evolved a complex cytoskeleton consisting of two classes of molecules: [49]

- Actin filaments, to resist distorting forces and convert chemical activity into mechanical motion. Actin made it possible for the membrane to grow and fuse. And through process of cytosis as an active transport mechanism, it moved large quantities of molecules in and out of cells. It also allowed cells to secrete substances through a process called exocytosis akin to kidneys secreting urine, and to bring them into the cell through another process called phagocytosis akin to mouth ingesting food [50].
- Microtubules to resist compressing and shearing forces and to act as tool to slide component parts through cytoplasm. They also helped cells in locomotion and in reproductive process of mitosis. In mitosis, the microtubules help to separate the duplicated chromosomes and then moving them [51].

2. The large Prokaryotes were capable of engulfing smaller Prokaryotes. With passage of time and through the process of evolution, the engulfed or phagocytosed aerobic Prokaryotes learned how to live within the host cell by;

   1. Wrapping itself with a double layered membrane made from the membranes of the host and the engulfed cells;
   2. Releasing the harmful oxygen and using it to form ATP-an essential component of cell metabolism. In this way the ingested cells survived inside, and using oxygen it metabolised the host cell's waste products and derived more energy some of which was returned to the host. Soon, a stable symbiosis developed between the host cells and the ingested cells.
   3. Over time, the host cells acquired some of the genes of the ingested cells, and the two kinds became dependent on each other; one living on the energy of the other and vice versa. This combination started to work as single Eukaryotic organisms, and the ingested cells became as

organelles such as mitochondria, chloroplasts and other bodies including nucleus, cilia, and flagella [52][53].

4. The organelles and organized DNA of Eukaryotes, unlike Prokaryotes, were able to create parts. The obvious examples are the flagella which are tail-like structures to help them move; or the cilia which are little hairs that help scoot the cells through the water. The list is endless. The anaerobe Prokaryotes base their metabolism on fermentation using organic molecules as raw material and energy source [54]. They do not use oxygen, which makes respiration possible and is more effective energy source for life than fermentation. So when the food supply from organic molecules decreased, some of the cells adopted sunlight as an energy source by establishing mechanism of oxygenic photosynthesis around 3 billion years ago. This type of photosynthesis used carbon dioxide and water as raw materials and with help of sunlight, produced energy-rich organic molecules such as carbohydrates, fat and proteins essential for future evolution [55][56].

These observations were confirmed through light microscopy for chloroplast by Schimpler in 1883, and for mitochondria by Walin in 1922. Lynn Margulis in the following years reconfirmed them through electron microscope adding further that the organelles were surrounded by two membranes - the inner one belonging to the engulfed cell and the outer one to the host cell. She also suggested that Prokaryote developed a membrane around its DNA which became nucleus of Eukaryote [57][58].

The observations became the basis of Endosymbiotic theory for the origin of the Eukaryotic cells [59][60][61]. Some authorities are not impressed with this theory arguing that the theory is based only on similarities between individual Prokaryotes and organelles of Eukaryotes. So they came up with an alternate hypothesis of 'Autogenous' according to which the eukaryotes were formed as a result of compartmentalization of ancestor Prokaryote by in-foldings of its plasma membrane making separate compartments for endoplasmic reticulum, golgi bodies, the nucleus, and the organelles [62][63]. To support this theory, the biologists are almost certain that Eukaryotes evolved from Prokaryotes because both use RNA and DNA as the genetic material, use the same 20 amino acids, have a lipid bilayer cell membrane and use L amino acids and D sugars. They are almost certain that eukaryotes evolved only once.

How do the Sufis look upon these theories which keep on changing with times while their beliefs remain static and unshaken. They say that though the scientific theories do change from time to time they still, in principle, fall in line with verses from the Quran when it says, "..with water did We create every living thing..." [64], or when it states, "...And surely, we created man from dry ringing clay made from stagnant blackish mud..." [65]. Verses such as these point at the beginning of life in 'Primeval Soup' and its onward journey through evolutionary stages up to formation of developed Eukeryote such as the present-day human being. The picture of water and clay, presented by the Quran, seems to be consistent with the mixture of inorganic materials becoming organic, as presented by science, which was followed by a dry stage to allow the organic material to develop irreversible strength as we saw it in our discussion earlier [66].

With passage of time, Prokaryotes and Eukaryotes continued to diversify and became more complex and better adapted to their environments. For example, around 1 billion years ago, some of Eukayotes accommodated themselves in divisions of specialized and multi-cellular cells living within the colonies and taking different roles according to the surrounding environment which led to the formation of plant, animals and fungi [67].

- Plant cells have a fairly rigid cell wall made of polysaccharide pectin, which provides the cell with structural support, protection, and a filtering mechanism. It also prevents over-expansion when water enters the cell. It has linking pores that allow the cell to communicate with the adjacent cells. Plant cells also have chlorophyllic pigment that gives plants their green colour and allows them to perform photosynthesis.

- Animal cells lack rigid cell walls; instead of pores, they have functionally analogous system of gaps which act like inter-cellular channels of some 1.5–2 nm in diameter linking adjacent cells. They do not have chloroplasts, and have smaller vacuoles. Also, due to lack of a rigid cell wall, they can adopt a variety of shapes, and being phagocytic, they can engulf other structures. There are many different animal cell types. For instance, human body has approximately 210 distinct cell types.

- Fungi cells are similar to animal cells with some exceptions. Their cell walls contain filamentous Chitin, and have porous partitions called septa which allow cytoplasm, organelles and nuclei pass through. Also with exception of some primitive fungi they do not have flagella.

The first multi-cellular Eukaryotes which emerged were the green algae plants at around 900 million years ago [68][69]. It was the same story with multi-cellular animals. No wonder that green algae which is a plant, resembles sponges which are multi-cellular animals. Both have bodies full of pores and channels that allow water to circulate through them for feeding and excretory purposes and have no nervous, digestive or circulatory systems.

This way of life which started as a single cell after creation of a membrane went through evolutionary stages shaping and reshaping its unicellular and multi-cellular structures. The important developments were the origin of muscular and neural cells and having hard body parts like skeletons which made the new form of life larger, complex, and more diverse leading to emergence of plants, fungi, animals and humans [70].

So, here we are at the juncture where four major life forms on earth have been living in communities according to their evolutionary statuses. It seems that irrespective of whether creation was by chance or by design, the evolutionists and the creationists agree on one major point that earth and everything on it including the life forms is a product of Singularity. Singularity as we understand is something with infinite nothingness as described by the physicists in their theories mentioned in earlier chapter.

Quran also gives messages on such nothingness and evolutionary diversity in creation when it says, *"I have indeed created you before, when you were nothing"*[71]. Then it says, *"Has there not been a long period of time, when man was nothing, (not even) mentioned?"*[72] Then it says, *"Say: travel in the earth and see how He originated the first creation, then God creates the latter creation; surely God has power over all things"* [73]. It further says, *"What is the matter with you that you fear not the greatness of God, when you see that it is He that has created you in diverse stages?"* [74]

It was verses like these which made the great Sufi Mawlana Rumi once utter;

"I died as a mineral and became a plant,
I died as a plant and rose to animal,
I died animal and I was a man.
Why should I fear? When was I less by dying?
Yet once more I shall die as man, to soar
With angles blest; but even from angelhood
I must pass on: all except God doth perish.
When I have sacrificed my angel-soul,
I shall become what no mind e'er conceived.
Oh, let me not exist! For non-existence
Proclaims in organ tones, To Him we shall return" [75].

This is the Sufi way of explaining the 'Theory of Everything' described by physicists which in Sufi language is called "Hama Oost". Mawlana Rumi goes one step further by asking a question as to what will become of us when we cross the stage of mankind.

This brings us to the discussion on mankind. But before that, I want to add three subjects which are relevant to the continuity of ongoing discussion and their effects on evolution of mankind. They are;

1. The concept of time.
2. The movements of the earth.
3. The movements of the moon.

REFERENCES

1. (Shapiro, Robert (1987). Origins: A Skeptic's Guide to the Creation of Life on Earth. Bantam Books. p. 110. ISBN 0-671-45939-2.)

2. (Dahm, R (Jan 2008). "Discovering DNA: Friedrich Miescher and the early years of nucleic acid research". Human genetics 122: 565–81. doi:10.1007/s00439-007-0433-0. ISSN 0340-6717. PMID 17901982.

3. (Elson D (1965). "Metabolism of nucleic acids (macromolecular DNA and RNA)". Annu. Rev. Biochem. 34: 449–86.)

4. (Oparin, A. I. (1924) Proiskhozhozhdenie zhizny, Moscow (Translated by Ann Synge in Bernal (1967)), The Origin of Life, Weidenfeld and Nicolson, London, pages 199–234.

5. (Oparin, A. I. (1952). The Origin of Life. New York: Dover. ISBN 0-486-49522-1.)

6. ...(Quran, 55:19)

7. ...(Quran, 25:53)

8. (Quran, 37:11).

9. (TV program; 'Life on Earth' by Sir David Attenborough).

10. (Woese, Carl (1967). The Genetic Code: the Molecular basis for Genetic Expression. New York: Harper & Row.)

11. (DNA AND THE BEGINNING OF GENETIC HISTORY - Google Groups).

12. (http://www.dnalc.org/view/16172-Gallery-3-Gregor-Mendel-Manuscript-1865.html)

13. (Title: The Naturalist's View Of Life Author: John Burroughs)

14. (Margaret O'Leary (2008) Anaxagoras and the Origin of Panspermia Theory, iUniverse publishing Group, # ISBN 978-0-595-49596-2)

15. (Zimmer C (August 2009). "Origins. On the origin of eukaryotes". Science 325 (5941): 666–8. doi:10.1126/science.325_666. PMID 19661396.]

16. (http://www.earthlife.net/prokaryotes/welcome.html)

17. (Microbiology, Principles and Explorations 5th Ed., by Jacquelyn G. Black 5th (2002)

18. (Liaisons with Life, by Tom Wakeford (2001)

19. (The Molecular Biology of the Cell, fourth edition. Bruce Alberts, et al. Garland Science (2002) pg. 808 ISBN 0-8153-3218-1)

20. (6Harold F (1 June 1972). "Conservation and transformation of energy by bacterial membranes". Bacteriol Rev 36 (2): 172–230. PMC 408323. PMID 4261111. http://www.pubmedcentral.nih.gov/articlerender.fcgi?tool=pmcentrez&artid=408323]

21. (Hall-Stoodley L, Costerton JW, Stoodley P (February 2004). "Bacterial biofilms: from the natural environment to infectious diseases". Nature Reviews. Microbiology 2 (2): 95–108. doi:10.1038/nrmicro821. PMID 15040259.)

22. (Lear, G; Lewis, GD (editor) (2012). Microbial Biofilms: Current Research and Applications. Caister Academic Press. ISBN 978-1-904455-96-7.)

23. (Karatan E, Watnick P (June 2009). "Signals, regulatory networks, and materials that build and break bacterial biofilms". Microbiology and Molecular Biology Reviews 73 (2): 310–47. doi:10.1128/MMBR.00041-08. PMC 2698413. PMID 19487730. http://mmbr.asm.org/cgi/pmidlookup?view=long&pmid=19487730.)

24. (Kok Gan, Chan; Atkinson, Steve; Kalai Mat hee; Choon-Kook Sam; Siri Ram Chhabra; Miguel Camara; Chong-Lek Koh & Paul Williams (2011). "Characterization of N-Acylhomoserine Lactone-Degrading Bacteria Associated with the Zingiber officinale (ginger) rhizosphere: Co-existence of Quorum Quenching and Quorum Sensing in Acinetobacter and Burkholderia". BMC Microbiology 11: 51. doi:10.1186/1471-2180-11-51. PMC 3062576. PMID 21385437. http://www.biomedcentral.com/1471-2180/11/51/abstract.

25. (Carey D. Nadell1#*, Joao B. Xavier2#, Simon A. Levin1, Kevin R. Foster2* 1 Department of Ecology and Evolutionary Biology, Princeton University, Princeton, New Jersey, United States of America, 2 Center for Systems Biology, Harvard University, Bauer Laboratory, Cambridge, Massachusetts, United States of America)

26. (12 Costerton JW, Lewandowski Z, Caldwell DE, Korber DR, Lappin-Scott HM (1995). "Microbial biofilms". Annu. Rev. Microbiol. 49: 711–45. doi:10.1146/annurev.mi.49.100195.003431. PMID 8561477. http://arjournals.annualreviews.org/doi/abs/10.1146/annurev.mi.49.100195.003431.)

27. (Shapiro JA (1998). "Thinking about bacterial populations as multicellular organisms". Annu. Rev. Microbiol. 52: 81–104. doi:10.1146/annurev.micro.52.1.81. PMID 9891794. http://www.sci.uidaho.edu/newton/math501/Sp05/Shapiro.pdf.)....(27A....http://m.

theepochtimes.com/n3/668208-is-there-a-physical-explanation-for-the-vibes-you-get-off-people/)

28. (Zimmer C (August 2009). "Origins. On the origin of eukaryotes". Science 325 (5941): 666–8. doi:10.1126/science.325 666. PMID 19661396.)

29. (Carl Woese, J Peter Gogarten, "When did eukaryotic cells (cells with nuclei and other internal organelles) first evolve? What do we know about how they evolved from earlier life-forms?" Scientific American, October 21, 1999.)

30. (Brown, J.R. (February 2003). "Ancient Horizontal Gene Transfer". Nature Reviews Genetics 4 (2): 121–132. doi:10.1038/nrg1000. PMID 12560809.)

31. (Forterre P, Philippe H (October 1999). "Where is the root of the universal tree of life?". Bioessays 21 (10): 871–9. doi:10.1002/ (SICI)1521-1878(199910)21:10<871::AID-BIES10>3.0.CO;2-Q. PMID 10497338.)

32. (Poole, Anthony, Jeffares, Daniel, Penny, David (September 1999). "Early evolution: prokaryotes, the new kids on the block". Bioessays 21 (10): 880–9. doi:10.1002/(SICI)1521-1878(199910)21:10<880::AID-BIES11>3.0.CO;2-P. PMID 10497339.)

33. (Woese C (June 1998). "The universal ancestor". Proc. Natl. Acad. Sci. U.S.A. 95 (12): 6854–9. Bibcode 1998PNAS...95.6854W. doi:10.1073/pnas.95.12.6854. PMC 22660. PMID 9618502. http://www.pubmedcentral.nih.gov/articlerender. fcgi?tool=pmcentrez&artid=22660.]

34. (Quran, 67:2-4)

35. (Quran, 15: 27, 29 & 34))

36. (Is a man eukaryotic)

37. (QURANIC CONCEPT OF EVOLUTION)

38. (Becker et al, Wayne M. (2009). The world of the cell. Pearson Benjamin Cummings. p. 480. ISBN 978-0-321-55418-5.)

39. (ref 7.....^ Shih YL, Rothfield L (2006). "The bacterial cytoskeleton". Microbiol. Mol. Biol. Rev. 70 (3): 729–54. doi:10.1128/MMBR.00017-06. PMC 1594594. PMID 16959967.)

40. (Kerfeld, Ca; Sawaya, Mr; Tanaka, S; Nguyen, Cv; Phillips, M; Beeby, M; Yeates, To (August 2005). "Protein structures forming the shell of primitive bacterial organelles.". Science 309 (5736):

936–8. Bibcode 2005Sci...309..936K. doi:10.1126/science.1113397. PMID 16081736.)

41. (Harold F (1 June 1972). "Conservation and transformation of energy by bacterial membranes". Bacteriol Rev 36 (2): 172–230. PMC 408323. PMID 4261111. http://www.pubmedcentral.nih.gov/articlerender.fcgi?tool=pmcentrez&artid=408323.

42. (Takemura, Masaharu (May 2001). "Poxviruses and the origin of the eukaryotic nucleus". Journal of Molecular Evolution 52 (5): 419–425. doi:10.1007/s002390010171. PMID 11443345.)

43. (What are the differences between prokaryotic Cells and eukaryotic)

44. (Ibid)

45. (Ibid)

46. (Animation: Phagocytosis - The McGraw-Hill Companies)

47. (Structures in All Eukaryotic Cells - Shmoop Biology)

48. (What are the differences between prokaryotic Cells and eukaryotic)

49. (Shih YL, Rothfield L (2006). "The bacterial cytoskeleton". Microbiol. Mol. Biol. Rev. 70 (3): 729–54. doi:10.1128/MMBR.00017-06. PMC 1594594. PMID 16959967.)

50. (Michie KA, Löwe J (2006). "Dynamic filaments of the bacterial cytoskeleton". Annu. Rev. Biochem. 75: 467–92. doi:10.1146/annurev. biochem.75.103004.142452. PMID 16756499. http://www2.mrc-lmb.cam.ac.uk/SS/Lowe_J/group/PDF/annrev2006.pdf. [dead link])

51. (Desai A.; and Mitchison TJ; (1997). "Microtubule polymerization dynamics.". Annu Rev Cell Dev Biol 13: 83–117. doi:10.1146/annurev. cellbio.13.1.83. PMID 9442869.)

52. (4141^ a b c d e f Fortey, Richard (September 1999) [1997]. "Dust to Life". Life: A Natural History of the First Four Billion Years of Life on Earth. New York: Vintage Books. ISBN 0-375-70261-X.]:60-61 [3838^ a b c d e f g h i j k l m n o Dawkins, Richard (2004). "All". The Ancestor's Tale: A Pilgrimage to the Dawn of Life. Boston: Houghton Mifflin Company. pp. 67, 95–99, 100–101, 160, 169, 194, 254–256, 293–296, 354, 483–487, 488, 536–539, 563–578, 564–566, 580. ISBN 0-618-00583-8.]:536-539)

53. (Andersson, Siv G. E.; Alireza Zomorodipour, Jan O. Andersson, Thomas Sicheritz-Pontén, U. Cecilia M. Alsmark, Raf M. Podowski, A. Kristina Näslund, Ann-Sofie Eriksson, Herbert H. Winkler, & Charles G. Kurland (November 12, 1998). "The genome sequence of Rickettsia prowazekii and the origin of mitochondria". Nature 396

(6707): 133–140. Bibcode 1998Natur.396..133A. doi:10.1038/24094. PMID 9823893. http://www.nature.com/cgi-taf/DynaPage. taf?file=/nature/journal/v396/n6707/full/396133a0_fs.html.)

54. (Dawkins, Richard (2004). "All". The Ancestor's Tale: A Pilgrimage to the Dawn of Life. Boston: Houghton Mifflin Company. pp. 67, 95–99, 100–101, 160, 169, 194, 254–256, 293–296, 354, 483–487, 488, 536–539, 563–578, 564–566, 580. ISBN_0-618-00583-8. 38]:564-566)

55. (45^ De Marais, David J.; D (September 8, 2000). "Evolution: When Did Photosynthesis Emerge on Earth?". Science 289 (5485): 1703–1705. doi:10.1126/science.289.5485.1703. PMID 11001737. http:// www.sciencemag.org/cgi/content/summary/289/5485/1703. (full text)

56. (Olson, John M. (February 2, 2006). "Photosynthesis in the Archean Era". Photosynthesis Research 88 (2 / May, 2006): 109–17. doi:10.1007/ s11120-006-9040-5. PMID 16453059. http://www.springerlink. com/content/g6n805154602432w/. Retrieved 2010-02-16.)

57. (Is it a plant? Is it an animal? No... - INTP Forum)

58. (Full Text (HTML) - Molecular Biology and Evolution - Oxford Journals)

59. ("Mitochondria Share an Ancestor With SAR11, a Globally Significant Marine Microbe". ScienceDaily. July 25, 2011. http:// www.sciencedaily.com/releases/2011/07/110725190046.htm. Retrieved 2011-07-26.)

60. (J. Cameron Thrash et al. (2011). "Phylogenomic evidence for a common ancestor of mitochondria and the SAR11 clade". Scientific Reports. doi:10.1038/srep00013.)

61. (The Endosymbiotic Theory first postulated by Lynn Margulis in the 1967. also...her 1981 book "Symbiosis in Cell Evolution").

62. (Kimball's Biology Pages, Cell Membranes 2^ a b Alberts B, Johnson A, Lewis J, et al. (2002). Molecular Biology of the Cell (4th ed.). New York: Garland Science. ISBN 0-8153-3218-1. http://www.ncbi.nlm. nih.gov/books/bv.fcgi?rid=mboc4.section.1864.)

63. (Budin, Itay; Devaraj, Neal K. (December 29, 2011). "Membrane Assembly Driven by a Biomimetic Coupling Reaction". Journal of the American Chemical Society 134 (2): 751–753. doi:10.1021/ ja2076873. http://pubs.acs.org/doi/abs/10.1021/ja2076873. Retrieved February 18, 2012.)

64. (Quran, 21: 3)
65. (Quran, 15: 27)
66. (QURANIC CONCEPT OF EVOLUTION)
67. (Chaisson, Eric J. (2005). "Ancient Fossils". Cosmic Evolution. Tufts University. http://www.tufts.edu/as/wright_center/cosmic_evolution/docs/text/text_bio_2.html. Retrieved 2006-03-31.)
68. .(Bhattacharya, Debashish; Linda Medlin (1998). "Algal Phylogeny and the Origin of Land Plants" (PDF). *Plant Physiology* 116 (1): 9–15. doi:10.1104/pp.116.1.9. http://www.iib.unsam.edu.ar/IIB-INTECH/html/docencia/BioVegetal/Evolucion03.pdf. (PDF)
69. (Dawkins, Richard (2004). "All". The Ancestor's Tale: A Pilgrimage to the Dawn of Life. Boston: Houghton Mifflin Company. pp. 67, 95–99, 100–101, 160, 169, 194, 254–256, 293–296, 354, 483–487, 488, 536–539, 563–578, 564–566, 580. ISBN 0-618-00583-8.)
70. ("Two Explosive Evolutionary Events Shaped Early History Of Multicellular Life". February 5, 2012. http://www.sciencedaily.com/releases/2008/01/080103144451.htm.)
71. (Quran, 19:9)
72. (Quran, 76:1).
73. (Quran, 29:20).
74. (Quran, 71:13-14)
75. (en.wikiquote.org/wiki/Rumi)

CHAPTER THREE

The concept of time

The concept of time has been baffling humans from time immemorial and continues to do so till present day. Three versions have emerged which kept the scientists, philosophers and the theosophists busy arguing with each other;

- the relative time,
- the absolute time,
- the imaginary time.

Relative time is taken with reference to a particular environment or situation in the universe.

Absolute time refers to universal standard time-frame which remains uniform at any point in the universe and cannot be comprehended. It resembles what some of us call the 'Hereafter'.

Imaginary time is complex as it is linked with quantum mechanics and is considered running at right angle to the direction of the relative time-flow in the space-time spectrum.

Initially it was Newton's theses regarding metaphysics of space, time and motion mentioned in his work 'Scholium' which paved the way for concepts of relative and absolute time. Keeping the nature of space and motion in relation to time in mind, Newton thought that relative time is measurable while absolute time cannot be measured. This is because he defined the true motion of a body to be its motion through absolute space and thus relevant to absolute time. This meant that absolute time remained constant while relative time was variable according to changes in the earth's rotation. Those who rejected Newton's theses thought that true motion could be analysed in terms of the specifics of the relative motions.

In plain words, the time which we experience is not absolute and is relative to our environment in the universe and depends on factors like mass in our vicinity and its speed in the space. It was Einstein who came up with subject of relativity of time in early 20th century and proved it with theories of relativity showing that time is dependent on mass and velocity. Until then, people generally did not know that time was a relative concept, and that it could change according to the environment.

Having said that, it is interesting to know that Sufis well before these theories knew about the relativity of time. They based their opinion on the Quranic verses which sates;

> "..A day with your Lord is equivalent to a thousand years in the way you count." [1]

Or,

> "He directs the whole affair from heaven to earth. Then it will again ascend to Him on a Day whose length is a thousand years by the way you measure." [2]

Or,

> "The angels and the Spirit ascend to Him in a day whose length is fifty thousand years." [3]

Not only that, the Sufis believe that people can perceive time differently at different occasions. They quote a conversation held between people during life in 'Hereafter', which goes like this;

> "He will say, 'How many years did you tarry on the earth?' They will say, 'We tarried there for a day or part of a day.

Ask those able to count!' He will say, 'You only tarried there for a little while if you did but know!" [4][5]

Thus, three viewpoints emerged which divided philosophers and scientists:

- According to the first view, time passes uniformly regardless what happens in the world as it is part of fundamental structure of the universe. Newton was supporter of this view. He theorized that mathematical (absolute) time passed by independently without disruption by other forces in the universe as he thought time was a dimension of the universe in which events occur in sequence. He called it realistic view of time. Essentially, he was saying that time was as real as the objects that it contains and it could be measured. According to this view, time travel becomes possible as various times behave like frames of a film strip spread out across the time-line. [6][7][8]

- The second view suggests that time is like an empty container in which events may be placed but the container itself exists independently of whether or not anything is placed in it. According to this view, time does not flow along with space and number and is part of a fundamental intellectual structure through which humans sequence and compare events. It is neither measurable nor can it be travelled. Gottfried Leibniz supported this view.

  Comparing the two views, it seems Newton was looking at time more as mathematician than a philosopher while Gottfried was scrutinising it more as a philosopher than a mathematician with regards to space and motion. [9]

- The third view seems to be interesting as it overlaps quantum mechanics with Sufis thinking. Imaginary time is a concept taken from quantum mechanics which is difficult to conceptualise. Theoretically, if we imagine "regular time" as a horizontal line running between 'past' and 'future', the imaginary time would run perpendicular to this line. Being part of space-time warp, imaginary time is dimension as if it were a dimension of space in which one can move forward and backward or move right and left. It is close to Sufis' thought because in term of understanding, imaginary time predicts not only effects we have already observed but also effects we have not been able to measure and yet accept them for other reasons. Imaginary time is also used in cosmology to help smooth out gravitational singularities in models of the universe and to resolve the question as to what happened before the Big Bang. Stephen Hawking popularized the concept in his book 'A Brief History of Time'. It is at this point that one finds a type of convergence between the quantum theories presented by physicists and Quranic verses narrated by the Sufis. [10][11]

Against these three viewpoints, time has become part of a measuring system; to compare the durations of events and intervals between them; to sequence the events; and to quantify rates of change in motions of objects. The measurements in such circumstances can be; spacial which are used to quantify the extent and distances between objects; or temporal which are used to quantify the durations between events.

This understanding is pretty close to Kant's philosophy. He thought of time as a fundamental part of an abstract conceptual framework, together with space and number, within which we sequence events, quantify their duration, and compare the motions of objects. According to him neither time nor space are substances but are elements of systematic mental framework that structure experiences. [12A]

Interestingly this philosophy touches Sufis' thought which says, "the intellect's relativity posits that the intellect's perception manner would render the relative perception of time. Like a key that fits the lock, our intellect also has the capacity of perceiving time and the universe. That is (1) time exists in the universe, (2) and the intellect is created with a priori abilities to perceive time and the universe. The two processes are coexistent, just like the coexistence of the world seen by us and the eyes." [12B] It shows how diversify is Sufism. On one hand it plays harmoniously with science on other hand it scrambles with philosophy.

Despite a major subject of discussion in science, philosophy and religions, time has always been difficult to conceptualise. That is why when it comes to defining it, it becomes puzzling. A simple temporal definition could be that as Einstein put it 'time is what clocks measure' [13A] but that is akin to a blind man touching a leg of an elephant and taking it as whole elephant.

According to temporal measurement, time takes two distinct period forms: the clock [13B] and the calendar, [14]. The clock is used for day-to-day life and the calendar for periods longer than a day.

Tracing the history of clock, we find that Egyptians made the first clock around 1500 BC, as a bent T-square to measure the passage of time from the shadow cast by its crossbar. The T was oriented eastward in the mornings and turned around at noon in the evening direction. In the following centuries markings were calibrated for hours according to local times. Improvement was made when water clocks or *clepsydra* were introduced one of which was found in the tomb of Egyptian Pharaoh Amenhotep I (1525–1504 BC). [15A]

The water clocks measured hours even at night. Arab inventors made more improvements in clocks in the Middle Ages. [15B][15C] It was in the 11th century when Chinese invented the first mechanical clocks driven by escapement mechanism. [15D] Today the most accurate timekeeping devices are atomic clocks which are accurate to seconds during millions of years. [15E}

Talking about calender, artefacts from the Palaeolithic period suggest that time was linked to the moon around 6,000 years ago. Accordingly, lunar calendars were fashioned which had either 12 or 13 lunar months (either 354 or 384 days) [16]

The first lunar calendar was devised by Sumerians in 3000 BC, basing it on the first day of new month. [17] It suffered from disadvantage of having 29.5 days a month, and twelve such months created deficiency of 11 days in a year. Thus constancy of time remained in fluctuation.

In an attempt to correct the inaccuracy, Julius Caesar, on advice of Greek astronomer Sosignes, put the Roman world on a solar calendar and introduced Julian calendar in 45 BC. [18] This calendar was based on 365.25 days a year. But the earth rotates around the Sun in about 365.2422 days. Therefore, the Sun passed through vernal equinox 8 days earlier after the lapse of 1000 years, bringing confusion for the Pope Gregory XIII, in Easter of 1582 AD. He, with help of astronomers, introduced Gregorian calendar, which was identical to the Julian calendar except that century years were not leap years, unless they were divisible by 400, such as the years 1600 and 2000. [19]

Even then, the accuracy of time cannot be maintained, because of gravitational effect of sun and moon over earth. This effect is visible in the form of Spring and Neap tides, which act like brake on rotation of earth, consequently the days are getting longer by 0.001 second every century. Though this number seems tiny, but because of this difference, 380 million years ago a day, known as Devonian day, would last for 22 of present hours, and there were 400 days in a year. [20] In addition to slowing down of earth rotation, the moon is being slowly pushed away from our planet by 2.5 cm (one inch) a year bringing a gradual change in timings of planet earth.

The Gregorian calendar was slowly adopted by different nations and today it is the most commonly used calendar around the world.

The Babylonians, Hinduism, Buddhism, Jainism, and the Native American Tribes have different notion of a wheel of time, in which time repeatedly runs in various cycles of ages as part of changing universe.

Ancient Greek philosophers, Plato, linked time with motion of the heavenly bodies and Aristotle defined it as the number of change with respect to before and after. [21] While a Greek Sophist, Antiphon in 5th century BC proposed that: "Time is not a reality (hypostasis), but a concept (noêma) or a measure (metron)." Parmenides, on other hand, went one step further maintaining that time, motion, and change were illusions. [22]

A French philosopher, Henri Bergson, postulated that time was neither a real homogeneous medium nor a mental construct, but it possessed what he referred to as duration which was creativity and memory that had been an essential component of reality. [23] According to him we do not exist inside time, "we are time". Hence, the relationship to the past is a present awareness of "having been", that allows the past to exist in the present. The relationship with future is different as it is a state of potential anticipation when it comes to thinking of a pending occurrence. This puts one not only "being ahead of oneself" but allows the future to exist in the present. In this way, the present becomes an experience, which is qualitative instead of quantitative enabling us to remember the past and project into the future. [24]

The Judaeo-Christian concept of time is based on the Bible, which considers it linear having a beginning as an act of creation by God and has an end at predestined event. According to this theology as time started by creation, the only thing being infinite is God everything else, including time, is finite.

When St. Augustine of Hippo was asked about time he replied, *'If no one asks me, I know: if I wish to explain it to one that asketh, I know not.'* However, he ended up calling it a 'distension' of the mind by which we simultaneously grasp the past in memory, the present by attention, and the future by expectation.' [25]

Sufis give reverence to time because God called himself 'the time' in Hadith narrated by Abu Hurarayra. [26] So they take the concept of time absolute when they find God calling himself as time or relative when they read God either taking oath on time [27]. or when they read Quran giving various versions of time. For example, they find that a day is equated to fifty thousand years sometimes and one thousand years at other. *'To Him ascend the angels and the spirit in a day the measure of which is fifty thousand years.'* [28] and *'He regulates all affairs from the heaven to the earth. Then they ascend to Him in a day, the measure of which is a thousand years as you count.'* [29]

They stress on the actual meaning of the Arabic word 'yawm' used for day in Quran. They say as there was no notion of 'day' comprising of 24 hours before the creation of universe, therefore, they take 'yawm' as a 'period' when Quran talks about creating universe and the earth in six yawms (days). [30][31][32][33][34][35]. Also according to them, when Quran compares a day of our time with a day (yawm) of that time it points to relativity of time. [36] To put it simply, when a 'day' is used in terms of universal happenings it points to absolute time, but when it is used in comparative term it points to relative time.

To bring inter-religious harmony between the three Abrahamic religions, Sufis find Quran giving continuity to the Biblical message regarding the concept of 'day' when Bible says, *"And on the seventh day God finished His work that He had done, and He rested on the seventh day from all His work that He had done."* [37] They also see Quran improving the Biblical version by saying that God does not get tired and so does not need rest, *"We created the heavens and the earth, and all that lies between them in six days, and no fatigue touched us"* [38]. In this way, Quran opened a window of opportunity for the Jews and Christians to understand Biblical account of creation of the world in six days which should be acceptable to modern science.

Sufis translate the 'periods' mentioned in Quran according to the geological finds which tell us how the universe and our world passed through various 'stages', from a gaseous state to galaxies, to the formation of the atmosphere surrounding the earth, and of waters and metals [39]. Even at human level such evolutionary 'stages' are mentioned in Quranic verse which is pertinent to time when it states, *"It is He Who created you from clay and then decreed a stated term (a reference time frame) for you and there is with Him another term (time frame different from yours). Yet you still doubt"* (this fascinating truth about your creation and the nature of time) [40]

According to psychologists, time seems to pass faster with age. For example, one day of an eleven-year-old boy is approximately 1/4,000 of his life, while one day of a 55-year-old man is approximately

1/20,000 of his life. Accordingly, a day would appear much longer to a young child than to an adult. [41]

The concept of time hit the science world when Einstein came up with 'General theory of relativity' and 'Special theory of relativity', according to which each object or body (including clocks) has its own clock which runs on its own "time". This meant that people travel at different speeds and that clocks run with different times placed in different places. He postulated that time runs fast in space and primarily linked it with two things; 'weak gravity' in space, and 'time dilation'.

'Time dilation' is an interesting phenomenon. [42] It amounts to slowing of 'time' with 'motion' and is taken as part of 'motion-time-dilation'. In simple terms, it means that time is dilated with motion and in the process it slows down. Some scientists consider 'motion-time-dilation' as a disguised form of 'gravity-time-dilation' because they believe, gravity in reality is a disguised motion. These two postulates fall in the Einstein's 'equivalence principle', which simply means that gravitation is equivalent to acceleration (motion). Putting it differently it also means that being at rest on the surface of the earth is equivalent to being inside a spaceship far from any sources of gravity and accelerated by its engines. The first state occurs when the mass in question is acted on by gravity, and the second when the mass is in a state of inertia when it resists forces and accelerations. According to Einstein's principle of equivalence, the given mass is equivalent in both states. [43]

Quran also points at 'time dilation' in a verse in which angels travelling at certain velocity appear to experience slower time than humans. It states, "*The angels and the Spirit ascend to Him in a day, the measure of which is fifty thousand years.*" [44] Here angels (consider them something like dark matter in space) experience 1 day which humans measure as 50,000 years. We should remember that Quran is talking about time vs time, and not, time verses distance. In that sense this verse points specifically at 'time dilation' and this can happen if angels (type of dark matter) accelerate to relativistic speed or they are in a weak gravitational field. Thus the verse agrees with

Einstein's theory of special relativity, which says that a faster moving object appears to experience slower time.

This part of Einstein theory deals with relativity of time in relation to the speed. But what about its relativity to the gravity?

Dealing with gravitational fields, the relativity theory demonstrates that time is slower in the fields of greater gravitation. For example, a man walking on the surface of the sun will find his clock running slow. This principle will apply to all his biological and anatomical functions at the level of his atoms.

Experiments conducted in the British National Institute of Physics by the researcher John Laverty proved these points when he synchronized two clocks indicating the exact time; one of which was kept at a laboratory in London; the other was taken aboard at a high altitude aeroplane shuttling between London and China. He established that the clock aboard the aircraft had a greater speed by one per fifty five billion seconds proving that time is conceived differently according to the medium, place and velocity. In other words, special relativity theory proves that velocity makes time relative and the general relativity theory proves that gravity makes time relative.

Einstein's general and special relativity theories not only changed the concept of time but of space also as he bracketed the two in 'space-time' rather than keeping them separate as 'space' and 'time'. His theories added time as the fourth dimension to already existing three dimensions of height, width, and length of space. This intimacy made him consider 'space' and 'time' elastic, so that when one expands the other shrinks. Similarly, he postulated that time is inversely linked to distances in relation to speed, so that distances appear compressed and time intervals appear lengthened for events associated with objects in motion relative to an inertial observer. Thus he rationalised time with regards to speed and distance in the following equation:

*speed (metres per second; **m/s**) = distance (metre;**m**) / time (seconds; **s**)*

Research work keeps going on to scientifically quantise time. In recent decades, for example, time is made a component ingredient of the International System of Units, which is derived from seven base units of measurement [45]. The system is based on the metre-kilogram-second and is an evolving system the unit definitions of which are modified by international agreements as and when required according to the technology measurement progress. It is the world's most widely practised system of measurement, used both in everyday commerce and in science [46].

To measure; i) temperature, ii) optical radiation, iii) mechanical and electromagnetic quantities, it was decided to devise an international system of six base units comprising of; 1) metre, 2) kilogram, 3) second, 4) ampere, 5) degree kelvin, 6) candela, in 10th General Conference on Weights and Measures (CGPM) held in 1954. Accordingly, these base units were given quantitative names of; length; mass; time; electric current; thermodynamic temperature; and luminous intensity. Four years later in 1960, the 11th CGPM named the system the International System of Units abbreviated as SI. In 1971 seventh unit, 'mole' with quantity name of 'amount of substance' was added to the list which is continuing till the present day.

It is interesting that Sufis also believe in similar SI units. They bracketed them in four groups in which; three international SI Units are placed in the first two groups; light is placed in the third group; and knowledge is added as an additional entity and is made as the fourth group. According to them these groups played essential role not only in creation of universe at the time of Big Bang but also at the making of consciousness at a later stage of evolution. Those groups will be discussed later in a chapter as the 'meeting plane', but for now, they are tabulated as follows.

- Wajood, which covers Length (meter), Mass (Kilogram) and Substance (Mole)
- Shahood, which covers Time (second), Electric current (Ampere), Thermodynamic temperature (kelvin-energy-force)

- Noor, which covers Luminous intensity (Candela)
- Knowledge which is divided into intuition knowledge and logical knowledge

The quantitative units are considered to be the building blocks of physics. Many other quantities can be derived out of their combinations. For instance; a speed is the ratio of a length by a time; acceleration is the ratio of a speed by a time; a force is the multiplication of an acceleration by a mass, and so on. In this way, conventional physics expresses everything against these basic quantities. But when it comes to quantum physics things change, when it challenges certain principles of convention physics.

For example, 'force' which is a pillar of quantum mechanics does not appear in SI 'base quantities'. Although we know that speed and acceleration which play essential role in making 'force' are mathematically derived from length, time and mass. So is "force" a fundamental constituent of the universe as asserted in the quantum physics, or a derived quantity of length, time and mass observed in the convention physics? In quantum physics 'force' has 'time' as its component, which seems to be a 'constituent' of the universe rather than a 'quantity'. Also 'force' seems to be a 'live phenomenon' in quantum physics rather than an 'inert quantity' in convention physics.

It is in contexts such as this that one can find commonalities between Sufism and quantum physics in perceiving the working of universe as both sometimes ignore the principles of convention physics based on mathematical-cum-logical assessments. In other words, logic or mathematics may not be used as the only tools to find reality all the time.

Coming back to time, as there is no physical interaction between time and corporeal phenomenon and as we cannot perceive time physically, we are unable to describe it accurately as an entity. To make it more confusing, time is expressed in terms of two of the seven basic quantitative units namely length and temperature according to the formula, "1 sec = 65 (1 meter) / square root of 1 degree Celsius". This creates doubt about time being a 'fundamental quantity'. In terms of units of SI, it is strange that time unit (second) can be expressed mathematically as a function of 2 other units, namely length (meter) and temperature (Celsius) [47].

Then, there is another way of perceiving time with regards to 'past', 'present', and 'future'. As time depends on the spatial reference frame of the observer, the past is actually the set of events that can send light signals to the observer; the future is the set of events to which the observer can send light signals. And thus the present becomes the light (Illumination) which is the 7th base quantity of SI system. This made scientists postulate an 'arrow of time' which means that time appears to have a direction - the past which is fixed and the future which is not necessarily fixed [48]. They justify 'arrow of time' through the 'entropy law', and 'entropy' is based on degradation of energy, which happens to be transfer of temperature over distance [49]. It is also called the 'dead end'. In this way, they express time as a function of distance and temperature which themselves are first and fifth quantitative units of SI system (time being the third). How can we quantise or rationalise this? Not even that, to make it more confusing physicists tell us that at the speed of light time stops, and temperature drops to absolute zero [50].

To add to the confusion, since 1967 the International System of Measurements has based the second, which is the unit of time, on the radiation emitted by caesium atoms. It thus defines a second as "9,192,631,770 cycles of that radiation which corresponds to the transition between two electron spin energy levels of the ground state of the 133Cs atom" [51] Now, how can that be translated into time we perceive socially when we say, 'I have no or plenty of time', or economically when we utter, 'time is money'; or for that matter even scientifically with vast difference in its concept between convention physics and quantum physics?

As opposed to this notion Standard Model of Particles and Interactions, suggests that time is not quantized. For example, Planck time ($\sim5.4 \times 10^{-44}$ seconds) is considered to be the smallest unit of time that the current physical theories fail to establish and doubt that it could ever will. It disconnected time from Singularity and made it as the starting point of the Big Bang. Writing about it in his book 'A Brief History of Time', and elsewhere Stephen Hawking addressed this issue by stating that time actually began with the Big Bang. Other scientists agree on descriptions of events that happened 10^{-35} seconds after the Big Bang, but what happened before one Plank time (5×10^{-44} seconds) after the Big Bang remain pure speculation.

Hawking received criticisms from philosophers such as Mortimer J. Adler who believed in logic of matter including time [52] To keep the philosophers and naturalist thinkers like Richard Dawkins with strong inclinations towards 'Darwinian logic' and 'Cause and Effect theory' less critical, Hawking expanded his statement carefully by saying that even if time did not begin with the 'Big Bang', nothing that happened then would have any effect upon the present time-frame. To strengthen his position further, he said the questions about what happened before the Big Bang were meaningless [53].

In a nutshell, there has been confusion about time in the fields of science, philosophy and religions. In middle of this confusion, there are tribes in Amazon such as 'Amondawa tribe' that has no abstract concept of time. It even does not have linguistic structure for it. The tribesmen recognise events occurring in time, but do not consider 'time' as a separate concept, so they do not have time periods such as "day", "month" or "year". The people do not refer to their age. They assume different names in different stages of their lives [54].

Finally, a word or two about 'time travel' which is the concept of moving backwards or forwards to different points in time. It is like moving through space, and is different from the normal "flow" of time on earth for an observer. According to this concept all past, present, and future points 'persist' in some unknown way. Time travel has been a subject in fictions since the 19th century. The central problem with time travel to the past is the violation of cause and effect principles and temporal or time paradox. Some scientists believe in probability of time travel in future by accepting the possibility of travel when they accept branch points, parallel realities, or universes [55].

Sufis believe in time travel though they link it with dreams. They quote Sura Kahf in which from three to seven people along with their dog went to sleep in a cave, when they woke up they found that 300 years had already passed. The three hundred years old sleep did not make them look old and they thought they slept for day or part of a day [56].

In short, one of the most important items in our life is time which itself is filled with confusion. Some of us ask questions why should we restrict ourselves to time and why not go back in history when there were no time restrictions? After all, there are tribes in Amazon which are living happily with no concept of time.

After discussing the concept of time let us move to 'the movements of the earth'

REFERENCES

1. (The Qur'an, 22:47)
2. (The Qur'an, 32:5)
3. (The Qur'an, 70:4)
4. (The Qur'an, 23:112-114)
5. (www.answering-christianity.com/time_relativity.ht)
6. (plato.stanford.edu/entries/newton-stm/)
7. (library.thinkquest.org/06aug/02088/newton.htm)
8. (Rynasiewicz, Robert : Johns Hopkins University (2004-08-12). "Newton's Views on Space, Time, and Motion". Stanford Encyclopedia of Philosophy. Stanford University. http://plato.stanford.edu/entries/newton-stm/. Retrieved 2012-02-05. "Newton did not regard space and time as genuine substances (as are, paradigmatically, bodies and minds), but rather as real entities with their own manner of existence as necessitated by God's existence... To paraphrase: Absolute, true, and mathematical time, from its own nature, passes equably without relation to anything external, and thus without reference to any change or way of measuring of time (e.g., the hour, day, month, or year).(Markosian, Ned. "Time". In Edward N. Zalta. The Stanford Encyclopedia of Philosophy (Winter 2002 Edition). http://plato.stanford.edu/entries/time/#3. Retrieved 2011-09-23. "The opposing view, normally referred to either as "Platonism with Respect to Time" or as "Absolutism with Respect to Time," has been defended by Plato, Newton, and others. On this view, time is like an empty container into which events may be placed; but it is a container that exists independently of whether or not anything is placed in it.")
9. (Gottfried Martin, Kant's Metaphysics and Theory of Science]... (Burnham, Douglas : Staffordshire University (2006). "Gottfried Wilhelm Leibniz (1646–1716) Metaphysics – 7. Space, Time, and Indiscernibles". The Internet Encyclopedia of Philosophy. http://www.iep.utm.edu/leib-met/#H7. Retrieved 2011-04-09. "First of all, Leibniz finds the idea that space and time might be substances or substance-like absurd (see, for example, "Correspondence with Clarke," Leibniz's Fourth Paper, §8ff). In short, an empty space would be a substance with no properties; it will be a substance that even God cannot modify or destroy.... That is, space and time are internal or intrinsic features of the complete concepts of things, not

extrinsic.... Leibniz's view has two major implications. First, there is no absolute location in either space or time; location is always the situation of an object or event relative to other objects and events. Second, space and time are not in themselves real (that is, not substances). Space and time are, rather, ideal. Space and time are just metaphysically illegitimate ways of perceiving certain virtual relations between substances. They are phenomena or, strictly speaking, illusions (although they are illusions that are well-founded upon the internal properties of substances).... It is sometimes convenient to think of space and time as something "out there," over and above the entities and their relations to each other, but this convenience must not be confused with reality. Space is nothing but the order of co-existent objects; time nothing but the order of successive events. This is usually called a relational theory of space and time.") (Mattey, G. J. : UC Davis (1997-01-22). "Critique of Pure Reason, Lecture notes: Philosophy 175 UC Davis". http://www-philosophy.ucdavis. edu/mattey/kant/TIMELEC.HTM.Retrieved 2011-04-09. "What is correct in the Leibnizian view was its anti-metaphysical stance. Space and time do not exist in and of themselves, but in some sense are the product of the way we represent things. They are ideal, though not in the sense in which Leibniz thought they are ideal (figments of the imagination). The ideality of space is its mind-dependence: it is only a condition of sensibility.... Kant concluded "absolute space is not an object of outer sensation; it is rather a fundamental concept which first of all makes possible all such outer sensation."...Much of the argumentation pertaining to space is applicable, mutatis mutandis, to time, so I will not rehearse the arguments. As space is the form of outer intuition, so time is the form of inner intuition.... Kant claimed that time is real, it is "the real form of inner intuition.") (McCormick, Matt : California State University, Sacramento (2006). "Immanuel Kant (1724–1804) Metaphysics: 4. Kant's Transcendental Idealism". The Internet Encyclopedia of Philosophy. http://www.iep. utm.edu/kantmeta/#H4. Retrieved 2011-04-09. "Time, Kant argues, is also necessary as a form or condition of our intuitions of objects. The idea of time itself cannot be gathered from experience because succession and simultaneity of objects, the phenomena that would indicate the passage of time, would be impossible to represent if we did not already possess the capacity to represent objects in time....

Another way to put the point is to say that the fact that the mind of the knower makes the a priori contribution does not mean that space and time or the categories are mere figments of the imagination. Kant is an empirical realist about the world we experience; we can know objects as they appear to us. He gives a robust defense of science and the study of the natural world from his argument about the mind's role in making nature. All discursive, rational beings must conceive of the physical world as spatially and temporally unified, he argues.")

10. (en.wikipedia.org/wiki/Imaginary_time)
11. (library.thinkquest.org/27930/time.htm)
12. A. Kant's Views on Space and Time (Stanford Encyclopedia of ...
12B (https://syedjehu.wordpress.com/2012/01/
13. A...(www.askamathematician.com/2009/11/q-what-is-time/)
13B .(HISTORY OF CLOCKS – HistoryWorld)
14. (A Brief History of the Calendar)
15. (15a)(www.thefreedictionary.com/clepsydra)(15b)(Ibn al-Razzaz Al-Jazari (ed. 1974) The Book of Knowledge of Ingenious Mechanical Devices, Translated and annotated by Donald Routledge Hill, Dordrecht / D. Reidel, part II.) (15c)(en.wikipedia.org/wiki/Al-Jazari)(15d)(Needham, Volume 4, 445; Needham, Volume 4, 448; Bodde, 140; Fry, 10.) (15e)(en.wikipedia.org/wiki/Atomic_clock)
16. (Rudgley, Richard (1999). The Lost Civilizations of the Stone Age. New York: Simon & Schuster. pp. 86–105).
17. (history-world.org/sumeria.htm)
18. (www.tondering.dk/claus/cal/julian.php)
19. (The Gregorian calendar - Time and Date)
20. (www.miguasha.ca/mig-en/a_devonian_day.php)
21. (Dagobert Runes, Dictionary of Philosophy, p. 318)
22. (Harry Foundalis. "You are about to disappear". http://www.foundalis.com/phi/WhyTimeFlows.htm. Retrieved 2011-04-09.) Time as an illusion is also a common theme in Buddhist thought. (Huston, Tom. "Buddhism and the illusion of time". http://www.buddhasvillage.com/teachings/time.htm. Retrieved 2011-04-09.) (Garfield, Jay L. (1995). The fundamental wisdom of the middle way: Nāgārjuna's Mūlamadhyamakakārikā. New York: Oxford University Press. ISBN 978-0-19-509336-0. http://books.google.com/?id=kfsyfoO1IlYC&pg=RA1-PR19&dq=The+fundamental+wisdom+of+the+middle+way+time#v=onepage&q&f=false.

23. (Bergson, Henri (1907) Creative Evolution. trans. by Arthur Mitchell. Mineola: Dover, 1998.)

24. (Martin Heidegger (1962). "V". Being and Time. p. 425. ISBN 9780631197706. http://books.google.com/?id=S57m5gW0L-MC&pg=PA425&lpg=PA425&dq=heidegger+sequence#v=onepage&q=heidegger%20sequence&f=false.)

25. (Augustine of Hippo. Confessions. http://en.wikisource.org/wiki/Nicene_and_Post-Nicene_Fathers:_Series_I/Volume_I/Confessions/Book_XI/Chapter_14. Retrieved 2011-04-09. Book 11, Chapter 14)

26. (Bukhari 6 Hadith 351)

27. (Quran, 103:1)

28. (Quran, 70:4)

29. (Quran, 32:5)

30. (Quran, 7:54,)

31. (Qurn, 11:7)

32. (Quran, 10:3)

33. (Quran 25:59)

34. (Quran, 32:4)

35. (Quran, 57:4)

36. (Quran 70:4, 32:5).

37. (Genesis 2,2).

38. (Quran, 50:38)

39. (Find out)

40. (Quran 6:2)

41. (Time perception - Wikipedia, the free encyclopedia)

42. (www.thebigview.com/spacetime/timedilation.html)

43. (rqgravity.net/TheEquivalencePrinciple)

44. (Quran, 70:4)

45. (Ian Mills (29 September 2010). "Draft Chapter 2 for SI Brochure, following redefinitions of the base units". CCU. http://www.bipm.org/utils/en/pdf/si_brochure_draft_ch2.pdf.).

46. (Official BIPM definitions). (Essentials of the SI: Introduction). (An extensive presentation of the SI units is maintained on line by NIST, including a diagram of the interrelations between the derived units based upon the SI units. Definitions of the basic units can be found on this site, as well as the CODATA report listing values for special constants such as the electric constant, the magnetic constant

and the speed of light, all of which have defined values as a result of the definition of the metre and ampere. In the International System of Units (SI) (BIPM, 2006), the definition of the metre fixes the speed of light in vacuum c0, the definition of the ampere fixes the magnetic constant (also called the permeability of vacuum) μ0, and the definition of the mole fixes the molar mass of the carbon 12 atom M(12C) to have the exact values given in the table [Table 1, p.7]. Since the electric constant (also called the permittivity of vacuum) is related to μ0 by $\varepsilon0 = 1/\mu0c02$, it too is known exactly.)

47. (does-time-exist.info/time-torn-to-pieces.html)
48. (en.wikipedia.org/wiki/Arrow_of_time)
49. (en.wikipedia.org/wiki/Entropy_(arrow_of_time)
50. (What happens at absolute zero? - physics-math - 17 February 2010)
51. (andersoninstitute.com/history-of-time-measurement-devices.html)
52. (Adler, Mortimer J., Ph.D.. "Natural Theology, Chance, and God". http://radicalacademy.com/adlertheology1.htm. Retrieved 2011-04-09. "Hawking could have avoided the error of supposing that time had a beginning with the Big Bang if he had distinguished time as it is measured by physicists from time that is not measurable by physicists.... an error shared by many other great physicists in the twentieth century, the error of saying that what cannot be measured by physicists does not exist in reality." "The Great Ideas Today". Encyclopædia Britannica. 1992.) (Adler, Mortimer J., Ph.D.. "Natural Theology, Chance, and God". http://radicalacademy.com/adlertheology2.htm. Retrieved 2011-04-09. "Where Einstein had said that what is not measurable by physicists is of no interest to them, Hawking flatly asserts that what is not measurable by physicists does not exist - has no reality whatsoever with respect to time, that amounts to the denial of psychological time which is not measurable by physicists, and also to everlasting time — time before the Big Bang — which physics cannot measure. Hawking does not know that both Aquinas and Kant had shown that we cannot rationally establish that time is either finite or infinite." "The Great Ideas Today". Encyclopædia Britannica. 1992.)
53. (Hawking, Stephen (1996). "The Beginning of Time". University of Cambridge. http://www.hawking.org.uk/index.php/lectures/publiclectures/62. Retrieved 2011-04-09. "Since events before the Big Bang have no observational consequences, one may as well cut

them out of the theory, and say that time began at the Big Bang. Events before the Big Bang, are simply not defined, because there's no way one could measure what happened at them. This kind of beginning to the universe, and of time itself, is very different to the beginnings that had been considered earlier.") (Hawking, Stephen (1996). "The Beginning of Time". University of Cambridge. http://www.hawking.org.uk/index.php/lectures/62. Retrieved 2011-04-09. "The conclusion of this lecture is that the universe has not existed forever. Rather, the universe, and time itself, had a beginning in the Big Bang, about 15 billion years ago.") (Hawking, Stephen (2006-02-27). "Professor Stephen Hawking lectures on the origin of the universe". University of Oxford. http://www.ox.ac.uk/media/news_stories/2006/060227.html. Retrieved 2011-04-09. "Suppose the beginning of the universe was like the South Pole of the earth, with degrees of latitude playing the role of time. The universe would start as a point at the South Pole. As one moves north, the circles of constant latitude, representing the size of the universe, would expand. To ask what happened before the beginning of the universe would become a meaningless question because there is nothing south of the South Pole.") (Ghandchi, Sam : Editor/Publisher (2004-01-16). "Space and New Thinking". http://www.ghandchi.com/312-SpaceEng.htm. Retrieved 2011-04-09. "and as Stephen Hawking puts it, asking what was before Big Bang is like asking what is North of North Pole, a meaningless question.")

54. (Mail Online dated Thursday, Apr 12 2012)
55. (Eternalism (philosophy of time) - Wikipedia, the free encyclopedia)
56. (Quran 18:1-110)

CHAPTER FOUR

The movements of the earth

---- ❖ ----

The earth is involved in various movements, each of which affects time, evolution and human development. These movements have also been changing the shape of the earth with the passage of time. For example, we know that the earth, with its elevation of 13 miles around the equator, is not truly spherical. Because of this bulge, it is flat at its poles [1].

It is for this reason, some Sufis consider it 'egg shaped' – as translated from the word '*daha*, used for earth in Quran – while others translate it as 'spread out'. But the correct meaning of the term, keeping in view its root '*d h a*', provides clear Quranic evidence in support of the 'spherical shape', for *dahâ* means "to shape like an egg", while its noun *dahiyah* is still used by Arabs to mean an egg [2][3].

We also know that as part of our Solar System, the earth is involved in four different movements;

1. It moves around the sun in elliptical orbit at speed of 66,600 miles an hour (18.5 miles/second) [4].
2. It rotates around its tilted axis of *23.5°* with a speed of about 1,000 miles an hour. The tilt is called the 'obliquity' [5].

The elliptical journey and the axial rotation of these two movements are counter-clockwise in direction. As a result of these motions, the sun rises from the east and sets in the west, lightening half of the earth, simultaneously bringing seasonal and other changes like day and night.

3. The third motion is called the 'nod'. Through this movement the earth changes its 'obliquity' angle, between 22.1° to 24.5°. This motion is also called 'nutation' and was discovered in 1728 by the British astronomer James Bradley. At present, this angle stands at 23.5°. This means the earth has just crossed the halfway point of the 'nod' by 0.4° [6].

4. The fourth motion is called 'wobble'. 'Wobble' is caused by the gravitational forces of the sun, moon and the other planets which not only make the path of the earth elliptical, but because of its protruding equator and the obliquity angle, makes it wobbles in a clockwise direction, just like a revolving top would wobble in its spin. This is called 'precession' [13].

As a result of these motions, the earth takes 24 hours to spin around its own axis; 365.26 days to circle the sun; and 41,000 years to 'nod' between 22.1° to 24.5°. So in all, the earth moves in space in four major directions by four different means. Every movement has seasonal effects on the earth and thus on its evolutionary processes [14].

The Sufis have been saying about the shape of earth and its movements in space for 1400 years supporting their argument by presenting Quranic verses which not only emphasize '*dahaha*' and its derivatives, but they also state that all celestial bodies are '*Yaa'rujoon*', which means 'travelling in orbits in space'. The Arabic words *Ma'arij*', *Urooj*', *'Arj*', *and Me'araaj*' all refer to "going in an orbital and curvy path" [7] or "gliding along smoothly in its orbit" [8].

In another place Quran says, "*He created the heavens and the earth with true (wisdom) He rolls the night over the days and rolls the day over the night, He has subdued the sun and the moon. All running for an appointed time*" [9]. The Arabic word '*Yukawwar*' has been used for rolling night over day. The word means to coil or to roll on an axis, pointing at the circular movement of earth on its axis. Furthermore, coiling or rolling of a thing happens only when that thing has spherical or circular shape [10]. Then at another place, the Quran says, "*And of his signs is this that the heaven and the earth keep to their (appointed) places i.e. to their orbits by His command*" [11]. Although Quran doesn't give the exact speed of the earth to be 66,600 miles per hour but it does say that, "*It is flying with the flight of clouds*" [12].

Coming back to the movements, let us take the cycle of 'precession' as an example. According to Graham Hancock [15], this important motion is our planet's characteristic 'signature' within the solar system. One such precession cycle takes 25,776 years to complete. During one cycle, the earth's polar axes point to specific stars in the celestial sphere in a regular and predictable manner which can be measured with mathematical accuracy. Thus, with help of computers, the knowledge of this motion makes it possible to calculate precisely the identity of the polar star (presently Alpha Ursae Minoris) at 10,000 BC or 10,000 AD. This find has a long lasting effect on our understanding about human history.

For example, if the age of an ancient monument could be accurately determined through these scientifically established movements, it would be possible to give validity to the pre historic writings linked to those monuments. This may also be applicable to myths and writings found in religious scriptures related to the chronology of such monuments [16].

Investigations such as this were also tackled by Professor Giorgio de Santillana of the Massachusetts Institute of Technology, along with Dr. Hertha von Dechend, in a book published in 1969, entitled 'Hamlet's Mill, An Essay on Myth and the Frame of Time'. The book focused on the connection between the mythological stories and the ancient observations pertaining to stars, planets and, most notably, the 26,000 years' precession of the equinoxes [17].

These and similar writings make it possible to link, pre-historical mythical, religious or scientific events and help eliminating misunderstanding created by its followers.

Among all the spinning, nodding and wobbling celestial movements of the earth, it is the elliptical movement which takes the sun furthest from the equator twice a year. This shift causes variations in the amount of heat created in different parts of the earth, affecting life forms thereon. Other important changes it brings on earth are the seasons. Depending on whether the sun is furthest from equator or nearest, four locations become cardinal in the cycle of precession. They are the two 'Solstices' and two 'Equinoxes', one each belonging to both summer and winter.

In the northern hemisphere, the 'summer solstice' falls on June 21, when the sun is furthest north from the equator and lights up the earth, making that day the longest and night the shortest of the year. Conversely, the opposite happens on this day in southern hemisphere where winter reigns supreme, and the day is the shortest and the night the longest of the year.

Similarly, the 'winter solstice' falls on December 21, when the sun is furthest south from the equator and throws the least amount of light on earth, making it the shortest day and longest night. Again, the opposite happens on this day in southern hemisphere where summer prevails.

These are two extreme positions of the sun, in which days and nights are stretched to their extremes. As opposed to this, twice in a year, day and night are equal in duration in both the northern and southern hemispheres. These are called 'equinoxes'. Thus, there is the 'spring equinox' which falls on March 21, and the 'autumn equinox' that falls on September 22 [18].

The two extreme positions of the sun result in sun rising and setting at two different positions in summer and winter making the direction of west and east variable to our naked eyes. Sufis open dialogue on this subject by quoting a verse from the Quran which says, *"He is the lord of the east and west, there is no God but He, take him therefore for {thy} disposer of affairs"*[19]. Then, it goes on to give various positions of sunrise and sunset, indicating the 'equinoxes' and 'solstices' when it talks of two easts and wests: *"He is the lord of the 2 Easts and 2 Wests"*[20]. It goes yet further to point at multiple locations between the two extremes of the 'solstices' when it says, *"He is the lord of all the easts"* [21] Or, when it says, *"now I do call to witness, the Lord of all the points in east and in west"* [22]. Then, pointing at the two 'solstices and equinoxes', the Quran also says, *"At length when such a one comes to us, he says to his evil partner, would that between me and you were the distance between 2 easts"* [23]. Finally, challenging the human psyche on the subject of Quranic knowledge, it says, *"verily we have brought humanity a scripture which we expound with knowledge"* [24]. We should remember that Quran mentioned this 1400 years ago.

It is pertinent to mention that these positions or points also move with the various movements of the earth. For example, if we look down on earth from the north pole, the equinoxes appear to be rotating in a clockwise motion, as opposed to all other counter-clockwise movements, completing a full circle in 25,800 years. In this way, the equinoxes move at a rate of about 50.27 arc seconds per year. This phenomenon is known as the precession of the equinoxes and plays important role in seasonal changes [25].

These changing positions were crucial for agriculture, astrology, and mythology in ancient times, as they are today in religious beliefs, in the spheres of science, mathematics, and astronomy. These positions were and still are significant because of their role in changing weather that effects agriculture and so the very survival of the human race. Moreover, the sunrise and the sunset became important directional links as east and west in the history of mankind.

It is clear from scientific and religious points of view that the movements of the earth played a fundamental role in the evolution of science and religions as part of the overall evolution of the planet earth. Quantum physics can be taken as the latest evolutionary phase from science and the Quran as part of the last organized religion of Islam. A large number of followers of Quantum physics in science and Quran in religions, are finding important converging points which if understood correctly will benefit human race.

It is interesting to find that common pedagogics of these two apparently diversifying subjects affect our day to day life without being noticed. And it is this ignorance in noting which has widened the gap we see today between science and religions. The question is what could be done to highlight those ignored common pedagogics? The answer lies in creating venues for opening discussions between scientists and religious custodians. Non-religious academicians and scholars can be added to the list to widen the scope of discussions for the good of humanity. Such venues would spread message of fraternal proximity.

This aspect will be discussed in the last chapter. For now, let us discuss the movements of the moon which has similar effects on our life.

REFERENCES

1. (*www.scientificamerican.com/article.cfm?id=earth-is-not-round*)
2. (*79:30*)
3. (3M. FATHÎ 'UTHMAN, *"Al-'ard Fî al-Qur'ân al-Karâm"*, *Proceedings of the First Islamic Geographical Conference*", Riyadh, 1404/1984, Vol. IV, 127; A. M. SOLIMAN, *Scientific Trends in teh Qur'ân*, London (Ta-Ha Publications), 1985, p. 16. (M. Mohar Ali, *The Qur'ân and the Orientalists*, Jam'iyat 'Ihyaa' Minhaaj Al-Sunnah 2004, p.75)
4. (www.physlink.com/education/askexperts/ae548.cfm)
5. (*https://en.wikipedia.org/wiki/Axial_tilt*)
6. (*en.wikipedia.org/wiki/Nutation*)
7. (Quran, 32:5, 34:2, 57:4, 70:3-4),
8. (21:34)
9. (39:6).
10. (Chapter V - The Quran and Science)
11. (30:25)
12. (27:88)
13. (*en.wikipedia.org/wiki/Milankovitch_cycles*)
14. (Earth's Rotation)
15. (Graham Hancock)
16. (FINGERPRINTS OF THE GODS - Meg Pugh)
17. (*en.wikipedia.org/wiki/Giorgio_de_Santillana*)
18. (Equinox and Solstice Guide)
19. (Quran,73:9).
20. (Quran,55:17).
21. (Quran,37:15).
22. (Quran, 70:40).
23. (Quran, 43:38).
24. (Quran, 7:52)
25. (The Earth, Sun, and Moon - Library)

CHAPTER FIVE

The movements of the moon

―――――――――― ✤ ――――――――――

The moon is as important to life forms on earth as the earth itself is. It plays a crucial role in making the earth liveable for mankind. Through that perspective, one can study about its origin, its effect on earth, its role in the evolution of earth, and what would have happened had there been no moon or what could likely happen if it disappears from the scene.

We know the earth did not have a moon initially. An object about the size of Mars, called Theia, collided with it at an oblique angle about 4.5 billion years ago. The cloud of molten rock raised as a result of impact formed the moon. The collision not only created the moon but it also had a profound effect on earth. It changed earth's axis and its rotation in orbit. It initiated the four movements of earth discussed in the last chapter and consequently changed its future evolution [1].

We have already viewed this scenario as perceived by the Sufis through verses of Quran.

The changes which followed were manifold. For example, the earth started rotating faster than the moon orbiting around it, and although the gravity of the moon was six times less than the earth [2], it's gravitational attraction pulled water on earth towards the moon causing tidal bulges. The pull created friction as the land rotated under the tidal bulge pulling the earth backwards and acted like brake, slowing down its rotation. As a result, the distance between the earth and moon is increasing, and the earth's spin is slowing down [3].

The tidal braking affected the moon also. It pulled the moon forward speeding up its rotation, which not only caused its orbit to slowly increase but also to move it away from earth at a rate of 3.82 cm per year. This was confirmed by experiments with laser reflectors left during the Apollo missions [4]. Because of these actions, the moon continues to slow down the rotation of earth by 0.002 seconds per century. Atomic clocks show that the earth's day lengthens by about 15 microseconds every year [5]. This seemingly trivial slowing down of the earth has prolonged the earth-day from 5 hours at the beginning to 24 hours today [6].

The moon is our closest neighbour in space and the brightest object in the night sky, which is gliding in its orbit at a distance of about 238,857 miles from earth. It takes six days to travel to and from the moon by rocket. In size, it is 2,160 miles across and has not changed much over millenniums. Its atmosphere has no air, wind, or vapours, while its soil has no water, making its surface lifeless and uninhabitable. The soil contains no fossils of plants or animals, but when the same was placed on the plants here on earth, plants grew even better than in ordinary soil from our planet. The sky, viewed from the surface of the moon appears black, while the stars are visible all the time.

The Quran mentions various celestial bodies, including the moon, taking different orbits and moving with different motions in space when it says, *"It is He who created the night and the day, and the sun and the moon, all (the celestial bodies) swim along, each in its orbit."* [7] Or when it says, *"The sun must not catch up the moon nor does the night outstrip the day. Each one is traveling in an orbit with its own motion"* [8].

It gives special attention to its brightness in relation to the sun, when it says, *"And made the moon a light (Noor) in their midst and made the sun as a Lamp (Siraja)"* [9]. It is pertinent to note that the Quran mentions the sun as *Siraj* which in Arabic means a mass of fire that produces light and uses the term *Noor* or light for the moon to highlight its brightness and portrays that moon does not produce light.

Because it is the brightest object amongst all other celestial bodies in the night sky, it has played an important role in the history of mankind; be that in relation to time, calendar, agriculture or other social activities that the Quran mentions with reference to the moon.

From earth, the surface of the moon appears smooth with dark and light patches of grey. In 1609, Galileo Galilei drew one of the first telescopic drawings in his book. Sidereus Nunciusand noted that it is not smooth but has mountains and craters [10]. The dark patches correspond to plains, called 'Maria' [11]. These were formed from flowing lava about 3.3 to 3.8 billion years ago [12]. The light spots are mountainous areas, called 'Terrae' or the 'highlands' [13]. There are countless craters on the moon made by impacts of meteorites. The largest crater is the Imbrium Basin, which is 700 miles wide. Its floor is covered by dark lava, forming the "eye" of the 'face' of the moon, which we observe from earth [14].

The far side of the moon which is also called the 'dark side' is not really dark. It is as often illuminated as the near side but we cannot see it during that period as the near side then is dark [15].

The gravitational attraction between earth and the moon stabilizes the crucial tilt of the earth between 22.1° and 24.5°. It stands at 23.5° today. This stabilized tilt gives earth its predictable climates and seasons. Because of this stability, the moon rotates around its tilted axis of 1.54° from west to east at the speed of 4.627 miles/second [16]. At the same time, it travels around the earth from west to east at 2,300 miles per hours in an elliptical orbit to cover 1.5 million miles of its journey. In doing so, it also circles the sun along with the earth. Since the orbit is elliptical, the moon is not always the same distance away from the earth. Because of this asymmetry, the point where it comes closest to the earth is called 'perigee' which is 221,456 miles, while the farthest point, 'apogee', is 252,711 miles [17].

Despite these asymmetrical motions and positions, we still see the same side of the moon, because it rotates exactly the same length of time as it takes to orbit the earth. So all we see is the same side changes from a crescent to a full circle and back. It is interesting that Quran talks of this movement in a very meaningful way when it says, *"And We have decreed set phases for the moon, until it ends up looking like an old date branch, dried up and curved."* [18] As one can see the verse uses the words *'old dried up date-tree branch'*. According to Arab traditions, when the date-tree branch gets old, it twists into a shape that resembles the English letter 'S'. Recent investigations have shown that the asymmetrical motion of moon is because it moves around earth in 'S shaped orbit'. It is this type of orbital movement which is one of the important reasons for the peculiar relationship that exists between earth and moon. It is also what present life forms on earth and ongoing evolution depend upon.

The changes we see as a result of such movements are due to different amounts of sunlight thrown at the moon and reflected at the earth, making different parts of the moon's surface visible to us as it moves around the earth. In this way, more and more of the moon's sunlit side comes to view each day until after 14 days, the moon moves to a position where the earth is between it and the sun, showing us its full face. Then the sunlit side begins to recede gradually, until it turns completely dark in another period of 14 days, getting ready for the next cycle.

Also, because of this stability, the moon completes a circle around the earth in approximately 27.3 days changing its position relative to the stars [19]. As there are 360 degrees in a circle, this movement comes to 13.2 degrees per day or just over half a degree per hour relative to the stars. It also means that it moves a few inches every night or one diameter every hour to the east among the stars.

It is also interesting that Quran links number 28 to the moon in a mathematical way. For example, the moon is mentioned 28 times; exactly the number of times and phases it appears to the inhabitants of earth. We know that it takes approximately 28 days for the moon to revolve around the earth and 28 days to rotate around its axis. It is pertinent to note that the Arabic word قمر, "moon" is mentioned directly and indirectly 28 times in 27 verses. So no matter how one looks at it, it seems that Quranic numbers 28 and 27 fall in some harmony with recently discovered number of 27.35 [20].

Although the moon and the earth both are moving eastward, due to the difference in their speeds we see the moon rising from the east and setting in the west. The same relative principle applies to moon's motion with other stars; as a result, the moon rises and sets a little later than other stars. And because of this disparity in the motions of celestial bodies, the moon rises and sets later and later every day, until it completes it circle in 27.35 days, when it is back in its original position.

Although the ancient Greek philosopher Anaxagoras (d. 428 BC) reasoned that moon reflected the light of the sun [21], most scientists, astrologists and the philosophers believed that moon was an illuminating object and was emitting light. For example, the astronomer and physicist Alhazen (965–1039) theorized that sunlight was emitted from every part of the moon's sunlit surface in all directions [22]. In the following centuries, scientists confirmed that moon reflects sunlight and does not emit it.

In this regard, the Sufis agree with the Greek philosopher, but they take the lead from a Quranic verse which states, *"Blessed is He who made constellations in the skies, and placed therein a lamp and a moon reflecting light"* [23]. According to the theosophist and religious scholar Dr. Zakir Naik in his video *'Is the Qur'an God's Word?'*, "The Arabic word for moon is 'qamar' and the light described there is 'muneer' which is borrowed light, or 'noor' which is a reflection of light" [24].

The gravitational pull of the moon on earth causes two tidal bulges seen as ocean tides. Because of variations in gravitational interplay between the moon, the earth and the sun which follow their own elliptical paths, the ocean tides appear; in twenty-four hours; in a month; and in seasons such as spring and neap tides respectively [25]. These tidal drags will continue until the spins of the earth and the moon are matched, which will also mean the end of the moon. However, before reaching that point, the end of the sun will likely occur first, when it starts bloating into a red giant, swallowing all the inner planets including the moon. According to scientists, "During the red giant phase the Sun will swell until its distended atmosphere reaches out to envelop the earth and moon" [26].

Sufis refer this event by quoting the Quran, which states, *"And He subjected the sun and the moon (to his law); each one runs its course for a term appointed."* [27]. And that appointed term is described as a time when,"...*the sun and moon are joined together"* [28][29].

Finally, what if we never had a moon? That is, if about 4.5 billion years ago, Theia had passed by without striking earth. Well, in that case, without the moon, the crucial regulatory tilt between 22.1° and 24.5° would not have existed and axis would have continued to wobble as does that of the moonless planet Mars, disrupting the solstices and equinoxes with disastrous consequences to the seasons we are used to. Also, without the moon, planet earth would have been subjected to the pull of the other planets as they orbited the sun, making it move haphazardly in different directions like a see-saw, leading evolution in a different direction from the one we are going through.

There most probably would have been a very long course of evolution with small changes in earth's environment. The earth would be a completely different place, where a day would last for only 8-10 hours. Having no moon to slow it down, the faster rotation would cause winds of 160-200 km to sweep the surface of the earth. The tilt axis of earth would wobble, resulting in dramatic changes in temperature. And although the seas would still be tidal, the tides would be much smaller, caused only by the sun. Life of some sort would probably exist as a result of minute adaptations that organisms make to their environment, but humans almost certainly wouldn't exist. I wouldn't be writing this book and you wouldn't be reading it.

This was a brief scenario of the earth without a moon. But what if, for some reason, the moon suddenly disappears? What would happen to earth, and for that matter, to us humans? In such a scenario, humans would have to evolve to survive an entirely different environment. These changes would occur over the course of thousands, nay, millions of years. During that period, the earth would develop extreme temperatures, high winds, small tides and short days. During the process of evolution, new life forms would emerge and many existing livings would become extinct. Similarly, because of temperature changes, the ice in the poles would melt causing the oceans to rise, changing coastlines all around the world, drowning countries in reachable regions such as the Netherlands and adjacent countries in the northern hemisphere as well as New Zealand and Australia in the southern hemisphere [30][31].

So we should be thankful to Theia hitting our planet and giving us moon which helped us-the humans, the way we are today.

With this, I will move to the history of mankind.

REFERENCE

1. (http://news.nationalgeographic.com/news/2007/12/071219-moon-collision.html)
2. (Moon's Gravity)
3. (Touma, Jihad; Wisdom, Jack (1994). "Evolution of the Earth-Moon system". The Astronomical Journal 108 (5)
4. (Chapront, J.; Chapront-Touzé, M.; Francou, G. (2002). "A new determination of lunar orbital parameters, precession constant and tidal acceleration from LLR measurements". Astronomy and Astrophysics 387 (2):)
5. (Ray, R. (15 May 2001). "Ocean Tides and the Earth's Rotation". IERS Special Bureau for Tides.)
6. (Touma & Wisdom, 1998).
7. (Quran 21:33)
8. (Quran, 36:40)
9. (Quran, 71:16)
10. (The Starry Messenger)
11. (Wlasuk, Peter (2000). Observing the Moon. Springer. p. 19.)
12. (Moon - Wikipedia, the free encyclopedia)
13. (G. Jeffrey Taylor (April 30, 2006). "Finding Basalt Chips from Distant Maria". Planetary Science Research Discoveries. http://www.psrd.hawaii.edu/April06/basaltFragments.html.)
14. (Mare Imbrium - Wikipedia, the free encyclopedia)
15. (Dark side of the Moon)
16. (Hamilton, Calvin J.; Hamilton, Rosanna L., The Moon, Views of the Solar System, 1995–2011)
17. (Quaest.io on Moon)
18. (Quran, 36:39)
19. (Ancient Timekeepers, Part 4: Calendars — World Mysteries Blog)
20. (Moon is mentioned 28 times in the Noble Quran, exactly as the)
21. (O'Connor, J.J.; Robertson, E.F. (February 1999). "Anaxagoras of Clazomenae". University of St Andrews.).
22. (A. I. Sabra (2008). "Ibn Al-Haytham, Abū 'Alī Al-Hasan Ibn Al-Hasan". Dictionary of Scientific Biography. Detroit: Charles Scribner's Sons. pp. 189–210, at 195.)
23. (Quran 25:61).

24. (Qur'an and Science: Moon Light is Reflected Light - Answering Islam)
25. (Lambeck, K. (1977). "Tidal Dissipation in the Oceans: Astronomical, Geophysical and Oceanographic Consequences".)
26. (Murray, C.D. and Dermott, S.F. (1999). *Solar System Dynamics*. Cambridge University Press. p.184.) (Will Earth Survive When the Sun Becomes a Red Giant?)
27. (Quran, 13:2)
28. (Quran, 75:8)
29. (The fate of the moon in the Holy Quran and science)
30. (Life without the Moon: a scientific speculation | Science in School)
31. Ptak Science Books | Out-of-Place Department: the Moon as Debris

CHAPTER SIX

History of mankind [1]

———— ◈ ————

How modern human surfaced from nowhere or somewhere in pre-historic period will always keep this mystery a controversy amongst evolutionists and creationists. We know that history of earth is divided in prehistoric and historic periods. The probable dividing line between the two is around 3200 BC. It is accepted that the events in historic part can be traced with some accuracy with the help of modern tools. But when it comes to tracing events in prehistoric times, it becomes difficult as tracing them with available tools is extremely difficult. In such circumstances they can rightly be termed speculative. Speculations invite disagreements which creates difference of opinion. In such circumstance, living in the 21st century, it is prudent for both sides to keep a space for the opposite views; or better still, fill the space with an alternate view that can bridge the gap between the two. It is in this context where one can see Sufism playing its role.

How?

Studying the speculative prehistoric events pertaining to mankind, it has been theorized that the fossil remains of first hominid, a man-like primate suggest that this creature known as Ramapithecus lived 12 million to 14 million years ago. It is presumed to be the ancestor of modern apes and lived on ground adapting itself to open grass [2]. Ramapithecus was followed by Australopithecus which appeared around 3.9 million years ago [3][4][5]. It went through evolutionary phases devising a series of species for another 3 million years. While passing through these phases, structural changes kept on appearing in its physique and social behaviour. Those changes were;

1. Its brain capacity increased from 450 cc to 525 cc,
2. Its average height increased from 3'-6" and to 5',
3. The prominent sagital crest on its skull with strong jaw muscles attached to it underwent gradual changes.
4. The heavier jaw bone with large molar teeth started receding with diminishing canine teeth,
5. It remained herbivorous and ate tough, hard to chew plants.
6. It became fully bipedal; the male stayed a little taller and heavier than the female because of their differing roles.
7. It gave no indication of speech capability.
8. And, somewhere along in its last million years' journey when it came out of forest into open grassland, it discovered club as defensive weapon to counter its predators.

As the events are related to prehistoric period, controversy exists on Australopithecus being the common ancestor of both ape and human. This speculation is based on a genome viewpoint, which suggests only 2 percent difference between modern man and the modern apes. On physical point of view, the greatest difference between the two is in locomotion. Humans walk upright which came about when hominid came out of jungle and adopted itself to plains. Its facial feature changed toward the modern appearance much later about 100,000 years ago. Before that, the face of earlier hominid was much more apelike [6].

From a social viewpoint, modern man and modern apes are quite similar in some aspects. For example, the sexual practices between the two are quite similar. Although homosexual activity is more common in apes than in human. This in case of human is about 10%.

Before 1972, most experts regarded Australopithecus as the forerunner of man. However, the situation became complicated when that year Richard Leaky discovered a skull and leg bones of a manlike creature in Kenya. It was about 2.5 million years old and was considerably advanced than Australopithecus. His leg bones and size of skull indicated that it was about 5 feet tall, could walk upright and probably more intelligent. It was labelled the `1470 Man' [7].

At the same time, another tool making creature, 'Homo Habilis,' was found in Tanzania. The implication of these findings is that as Australopithecus co-existed with `1470 Man' and 'Homo Habilis', and was less advanced than either of them, it cannot have been man's ancestor. Because of such findings, some authorities call Australopithecus an evolutionary `dead end'. The controversies continue.

Despite the controversies, the evolutionists speculate that evolution carried on in following manner.

Homo Habilis: It is generally believed that Australopithecus was followed by Homo Habilis which lasted between 2.4 million to 1.2 million years ago. The species is also called the '*handy man*' because tools were found with its fossil remains. Its brain size rose from 500 cc to 800 cc during its evolutionary life and the shape of its brain suggests that it might have developed some speech capabilities. With the height of about 5 feet, it weighed around 100 pounds. Some scientists believe that Habilis is not separate species, but it is late Australopithecus or an early Homo Erectus [8].

Homo Erectus: It lived between 1.8 million and 300,000 years ago. Being a successful species for about a million and a half years, its brain expanded from 800 cc to about 1200 cc. It developed speech capabilities and made tools, weapons for hunting and discovered fire for cooking. Such needs made him to travel out of Africa into China and South-east Asia and, in the process, developed clothing for northern cold climates. Like Habilis, it had large jaw bone with huge molars, no chin, thick brow ridges, and a long low skull [9].

Homo Sapiens: Homo Erectus was followed by three successive species of Homo Sapiens; Archiac, Neanderthal, and Sapiens;

1. Homo Sapiens Archiac is considered as a bridge between Homo Erectus and Homo Sapiens during the period between 500,000 to 150,000 years. Its brain averaged about 1200 cc

and had definite speech capability. Its skull was more rounded and had smaller features, such as its molars and brow ridges were smaller. The skeleton was well proportioned but stronger than the modern man [10].

2. Homo Sapiens Neanderthals lived in Europe and the Middle East between 150,000 and 35,000 years ago. It coexisted with Homo Sapiens Archaic and early Homo Sapiens Sapiens. It is not known whether it was of the same species and disappeared into the Homo Sapiens Sapiens gene pool or was crowded out of existence by the Homo Sapiens Sapiens. Recent DNA studies have indicated that the Neanderthal was an entirely different species and did not merge into the Homo Sapiens Sapiens gene pool [11].

3. Homo Sapiens Sapiens first appeared about 120,000 years ago and evolved into a form almost indistinguishable from modern man around 40,000 years ago. There has been no change in his appearance ever since. The brain of the modern man has an average size of 1350 cc [12].

The last 40,000 years are important in history of mankind as this period is filled with controversies for Homo Sapeins Sapiens in mythologies, religions and science. The controversies became prominent because during this period non-recordable pre-history events were separated from recordable historic events. The stories of separation have been especially highlighted in the last three centuries of geological upsurge and technological developments as a result of industrial revolution. In simple words, there are no written records from human prehistory as clear techniques for dating were not well-developed until the 19th century [13].

Before going further, let us see what the Sufis say about history of mankind so far. They take their understanding from Quran and authentic Ahadith. As mentioned before, they insist that Quran is not a book of science or history but is a book of 'signs' presented by a prophet 1400 years ago. He had no conventional education but developed immense spiritual powers through meditation in solitudes in 'Ghar-e-Hira' (cave of Hira) for forty years. According to Sufis, Quran is known to have several layers of understanding. It is for this reason its readers take scholastic views according to their understanding and explain them accordingly.

Thus one finds scholars like Haroon Yahya, who is against theory of evolution, proving his point of views by giving verses from Quran, while same or similar verses are presented by other scholars like Hassan El-Najjar who support evolution according to his understanding. The latter group suggests that universe was created by God who let it go through a process of evolution through natural selection without interference.

Sufis take slightly different view. They believe that Singularity was exploded by 'Kun' of God and then let it pass through a 'controlled' evolution. By controlled evolution they mean that God acts as a force letting species go through process of evolution and in the process some species get extinct while other progress according to their surviving capabilities. The evolutionists call it intervention by 'nature' labelling it as 'survival of the fittest.' So in a way both evolutionists and Sufis are on the same page except they give different name to the intervening force.

Sufis get their understanding from the same verses of Quran, the other theosophists get with exception that Sufis read them in spiritual realm. For example, they quote a verse which in its unique style challenges those who do not believe in human's pre-life of non-existence, *"Doth not man remember that We created him before, when he was naught?"* [14] How did human appear from 'non-existence' to 'existence' and then went through evolutionary stages? It is explained by the Sufis through verses of Quran. They put forward those verses in chronological order of human development as part and parcel of evolution of solar system and earth.

For example;

1. Quran says human was created from dust. This is the earliest part of history when life did not exist and our solar system was

in the form of swirling dust. *"And of His signs is this: He created you of dust, and behold you human beings, ranging widely!"* [15]

2. Then the dust started to solidify turning into something like clay which floated in space with thundering noise. Pointing at this phase of evolution Quran states, *"We created man from sounding clay, from mud molded into shape"* [16]. Sufis call this phase of human development as 'Jamadaat'.(matter)

3. The evolution continued as the earth was taking rocky and mountainous shape covered with clay. Quran at this stage talks of man created out of clay, *"Allah is He who has made everything He created better, and He began the creation of the human (being) out of clay"* [17]. Or it says, *"He is Who has created you from clay, then he spent a term of time (away from you), and (it is) a specific term he determined. Yet, you doubt (his ability)!"* [18] The important point in this verse is that it uses the Arabic word *'bada'a'* which means that human creation happened in a process that had a beginning not just at once thus pointing at evolutionary process. The same meaning is found in another verse which says, *"Were We then fatigued with the first creation? Yet are they in doubt with regard to a new creation"* [19]. All these evolutionary phases are part of pre-life state of 'Jamadaat' (matter) described by Sufis

4. As the evolution carried on, water and seas appeared on the scene. The geologists tell us that life appeared in water at the bottom of sea in the sticky clay of 'Primordial Soup'. As we discussed in early chapters, Quran also talks of life appearing in water at the bottom of sea where an impermeable barrier was created between 'sweet and sour water' identical to cell membrane. That was the beginning of life of unicellular organism. Quran refers to that phase of evolution when it says, *"...and We made every living thing out of water? Will they not then believe?* [20] Talking about the life in sticky clay of 'Primordial Soup' Quran states, *"...Indeed, We created men from sticky clay"* [21]. Or when it says, *"We created the human being from stinking, smooth, (and wet) clay."* [22]

5. The evolution continued and water started to play important role in the origin of human life. Quran mentions it clearly by saying, *"And He it is Who hath created man from water"* [23].

6. As the evolution continued, life in water flourished and in the process plants appeared. Sufis link plant life as part of their life in evolutionary process and call it 'Nabataat'. They refer it to Quranic verse which says, *"And Allah has caused you to grow out of the earth like plants"* [24].

7. Then, Quran talks of creation of animal life in water, categorizing animals and taking them out of water onto the surface. Sufis link their life to this phase of evolution calling it 'Haywanaat'. *"Allah has created every animal out of water. Of them (is a category which) walks upon its belly, (another which) walks upon two legs, and (a third which) walks upon four. Allah creates what He wills. Allah is Able to do everything (he wants)"* [25]

It is this factor or force in process of evolution which Sufis call 'Allah' and evolutionists call 'The Nature'.

8. These three stages of human evolution from 'matter' to 'plant' and unto 'animal' has been mentioned by the great Sufi poet, Rumi in his 'Masnavi' when he says,

"I died from minerality and became vegetable;
And From vegetativeness I died and became animal.
I died from animality and became man.
Then why fear disappearance through death?
Next time I shall die
Bringing forth wings and feathers like angels;
After that, soaring higher than angels -
What you cannot imagine, I shall be that" (26).

Thus, it seems Sufis are inclined in their beliefs towards evolution of human. Before going further let us recap it up to this point by quoting

Quranic verse which states, *"It is He Who created you, fashioned you perfectly, and made you with the right proportions (straightened you up, to walk in an upright position)"* [27].

In this verse Quran uses three verbs; first 'khalaqa for creation; second 'sawwa' for fashioning perfectly; and third 'adala' for making walk in upright position. First is linked with living cell; second is pointing at change from unicellular prokaryote organism to multi-cellular eukaryote animal; and third is hinting at human departure from animal phase by walking straight as Homo Erectus.

Ibn Kathir explains this verse using a Hadith from Prophet Muhammad which says that God created humans in the best image and the right proportion and made them walk in a balanced way, in an upright position, which allowed them to walk between the two cold places such as North and South Poles [28]. This is a direct reference to the Homo erectus, which marked a major departure of humans from their closest kinship in the primate family. It also points to evolutionary progress which made humans to explore, migrate, and ultimately live in all regions of the earth between the two cold areas [29].

After separating hominids from animals and starting upright walk on two legs as Homo erectus, two further evolutionary changes appeared. First, alteration in structure of its skull, second expansion of its brain. These two changes played essential evolutionary role in separating humans (Homo Sapiens sapiens) from hominids (Homo erectus). The expanded brain of modern man (Homo sapiens sapiens) became vital towards achieving knowledge and using it to his benefit.

With passage of time and in process of evolution modern man developed coordination between 'hearing', 'seeing' and 'speaking' to help attain knowledge. According to human development 'hearing' appears in the womb followed by concentration of sight a few days after birth and learning to speak a few months later. The Quran mentions these essentials of knowledge and place them according to their embryological development and tie them to heart instead of the intellect to give it spiritual uplift when it says, *"Then He shaped him (in due proportions), and breathed in him of His Spirit, and made for you hearing, sight, and hearts; little thanks you give"* [30].

Some Sufis see a link between hominid (Homo erectus) and modern man (Homo sapiens sapiens) by referring Quranic verse which says, *"O mankind, what has deceived you concerning your Lord, the Generous, Who created you, proportioned you, and balanced you? In whatever form (image) He willed, He put you together (assembled you)"* [32]. They argue that the Arabic verb, 'rakkaba', used in this verse can be translated into 'putting together' or 'assembling'. Thus, the word may refer to assembling human beings by using genetic materials from other organisms, in order for humans to be better than their closest animal relatives, the primates. They compare such 'assembling' by God, to the scientists using genetic engineering and introducing changes in existing organisms.

Ibn Kathir explains the Arabic word 'rakkaba' by saying that the fertilized egg carries all the genetic characteristics of humans all the way from the first creation [33]. Ekremah, Abu Saleh, and Quotada added that some people may even have a feature of animals as their faces may look like monkeys pointing to the fact that human being is the product of a long line of genetic traits [34].

Tracing the history of mankind further and referring to Quranic verses, Sufis say that a competition based on knowledge took place between various types of livings including the humans. It was won by human making him the viceroy of planet earth to govern it according to his intellectual acumen [35]. *"And We created you (humans, in plural form), then fashioned you (made you in the image you are, also addressing humans in plural form), then said to the angels: Prostrate to Adam! And they prostrated, all except Iblis (another name for Satan), who was not of those who made prostration"* [36].

A few points are important in this verse;

First, God uses humans in plural with regards to their creation (khalaqa) and fashioning their image (sawwara) but when it comes to wining the competition, God mentions one human-Adam.

Second, the word 'then' is used between 'khalaqnkum' and 'sawarnakum' which indicates period of time between the two events during which humans went through stages of creating life, then passing through its increasing complexity and finally bringing it to the human stage which is higher in rank than other livings.

Third, the word 'then' is used again between 'sawarnakum' and ordering to accept Adam's superiority which shows another period was given to Adam amongst humans in which he acquired knowledge. This is confirmed in another Quranic verse which says,"*He taught Adam all the names. Then He introduced (some intelligent beings) to the angels, asking them to tell Him the names of these beings, if the angels were true to their claim (that they more deserved to be His deputies on earth*" [37].

Fourth, it also shows that human superiority on planet earth is related to knowledge because of which Adam won the competition. After winning, he was given tasks to perform his duties with responsibility. This verse gives support to the argument of creating humans through stages of creation, fashioning, and education [38].

After human was isolated from other hominids and became a 'modern man (Homo sapiens sapiens) and before he took the responsibility of becoming viceroy of planet earth at the end of this competition, Quran gives some details of his embryological development. This type of knowledge was not known 1400 years ago. It starts by saying, "*We placed it as a nutfah (fertilized egg) in a safe (deep) lodging; Then, We created the nutfah into an alaqa (a fertilized egg sticking to the womb sucking nutrients from it like a leach). Then, We created the alaqa into mudghah (a little lump, like a chewed substance). Then, We created the mudghah into bones. Then, We clothed the bones with flesh. Then, We produced it (the human being) as another creation. So blessed be Allah, the Best of creators!* [39]

A 'nutfah' is the Arabic word for a fertilized egg-a zygote. While 'alaqa' is the Arabic word for a leech symbolizing a fertilized egg sticking to the womb wall and sucking nutrients like a leech. This type of medical information about developmental stages of foetus in uterus has only come to light recently. Sufis link this information to the spiritual knowledge and wisdom of Muhammad who had no formal education.

In this way, Quran gives step by step development of human from the time when earth was in the form of dust to the final stage of human development as embryo in uterus. As the notion of time in Quranic knowledge is cosmological and not what we have created for ourselves on planet earth, these steps at times are millions years apart. Once we understand this point, it becomes easy to understand human's social and cultural development as described by the naturalists such as Sir David Attenborough who worked hard in investigative field of fossils related to prehistory periods and historic eras.

Lastly, after bringing the evolutionary process to modern man (Home sapiens sapiens) Quran hints at spiritual insight of human being by stating *"O humans! Be pious (careful of your duty) to your Lord, Who created you from a single soul, and from it He created its mate, and from them He has spread a multitude of men and women"* [40].

As 'soul' plays vital role in spiritual journey, this verse points at spiritual development of human beings in future. This aspect of human is important for uplift of societies at local, regional, and global levels. This topic will be discussed later in the relevant chapter.

Now that we have found minimum differences about the history of mankind between the scientists and Sufis, let us proceed further and follow humans' cultural and social development as presented by the naturalists through their investigative work on fossil finds from prehistory and cryptographic records from historic periods. It is pertinent to note that the end of prehistory which is related to the time when relevant written historical records as hieroglyphics became source of information, varied from region to region. For example, it is generally accepted that Egyptian prehistory ended around 3200 BC, whereas in New Guinea the end of the prehistoric era is set at around 1900 AD. It was the same story in Europe and elsewhere [41].

It is also pertinent to mention that knowledge of prehistory became important part of 'evolutionary psychology' which deals with human characteristics as adapted in the prehistoric environment during the long Palaeolithic period [42]. According to geologic findings, the actual human prehistory started in the Palaeolithic Era, or "Early Stone Age" around 2 million years ago when hominid started making crude stone tools. It progressed successively during the period of Homo sapiens sapiens passing through the 'New Stone Age' of Neolithic Era at the end of the Ice Age around 10,000 years ago, and ended around 5,000 years later when the Bronze Age began.

Prior to the appearance of Homo sapiens sapiens the hominids changed from being herbivorous to mainly meat eater and hunting became its major means of survival. Accordingly, the defensive weapon of hominid-the club, changed to offensive weapon of man-the spear and flint. It was during the period of Homo sapiens sapiens, when humans left caves and settled in huts made of branches, stones, or bricks, depending on the available resources. In this way, the first isolated human settlements appeared as gathering of small huts in shape of small villages which could easily be defended.

One of the most important events of the prehistory was the Agricultural Revolution which started during the Neolithic Age between 8000 and 5000 BC. As part of and as a result of that revolution following changes appeared in the history of mankind;

1. Humans started taming, domesticating and breeding animals and growing grains for feeding purposes. As all this needed water, the settlements appeared along the river banks; the major being along the rivers Euphrates and Tigris in Mesopotamia, around 3500 BC [43], river Nile in Egypt around 3300 BC [44], and the Indus River in India around 3300 BC [45]. Similar habitations appeared along the banks of major rivers in China.

2. As the sizes of settlements increased they changed into towns and cities. In this way, elaborate cities grew up with high levels of social and economic complexity seemingly different from each other because of infrequent links between the people living there. As part of evolutionary processes, the need to store food between seasons enabled people in division of labour. They started getting differentiated according to their trades such as farmers, shepherds and craftsmen etc. They exchanged food, pottery, baskets and various items in

markets as part of barter trade. Such trade not only made way to expand the sizes of villages, towns and cities but it also increased the chances of creating human classes thus giving various shapes to societies and civilizations. The growing complexity of societies necessitated systems of accounting, which led to writing. and that became not only essential part of trade to meet the needs of societies but also an essential tool for record keeping paving the way for converting prehistory era into historical period [46].

3. Agriculture being the main source of living, people linked their timetable of days and months of the year with sowing and harvesting of crops which paved the way for making calendars as discussed earlier.

4. The use of clay appeared when Neolithic people started using it for dwelling, making clay pots, and human or animal figurines. They not only used pots for storing grains, food items or water but they also started painting them with images of humans, animals and plants. That was the leisurely and aesthetic aspect of human evolution [47].

5. From clay they went for wooden technology and started using sticks to catch fish in shallow waters. With passage of time, they made the first 'vessels' in shape of canoes built of carved tree trunks or skiffs made of scaffolds of tree branches covered by tarred skins. In this way, they started using them for fishing and navigation through shallow waters [48].

6. Metallurgy was another important item that appeared at the tail end of Stone Age. Around 8000 years ago, the first processed metals were copper, tin, silver and gold. Near the end of the last Stone Age, about 6,300 years ago, people from Indus Valley to Central Asia started to process copper. Thus metallurgy brought gradual improvement in the living styles of humans as they started to make new metal tools, adornments and weapons ending the era of the 'Stone Age' around 5,000 years ago [49].

7. Thus stone as major tool was replaced in the following millenniums by bronze opening the gate to the 'Bronze Age'. Bronze became part of life used in agriculture, social life and warfare. Up until around 3000 BC, agricultural settlements had been almost completely dependent on stone tools. Sometimes in that millennium, copper and bronze tools, decorations and weapons took over the stone tools in Eurasia. Invention of writing is also linked with the beginning of the Bronze Age [50].

In the following centuries roughly corresponding to the "Axial Age" at the beginning of 7th century BC, iron tools and weapons replaced the bronze in the Eastern Mediterranean region, Middle East and China. The era saw not only a set of independent transformative philosophical ideas but religious too in various locations. For example;

- In philosophical fields, Socrates [51], Plato [52], Aristotle [53], and other philosophers laid foundations of Ancient Greek philosophy in the 5th century BC.
- In 6th century BC; Chinese Confucianism as philosophy and Taoism as spirituality [54]; Indian Buddhism and Jainism as religio-spirituality; Persian Zoroastrianism and Jewish Monotheism as religions were getting organized.

In this way, the history of mankind came out of pre-historic period and entered the historic period bringing theology, philosophy and spirituality in social life of modern man.

This brings us to the topics of;

- Mankind and Theology,
- Mankind and Philosophy,
- Mankind and Spirituality.

Let us take them one by one.

REFERENCES

1. (Addewid - Earth-Side Timeline)
2. (Was Ramapithecus one of the earliest humans? - Curiosity)
3. (Australopithecus - Wikipedia, the free encyclopedia)
4. (Australopithecus – Ecotao)
5. (Stages Of Man Evolution – Creation)
6. (The Earliest Hominids)
7. (Richard Leakey's Skull 1470 - Institute for Creation Research)
8. (Homo habilis)
9. (Homo Erectus)
10. (Archaic humans - Wikipedia, the free encyclopedia)
11. (Neanderthal - Wikipedia, the free encyclopedia)
12. (Paleolithic - Human Past Index)
13. (8.Graslund, Bo. 1987. *The birth of prehistoric chronology.* Cambridge:Cambridge University Press.)
14. (Quran, 19:67).
15. (Quran, 30:20)
16. (Quran, 15:26)
17. (Quran, 32:7).
18. (Quran, 6:2).
19. (Quran, 50:15)
20. (Quran, 21:30)
21. (Quran, 37:11)
22. (Quran, 15:26)
23. (Quran, 25:54)
24. (Quran, 71:17)
25. (Quran, 24:45)
26. (Poems by Rumi: I died from minerality)
27. (Quran, 82:7)
28. (Tafsir Ibn Kathir, Volume 4: 267)
29. (Creation and Evolution in the Holy Qur'an By Hassan El-Najjar)
30. (Quran, 32:9)
31. (Spirituality-a new dimension P.30)
32. (Quran, 82:6-7-8)
33. (Tafsir Ibn Kathir, Volume 4: 267-268)
34. (Creation and Evolution in the Holy Qur'an By Hassan El-Najjar)
35. (Spirituality-a new dimension: P 53)

36. (Quran, 7:11)

37. (Quran, 2.13)

38. (Creation and Evolution in the Holy Qur'an By Hassan El-Najjar)

39. (Quran, 23: 12-14)

40. (Quran, 4:1)

41. (Who's? Right: Pre-Historic Mankind)

42. (The Handbook of Evolutionary Psychology (2005), David M. Buss, Chapter 1, pp. 5-67, Conceptual Foundations of Evolutionary Psychology, John Tooby and Leda Cosmides)

43. (Ascalone, Enrico. Mesopotamia: Assyrians, Sumerians, Babylonians (Dictionaries of Civilizations; 1). Berkeley: University of California Press, 2007 (paperback, ISBN 0-520-25266-7] [35^ Lloyd, Seton. The Archaeology of Mesopotamia: From the Old Stone Age to the Persian Conquest.] [9^ McNeill, Willam H. (1999) [1967]. "In The Beginning". A World History (4th ed.). New York: Oxford University Press. p. 15. ISBN 0-19-511615-1.]

44. (Baines, John and Jaromir Malek (2000). The Cultural Atlas of Ancient Egypt (revised ed.). Facts on File. ISBN 0816040362.] 11^ Bard, KA (1999). Encyclopedia of the Archaeology of Ancient Egypt. NY, NY: Routledge. ISBN 0-415-18589-0.] [12^Grimal, Nicolas (1992). A History of Ancient Egypt. Blackwell Books. ISBN 0631193960.)

45. (Allchin, Bridget (1997). Origins of a Civilization: The Prehistory and Early Archaeology of South Asia. New York: Viking.] [37^ Allchin, Raymond (ed.) (1995). The Archaeology of Early Historic South Asia: The Emergence of Cities and States. New York: Cambridge University Press.[13^ Allchin, Raymond (ed.) (1995). The Archaeology of Early Historic South Asia: The Emergence of Cities and States. New York: Cambridge University Press.] [14^ Chakrabarti, D. K. (2004). Indus Civilization Sites in India: New Discoveries. Mumbai: Marg Publications. ISBN 81-85026-63-7.] [15^ Dani, Ahmad Hassan; Mohen, J-P. (eds.) (1996). History of Humanity, Volume III, From the Third Millennium to the Seventh Century BC. New York/Paris: Routledge/UNESCO. ISBN 0415093066.)

46. (Schmandt-Besserat, Denise (January–February 2002). "Signs of Life". Archaeology Odyssey: 6–7, 63. https://webspace.utexas.edu/dsbay/Docs/SignsofLife.pdf.)

47. (Neolithic: the New Stone Age – Softpedia)

48. (Chapter 1 – bornemania.com)
49. (HISTORY OF METALLURGY)
50. (FC8: The Birth of Metallurgy and its Impact - The Flow of History)
51. ("Socrates". 1911 Encyclopaedia Britannica. 1911. http://www.1911encyclopedia.org/Socrates_%28philosopher%29)
52. (Stanford Encyclopedia of Philosophy: Plato)
53. ("The Internet Encyclopedia of Philosophy". Utm.edu. http://www.utm.edu/research/iep/a/aristotl.htm. Retrieved 2009-04-18.)
54. (Ch'u, Chai; Winberg Chai (1973). Confucianism. Barron's Educational Series. p. 1. ISBN 9780764191381.) 2, (Nystrom, Elsa A. (2006). Primary Source Reader for World History: To 1500. Thmpson, Wadsworth. p. 46. ISBN 9780495006091.)

CHAPTER SEVEN

Mankind and theology

— ❖ —

The word religion is extracted from the Latin term 'religio' which means tying together. The question arises as tying what together? Studying the world religions, we come to know that religions are the product of three basic ingredients with varying distribution of the three. They are theology, philosophy and spirituality. It is these three ingredients which are tied together to play two important roles. First, to form organized religions. Second, to play vital role in restructuring societies.

History tells us that primitive religions evolved systematically where these ingredients played individual part paving the way for organised religions in coming millenniums.

History of religion also reveals that theology, like the other two ingredients, elevated societies by introducing discipline amongst humans. The knowledge of theology is considered to be intuition, which explores the world of the unseen and its three entities - godhead, spirit and soul. This knowledge is usually projected as the 'sixth sense'. It is beyond logical grasp and cannot be taught in the conventional manner in schools.

Exploiting theology, the custodians of religions effectively used fear, sacrifices, and rituals to control and subjugate societies. In this way, they held power in their hands and ruled for centuries. To maintain their hold over power, they boasted about their faith, created misunderstandings by demeaning other faiths and initiated religious wars. In the process of keeping dominance and holding a grip on the power, they developed an attitude where they;

- Failed to gain optimum knowledge about their own faith.
- Failed to study other faiths.
- Failed to understand other faiths and looked down upon them.
- Failed to realise the concepts of godhead, spirit and soul.
- Failed to know the working of the world of the unseen.
- Failed to see the links between this world and the unseen world.
- Divided godhead according to their understanding (which in reality was/is misunderstanding) and boasted that their god (s) was (were) superior to others'.
- Soiled religious beliefs with their egos.
- Failed to evolve their thought process according to societal progress.

The question is how did theology-the first ingredient of religion-appear on the scene?

Going back in the history of mankind, one finds that death immensely influenced human psyche by inspiring fear and awe in mind of the living. Anthropologists tell us that prior to the origin of organized societies, when humans lived as solitary hunters, they believed in a great unknown power which controlled the dead. They postulated this theorem on the basis of seeing and talking to the dead in their dreams. The fear of death thus became an important component of basic human instincts which played its due role in evolution of religions. Archaeological finds confirm that prehistoric people collected human skulls in caves and placed them in semi-circular formations. This placement of skulls points to a kind of ritual and to a notion that unknown powers resided in skulls. It is said that primitive humans ate brains of the deceased in order to acquire their strength, and then kept their skulls in an orderly fashion to protect themselves from their curse [1].

This was the beginning of religion based primarily on its first ingredient-the theology. Such primitive religion consisted of:

- The concept of a super-entity which lived in skulls.
- The continuity of life by interacting with the dead in dreams.
- The superior power of the dead by noting what the dead could do in dreams.
- Obtaining personal empowerment by eating brains of the dead.
- Rituals of placing skulls in an orderly fashion for self-protection.

This was theology in its most pristine form which was run on basic human instincts. Those instincts are also called 'Id' or 'Triebe' and were built on the;

1. Fear of death
2. Need to survive;
3. Urge to eat;
4. Desire to mate;

With passage of time human thinking advanced and rationality of logic set in to evaluate basic instincts philosophically. The struggle to fulfil basic instincts with help of rationality led mankind to advance in theological thinking and in social behaviour in the millenniums that followed. This also meant that human psyche had to face not only basic instincts but rationality too. In doing so their religious belief which was up until then based on theology was exposed to philosophy.

This exposure created a problem as there was major difference between instinct and rationality. The instinct remained unchanged and to this day we possess those very instincts, which we inherited from our ancestors in unaltered form [2].

Rationality, on the other hand, was connected with intellect of the developing brain, which brought reasoning to mankind's instinctive traits. So, as opposed to the unchanging nature of instincts, reasoning progressively changed as human intelligence advanced [3].

It was the rationality which became an evolutionary tool in religious growth. It is for this reason that, the second half of the 19th century and first half of the 20ᵗʰcentury gave rise to a few theories which shed light on the origin of the theological aspect of religions. For example:

1. In 1871, E. B. Tylor put forward a theory stating that primitive people thought they were inhabited by an entity which brought dreams and visions. Tylor called this entity 'anima' which became the focal point of future religious build-up [4].

2. In 1890, James Frazer came up with a theory which corresponded with Charles Darwin's theory of evolution. Frazer said that magic was the first stage of human intellectual development, in which a person could influence their own life and those of others by means of magical objects and sorcery. With the advancement of mental aptitude and frequent occurrences of unexplained failures of magic, they turned their rational thinking to other supernatural entities. This became the basis of religion [5].

3. In 1898, Andrew Lang in the 'Making of Religion' suggested that the concept of one supreme being existed in the earliest theological beliefs. He put forward his theory after studying the aborigines of Australia [6].

4. In 1899, R.R.Marett postulated that primitive people did not, at first, conceive of an individual soul but believed in an impersonal force which animated the world. He called it 'animism' which merged with future religious practices [7].

5. In 1912, Wilhelm Schmidt, like Marett, influenced by the Genesis story, conducted an extensive comparative study of primitive cultures, and concluded in 'The Origin of the Idea of God' that a belief in god existed among the most primitive peoples which might be called the earliest form of religion [8].

6. In 1912, Émile Durkheim published his major work, 'The Elementary Forms of the Religious Life' in which he theorized that religion was the product of society and that

certain ongoing practices in society became a pattern of worship [9].

7. In 1913, Sigmund Freud said that in prehistory, jealous sons killed their fathers for having full control over womenfolk. Their guilt in later life made them worship their ancestors [10].

8. In 1922, Lucien Levy-Bruhl advanced the theory of primitive mentality and claimed that primitive people used pre-logical thinking (probably based on instincts) in originating and accepting religion as it was at the time [11].

9. Herbert Spencer, a contemporary of Tyler, suggested that religion had its origin in visions or appearance of ghosts of the dead. These ancestors were worshipped as gods and that such theories about primitive religion were conjecture and could not be proven [12].

10. Mircea Eliade, the Romanian authority on religions, stated that modern historians know very well that it is impossible to determine the origin of religion, so it is better to accept it and study its progress and its effect on human life [13].

Notwithstanding many theories and hypotheses, the fact remains that it is impossible to know precisely how theological virtues evolved other than to conclude that it was the fear of the dead and the unknown power which controlled them. This appears to be what triggered the development of religion. Because power was attributed to the dead, disturbing the dead was regarded with fear. To avoid their curse and keep the supernatural power happy, rituals involving human sacrifices were introduced. Those rituals became deep-rooted, taking different forms as time passed and theological aspects of religions evolved.

In the process of theological evolution, occasional deficiencies in rational explanation made humans dependent on someone or something. And what better than the mighty entity which lived in the skulls and controlled the dead? But how to establish contact with this mighty force remained a mystery. Soon, the answer was provided by the magician who displayed his powers through skilful, showy tricks.

Thus the magician introduced magic to religion and mingled it with prehistoric theology. He practised magic by chanting words and performing tricks. To win the faith and awe of his audience, he had to resort to honing his acting skills. As time passed, the magician earned the reverence of the people. He projected himself as a healer, a fortune-teller and someone foreclosing disasters rationally. During his performances, he seemed to call upon the supernatural power of the dead to perform great feats [14].

He kept playing on that power until people realized that he was not always right in what he did or said. His failure raised doubts, which made them believe in existence of a second power which was beyond even the reach of the magician and his skills. Thus they logically started searching for another source of power, so great that it could control people from outside. This belief sowed the seed of transcendence theology, taking root in theological concepts of religions in primitive societies that emerged in the proceeding millenniums [15].

Meanwhile, in many regions, religion and magic remained intimately intertwined and, at times, it became impossible to distinguish between the two. This can be seen in certain sacrificial or ritualistic ceremonies of different religions to this day [16].

With advancement in intellectual faculties in advancing millenniums, a third supernatural power appeared in human psyche. According to its proponents, this power resided in bodies, not specifically in skulls. Some thought, it existed in abdomen, most probably in or around liver and the inner strength of individuals depended on this power.

Thus we find three phantasmal powers appearing during the evolution of theology [17]:

1. The first power was linked to the dead, which made them powerful. It supposedly lived in skulls and became known as the present-day 'spirit'.

2. The second power was more powerful than the first. It supposedly gave continuity to life after death and controlled humans. It lived outside the body and was unapproachable by the magician. This power is considered to be the present-day 'godhead'.

3. The third power, which also lived in the body but not necessarily in the skull. Its power varied from person to person and can be identified as the present-day 'soul'.

These three powers remained indistinguishable from each other for a long time. The important difference was that 'godhead' did not live in human body, while the 'spirit' and 'soul' did. As human intelligence advanced, 'godhead' surpassed 'spirit' in its importance and power. We have no evidence as to when this change occurred. All we know is that one of the oldest religions in the world, the Huna of Polynesia, still believes in a high spirit called 'Aumakua' which lives outside our body. That religion does not talk of god. Though it believes in two other powers called 'Unihipili' and 'Uhane' living within the body [18].

The study of theology also tells us that a distinction between spirit and soul has remained obtuse till present day. As a result, the learned theologians of the most advanced and organized religions take one for the other, keeping the identities and so interrelationship between the two hazy. This obtuse relationship has been trickling down for millenniums, from when humans lived in caves in the Mesolithic era, around 14,000 years BC. This obliquity is evident in the paintings on the walls from that era. They typically used the red colour, for its resemblance to blood, which purportedly reflected the image of life and spirit. The chief subject was hunting, depicted by animals and humans. Birds appeared later [19]. They painted, not to fulfil their recreational needs, but it had a marked theological significance as they believed that whoever painted an image would get the strength, the 'inner powers' (present-day, spirit and soul) of the painted figure.

To illustrate this point, an interesting painting from Mesolithic era (around 13,000 BC to 14,000 BC) known as 'The Sorcerer', in the cave of Les Trois Frères in France, is worth describing. It depicts a hybrid creature with the eyes of an owl, antlers of a stag, paws of a bear, tail of a horse and bearded face of a man. Besides others, this painting points at two things: first, it indicates different species sharing and thus enhancing their 'inner powers'; second, it alludes to sorcery, through which the painter could increase his own powers by extracting 'inner powers' of different species from a single painting [20].

Such sorcery was also visible in burial rites, when corpses were painted red by magicians of that era. The practice was indicative of a theological belief that, in doing so, the powers of the dead were kept intact, granting departed spirit eternal happiness [21].

Thus godhead, spirit and soul were established as primary entities in the realm of theology. Their powers and positions varied from region to region and theology to theology, but largely, the spirit and soul yielded to the supremacy of godhead. The spirit remained incomprehensible, and was considered higher than the soul. Meanwhile, the soul came to be known as the inner strength of man. Despite having various powers and positions, the three remained elusive for millenniums.

With the appearance of agriculture and emergence of complex societies, godhead flourished, redefining its shape, power and form. In the process, it was divided in three groups: the first was related to agriculture, the second to nature and the third to an unknown world:

- The gods linked with agriculture were called the 'primary gods'. They were four in number;
- The sky god (Anu) [22],
- The earth goddess (Ki) [23],
- The air god (Enlil) [24],
- The water god (Ae) [25],
- The gods attached to the nature were called the 'secondary gods'. They were three in numbers:

1. The sun god (Shamas) [26],
2. The moon god (Sin) [27],
3. The fertility god (Ishtar) [28].

- The gods associated with the unknown world were the most powerful. Their abode and nature were beyond the human mental grasp. Some called them Annunaki. Others thought they had a hierarchy among them which trickled down to the gods of other groups. The chief god was labelled by some as Nergal who was the strongest and kept his identity secret [29].

In the following millenniums, most evolving societies maintained the concept of multiple godhead with their varied powers, while the notion of spirit and soul remained elusive.

For example:

1. In Egyptian society, the belief in multiple godhead persisted until the arrival of Christianity. The Egyptians also believed in spirits of the dead, which played an important role in their daily lives. They also believed in two inner powers called 'Ba' and 'Ka'.

'Ba' was known to be selfish, creating restlessness and resided in abdomen.

Ka represented the intellectual aspect of personality and enjoyed aesthetic beauty. It had two elements— 'ikhui', and 'khabit' [30].

2. In Greek society, the gods of nature were given preference. These gods were personalized in the following centuries. With the appearance of philosophy, rationality was introduced to religion, shifting focus from divinity to politics. At the same time, the concept of 'inner power' resulted in mysterious cults and at times these powers became so great that they took over the strongest gods of religion. As the spirits of the dead were

not given primary importance, the fear of the unknown did not play on the Greek psyche as seen in other theologies of the world at that time [31].

3. Romans initially believed in an 'inner power' called 'numen' which at times, identified itself male virility (Genius) and female sensuality (Geno). But this belief was invaded by the foreign godhead of agriculture and nature. As a result, the 'numen' was amalgamated with godhead, attributing different powers to deities. The Greek influence brought personification to these gods. This influence also reduced the fear of the dead in the believers' psyche [32].

4. In India, concepts of multiple godhead and spirits of the dead prevailed in society. Brahmins, or the priestly cadre, took full advantage of those concepts to widen the gap between the castes for their own benefit around 10thcentury BC and ultimately changing Hinduism to Brahmanism. In 5th century BC Buddha and Mahavira rejected the Brahmin concept of religion and introduced a novel idea of self-improvement by awakening the 'inner power' ('soul'). Buddha side-lined godhead and awe of the spirits of the dead. Instead, he emphasized on good deeds, which he said were the key to awaken the 'inner power' ('soul'). According to him, one could reach the unseen world of spirits and godhead (Nirvana) by energizing soul through self-discipline. This was the first time divinity was given a new shape marking the appearance of true spirituality. It was this type of spirituality which was going to be taken up by some of the world's major religions in the coming centuries [33].

5. In China, religion started with concept of super-entities equivalent to godhead, living in heaven as well as on earth. They kept contact with humans through emperors via invisible links to maintain harmony. This concept was overshadowed by Taoism in 3rd century BC which based its teaching on 'Te' as the inner power. There was no concept of godhead in

original Taoism, but in later centuries, local godhead entered its fold [34].

6. In Japan, theology of Shinto had multiple godhead of nature whose powers were transmitted to different things making them 'kami'. The Shinto attitude towards the dead was one of fear of pollution rather than awe. That is why they quickly disposed dead bodies and then washed themselves to become clean. Sometimes they left homes where death occurred and built new dwellings to live in. There was no concept of 'soul' in original Shintoism. But after Japan opened to foreign theologies in the first century of the last millennium, it was introduced to Buddhism. This brought the concept of soul to Shintoism and thus the appearance of 'double' or 'mixed' Shinto. After its separation from Buddhism in the middle of the 19th century, the concept of soul faded in this theology [35].

7. The Aborigines of Australia and the Maoris of New Zealand have remained primitive in their concept of superhuman powers. They believe in spirits but not godhead. Some of them also believe in an inner power called 'Mana', which is equivalent to the 'soul' [36].

8. The Huna theology of Polynesia believes in one high spirit called Auamakau, which is common to all living things. In addition, every human has two powers: Unipihili, which mimics the soul in its concept; and Uhane, which is equivalent to a second soul or spirit. There is no concept of godhead in this religion. That is why it is sometimes referred to as a system rather than a religion [37].

9. Natives of South and North America are strong believers in nature spirits. There is a hierarchy among the spirits, but no concept of godhead or soul. Inner strength is gained through the spirits rather than the soul [38].

10. Mayans in Latin America believe that the power of nature spreads to every human being. Light plays important role in this power sharing. They also believe in multiple godhead

and spirits of the dead. There is no concept of soul in the usual sense, but light could well be equated with the soul or spirit [39].

11. The Pygmies, Hottentots and Bushmen of Africa believe in godhead of nature and spirits of the dead. The concept of soul is non-existent [40].

12. The theology in Mesopotamia went through commotions which affected a major population of the world in the coming millenniums. It all started around 10,000 years ago, when Mesopotamian society was consolidating and, accordingly, multiplication of godhead was bringing changes in their divine statuses. Most probably, during this period, a mythological notion emerged amongst theological custodians about a competition which took place between three groups of lower deities in the 'unknown world';

The first group had light in their nature. They were obedient and known for keeping good record in performing duties.

The second group had fire in their nature. They had administrative capabilities and were known for belligerent qualities.

The third group was made of clay. They had resourceful intellect and were good in conveying messages.

According to Mesopotamian theological belief, the competition was arranged by the highest god of the 'unknown world'. Knowledge was what they had to compete with to establish supremacy. The challenge was deemed to have been won by a member of the third group. The first group accepted the defeat and was classed as angels. The chief of the second group rejected the result and became the devil. The winner from the third group was refashioned giving him a new shape and was sent to a lucrative place in the 'world of the unknown' equivalent to the present day notion of 'paradise'. Also, he was awarded a female companion.

Having an inquisitive mind, he was easily persuaded by his companion to disobey the highest god. As punishment for his disobedience, he was turned into a messenger human named Adam and banished to earth, which had cooled down by then and was suitable for human existence. Did 'Adam' go through a paranormal (spiritual) experience during the competition, we will never know. All we are told is that he started a new life with his companion, Eve, spreading the theology of one god and sowing the seed of prophetic theology, which became the core of prophetic religions of Mesopotamia [41].

As the history of religion reveals, his theology was not implemented effectively because the region was ruled by kings and rulers who considered themselves as its custodians. They implemented their own theological concepts using brute force, human sacrifices, widespread fear or convincing magic. One can come across the occasional prophet like Enoch, Noah, Hud and Salih, who emerged to convince people to follow the theology of one god. But largely, belief in multiple godhead ruled Mesopotamian societies. Noah, whose name is associated with floods, is given the name of 'Utnapishtim' in old Mesopotamian mythologies [42].

Then, around 1900 BC something extraordinary happened which brought remarkable changes in Mesopotamian theology. The working of prophetic religion, the concept of godhead, and the attitude of ordinary man all changed. This was the century which gave us a wandering man from Ur of Sumer. He set out five major milestones in the theological aspect of religion.

1. First, he particularized the concept of one god and brought rationality in notion to align mankind in one direction.
2. Second, he produced a divine scripture as proof of his prophethood and used reasoning in his discourses to bring people into direct contact with the highest god of the 'world of the unknown'.
3. Third, he instituted the notion of a Day of Judgement after death in order to discipline mankind in this life.
4. Fourth, he changed human sacrifice to animal sacrifice to give dignity and respect to humanity.

5. Finally, he upgraded the status of ordinary man by giving him a chance to represent god as his prophet and took away religious custodianship from kings and rulers.

This wandering man was the prophet, Abraham, the grandfather of Israel and great-great-great- grandfather of Moses and Mohammed. The fundamental pillars introduced by him to theology became the foundations of Judaism, Christianity and Islam.

We find that Abraham inspired theology and in the following decades and centuries, the prophetic religions saw a series of prophets such as Ismael, Isaac, Jaqub, Solomon, Josef, Lot, Job, and Jethro, all stressing on the concept of one god. In the process of evolution, the theology of one god El changed to Eloha.

Occasional archaeological finds confirm the existence of these prophets. For example, the archaeologist K. Politis, on September 15, 1991, excavated the supposedly burial site of Lot, at the south-eastern shore of the Dead Sea, in the Jordan River valley, near the Biblical city of Zoa (the modern-day town of Sai). During excavations, he came across a stone with a Greek inscription, mentioning a cave where Lot and his daughters took refuge. Many more biblical figures are buried in various locations in Mesopotamia [43].

Then around 1200 BC, Prophet Moses came and revolutionised the prophetic religion of Abraham by changing Eloha to YHWH as divine unity and created Judaism. He formalized the new religion by giving his people the Ten Commandments as divine scripture [44]. After Moses, the prophetic religion passed through the Axial age until the arrival of Jesus Christ around 8 BC. Jesus Christ added an important pillar of spirituality to the existing pillars of theology and nascent philosophy erected by Abraham and Moses.

During this time of evolutionary stages in theology, we find that though the notion of godhead became somewhat clearer, the concepts of spirit and soul continued to be obscure. This obscurity remains till the present day despite their acceptance by vast majority of populace we call the believers. The majority of those believers are still not clear about the actualities and workings of godhead, spirit and soul.

I usually give the following example to clarify the concepts of the three entities to some extant;

A person 'A', gives his personal attire 'B' with the pockets filled with cash 'Ca', to a second person 'D' and tells him to spend the cash carefully on shopping 'Cb' for one day 'F'. 'A' also tells 'D' to return his attire unspoiled at the end of the day and to give him an account of how he spent the cash and what he bought.

This example can be translated as follows:

- 'A' may be taken as 'god',
- 'B' as 'spirit',
- 'Ca and 'Cb' as different forms of 'soul' changing its shape from 'Ca' to 'Cb'
- 'D' as human
- 'F' as lifespan of 'D'.

The example highlights the following points;

- God gives two of his belongings, i.e. 'spirit' and 'soul' to man.
- The 'spirit' returns back in its original shape at the time of death.
- The 'soul', accompanying a human at birth is different (cash) from the one at the time of death (shopping) as it changes with life experience. Depending on how humane the man is during his lifetime his soul might end up contented or dissatisfied at the time of his death.

To summarize, it appears that godhead, spirit and soul played pivotal roles in theology of religions. Among the three, godhead made itself known to humans step by step in line with the development of their intellectual acumen. First, god manifested itself in the fear and awe of the 'spirit' in early human history. Later, it let itself be known through the 'soul', by stimulating man's inner self through disciplining him and letting him appreciate human values.

The Sufis go one step further by saying that the same god is appearing now as a formidable force presented by scientific theories of quantum physics equating the religious forces of 'spirit' and 'soul' with subatomic forces of science. This topic will be taken up later in appropriate chapter.

REFERENCES

1. (Origin of Religion)
2. (Sigmund Freud - My Webspace files)
3. (Spirituality-a new dimension P.5)
4. (Edward Burnett Tylor - Wikipedia, the free encyclopedia)
5. (James G. Frazer - College of Arts & Sciences)
6. (Origin of Religion)
7. (Ibid)
8. (Ibid)
9. (Émile Durkheim - Wikipedia, the free encyclopedia)
10. (Freud Sigmund - World History Timeline)
11. (Lucien Levy-Bruhl - New World Encyclopedia)
12. (Origin of Religion)
13. (Ibid)
14. (Chapter 4. Magic and Religion. Frazer, Sir James George. 1922
15. (Spirituality-a new dimension P.6-7)
16. [MAGIC/RELIGION]
17. (Spirituality-a new dimension P.8)
18. (Huna (New Age) - Wikipedia, the free encyclopedia)
19. (Origin of Religion)
20. (The Sorcerer (cave art) - Wikipedia, the free encyclopedia)
21. (Paleolithic religion - Wikipedia, the free encyclopedia)
22. (Anu (Mesopotamian god) -- Encyclopedia Britannica)
23. (Sumerian Goddess and Gods: Ki the Sumerian Goddess of the Earth)
24. (Enlil (Mesopotamian god) -- Encyclopedia Britannica)
25. (Ea (Mesopotamian deity) -- Encyclopedia Britannica)
26. (Shamash (Mesopotamian god) -- Encyclopedia Britannica)
27. (Sin (Mesopotamian god) -- Encyclopedia Britannica)
28. (Who is Goddess Ishtar)
29. (Anunnaki - Wikipedia, the free encyclopedia)
30. (Spirituality:a new dimension; P.43)
31. (Ibid P. 68)
32. (Ibid P.73)
33. (Ibid P.129)
34. (Ibid Page. 14)
35. (Ibid P.160)

36. (Ibid P.155)
37. (Ibid P.147)
38. (Ibid P.87)
39. (Ibid P.93)
40. (Ibid P.83)
41. (Ibid P.11)
42. (The Flood of Noah and the Flood of Gilgamesh)
43. (List of burial places of biblical figures - Wikipedia, the free)
44. (The Ten Commandment)

CHAPTER EIGHT

Mankind and Philosophy

— ❖ —

Philosophy works best when it is applied to understand the world of the seen around us. This knowledge nourishes on reasoning which arises in response to doubt expressed by an enquirer. In a way, it is an egoistic war of intellect between two parties, not only to satisfy self-esteem but to find truth. Some people compare it with the peeling of an onion. Others call it an open ended knowledge. The rationalists apply this knowledge to understand the working of the world of the unseen and its entities such as godhead, spirit and soul. It is akin to giving reading glasses to a blind person and expects him to read. Applying philosophical knowledge to understand the working of the world of the unseen creates rift between the logicians and theologians.

Major sources agree that philosophy flourished in Greece and India in 1st millennium BC. Prior to its establishment, the early humans with inquisitive mind and limited intellectual acumen must have been asking questions about the working of the world and thus sowing the seeds of future philosophy. It is for this reason some believe that philosophy in a primitive form appeared in prophetic religion of Mesopotamia when prophet Abraham started to ask pertinent questions about godhead in 1900 BC [1]. It was the same story in other parts of the world where societies and theologies were growing side by side.

For example, in India philosophy showed its face in scriptures such as Upanishads in the 1st millennium BC. In Greece it became a hub in that millennium and in a short span of decades' thinkers and philosophers appeared who challenged theology [2]. So what exactly is this philosophy which challenged theology and changed the world in just a few centuries? Dr. Ralph Barton Perry Ph.D, Assistant Professor of Philosophy in Harvard University, reflected it by stating, 'Philosophy is neither accidental nor supernatural but inevitable and normal' [3].

According to the Greek definition, philosophy is seen as "the love of wisdom and pursuit of knowledge for its own sake." L.T. Hobhouse stated [4], "Philosophy is the attempt at a rational interpretation of reality as a whole." F.C.S. Schiller [5] said, "Behind all philosophy lies human nature and in every philosophy there lurks a man." Immanuel Fichte [6] said, "The kind of philosophy a man chooses depends on the kind of man he is." he further said, "By philosophy the mind of man comes to itself, and from henceforth rests on itself without foreign aid, and is completely master of itself, as the dancer of his feet, or the boxer of his hands."

A Sufi might put it in a more simplistic way by saying that philosophy is knowledge wrapped up in doubt and unwrapped by reasoning and in the process not only truth is revealed but also more doubts appear and thus the search goes on.

Generally speaking, philosophy is divided into three areas:

1. Ontology: the study of the ultimate nature of being or reality. This is a field of knowledge concerned with the essence of things in abstract [7].
2. Epistemology: the study of the ultimate nature, validity and limitations of human knowledge [8].
3. Axiology: the study of the ultimate nature, reality and significance of values [9].

At its zenith, in the 1st century BC in Greece, philosophy involved in five fields of studies: aesthetics, ethics, metaphysics, politics and logic.

1. Aesthetics and ethics are part of axiology. It is the study of form and beauty which is related to mental tranquillity, bringing individual sobriety, ease and intellectual wealth. This study leads one to the peak of perfection in art. The Greeks, with their developed intellectual aptitude and leisurely living, appreciated the philosophical refinement in these fields. The aesthetic philosophy began more or less at the same time as politics and was furthered by the Romans in the following centuries [10].

2. Ethics is the study of ideal human conduct. It is involved in the knowledge of good and evil and elucidation of wisdom [11]. In Sufism, it becomes visible on the 'path of knowledge' which will be taken up in the next chapter.

3. Metaphysics is the study of matter and mind and their interrelation vis-à-vis their perception and erudition. It became part of ontology and epistemology [12].

4. Politics is the study of social organization, monarchy, aristocracy, democracy and anarchism. It became popular amongst the ruling elites. The Greek philosophers prioritized this subject ignoring theology and by 500 BC they were arguing about aristocracy and democracy as against monarchy. Around 300 BC, the proponents of democracy divided Greek society into 42 sub states, with detrimental results for Greek civilization and unity.

5. Logic, among other things, became the basis of science. It involved; thought and research; deduction and induction; experiments and analysis. This study helped promote science in years to come. It also helped the future Sufis identify the realms of Nafs (soul), Qulb (mindfulness) and Ruh (the spirit) which will be discussed later.

Although the earlier Greek philosophers, such as the Sophists, Parmenides, Heraclites, Zeno and Anaxagoras, put society on the path of knowledge and civilization in an equitable direction, it was the bald, moon-faced and plumpish Socrates who changed the concept of philosophy in the 4th century BC. He picked up the spade of reasoning and started digging the ground of knowledge, removing the mounds of doubts to find the treasure of truth and riches of wisdom. It was his very modest but effective approach which became part of his lifestyle. "One thing only I know, that I know nothing," he, once, said [13].

In this way, he introduced philosophy to mankind and became the first martyr of knowledge, when he refused to denounce aristocracy and was condemned by the Athenian authorities to accept death by drinking the killer hemlock. After his death, the legacy of his nascent philosophy was passed on to his able pupil, Plato.

Plato became a staunch opponent of democracy and strong supporter of aristocracy, propagating the concept of a wise ruler, or 'philosopher king'. The idea of 'philosopher king' was translated into 'wise khalifa' by Sufis in coming centuries making it the principle of 'Khalifat' (kingship) in Islamic society [14]. Plato said that the real human virtues are courage ('andrania') and moral thought ('phronesis') which became the basic principle of future Sufism. Sufis believe in benevolent dictator to rule a society and so a state. Plato combined philosophy with poetry, and science with art. His notion of utopian statehood took him to Sicily, after receiving an invitation from the ruler, Dionysius, but was disappointed to find that the emperor was not a wise person. Annoyed by his reasoning, the king sold him as a slave. This morally wise philosopher died peacefully in his sleep in 347 BC. He nurtured infant philosophy and nourished it to adolescence than handed it over to one of his able students, Aristotle [15].

Aristotle [16] was a handsome, brave and intelligent aristocrat. He became the tutor of Alexander the Great. But, as Will Durant put it, "Alexander left philosophy after two years to mount the throne and ride the world." In doing so, he took the virtues of courage and intelligence along with him. Aristotle added mathematical, speculative and political knowledge to the inherited philosophy, but, most importantly, he introduced logic in elucidation.

It simply meant the art and method of correct thinking, but by definition it signified general characteristics of individuals and specific differences between them for rational comparisons. This was an advance on philosophies of Socrates and Plato by stressing on individuality rather than generality. He said, "Men come and go but man goes on forever." How right he was! Ernest Renan once said, "Socrates gave philosophy to mankind, Aristotle gave it science." Both these thinkers made tremendous advances which were taken up by future theosophists mingling it with theologies.

Aristotle also stressed on interlinking matter with form, saying that everything is moved by an inner urge to become something better than it is, to acquire a new form. This concept was taken up by the Sufis to suppress selfish ego (*Nafs-e-Amara*) through meditative techniques (*Tariqat*) in the following centuries. He observed that matter embodies the possibility of form and form is the actuality of matter creating a close link between possibility and reality. This notion helped future Sufis to identify the two paths of knowledge and deeds (*'Ilm' and 'Amal'*) in the following centuries. This subject will be discussed later.

In later years, Aristotle shifted his thinking from science to moral conduct and character, stating that they produced the quality of goodness and goodness brought happiness. In his notion happiness was the life of reason, and reasoning brought the 'golden mean' between the two extremes of excess and deficiency. Unlike the mathematical mean, golden mean brought flexibility in conduct and maturity in character. He stayed away from prayers and the sacrifices of theology.

After the death of Alexander the Great in 323 BC, Aristotle was made a target by the democrats. It is said that he committed suicide by drinking the same hemlock which took the life of his master's master, Socrates.

With his death in 322 BC, Greek philosophy took a political turn from aristocracy to democracy and soon Greece was divided into 42 political sub states as part of a democratic process. But at the gross root level, philosophy was spreading its wings in social organs and soon thinkers, theorists, and poets surfaced in the fertile field of the intellect. Their participation in regularly-held festivals changed the dry, unattractive and 'godly' ceremonies inspired by theology to philosophically inspired pleasing human gatherings. People all around the country would flock to the towns and enjoy old-time magic, new refreshing poetry, creative theatrical entertainments and absorbing philosophical discourses.

In these gatherings, poets, thinkers and scholars would voice their concerns on non-philosophical divine indulgences and blind obedience to the gods. They would pity the grief-stricken, helpless and feeble humanity which was thrown to earth by the non-pitying gods. Through their discourses, they would try to divert the attention of the public from religion to politics of aristocracy and democracy. Repeated outbursts of such revolutionary thinkers started to change the psyche of people and they found themselves detaching from theology of religion and tilting towards politics thus separating religion from politics. In coming centuries this trend was reversed by Christian clergy till the Bastille revolution when church was separated from state [17].

While the Islamic theosophists and Sufis still believe in non-separation of politics from religion [18A]. A well-known Sufi poet and thinker of Indian subcontinent, Alama Iqbal once said *"jalaal-e-paadshahi ho ya jamhoori tamasha ho; juda ho deen siyasat se tu reh jati hai changezi"* (whether it is the grandeur of monarchy or the game of democracy, when religion is removed from politics it is left with Mongolism.) [18B]

The fallout of Greek philosophy was felt in all walks of life in coming decades and centuries in Europe. For example, Roman society, by nature, was trained to be strict in discipline as people confined themselves in letter and spirit to obeying theology with or without any affection. This psyche was transmitted to political ceremonies too, where the official functions of the state looked like religious ceremonies and vice versa showing total mingling of theology with politics.

With extension of Greek influence, Rome was exposed to poetry, aesthetics and philosophy creating a kind of confusion in which, over the years, the priests lost control over religion and religion lost theological values. In the process, a split appeared between state and religion. For the public, the social events became more important than religion.

Then, in 45 BC, Julius Caesar was killed and his adopted son, Octavian, took over the affairs of state changing the republic into an empire and made himself Augustus, the emperor. In doing so, he declared himself god through the Senate in 42 BC, bringing godhead in line with statehood and slowing down Greek philosophical influence of separating religion from politics.

This did not stop Greek philosophy diffusing gradually in other European and American societies in the following centuries. Its philosophical teachings also spread to the Middle East in the 4th century BC through the conquests of Alexander the Great [19]. As a result of this diffusion, two schools of thought stood prominent in 18th and 19th centuries in Europe. Similarly, an upsurge in rational approach brought changes in Chinese culture through three schools of thought in China.

The two philosophers who changed the European mind-set were Rousseau and Nietzsche. They opened the doors to Rousseau and Nietzsche Schools of thought respectively. These schools affected individuals, communities, and societies at educational, political, theological, and spiritual levels in Europe, America and Russia.

In China, on the other hand, Confucianism, Legalism, and Taoism schools of thought affected Chinese society.

Let us take them one by one:

1) Rousseau School of thought [20].

The founder of this school, Jean-Jacques Rousseau, also known as the father of government schools, was born on 28 June 1712 in Geneva and died on July 1778 in Ermenonville, France, at the age of

66. His paradoxical personality both reflected and contradicted the 18th century rationalism of enlightenment through his thoughts. Four of them made history in following years. They were;

1. Progressivism;
2. Romanticism;
3. Collectivism;
4. Nationalism.

He linked progressiveness with the latter three in his teachings which appealed to the scholars, educationalists and academicians in Europe, America and Russia in coming decades.

Progressivism

Jean-Jacques Rousseau's progressivism was an exploratory effort to educate children at a new level that stressed on idea that a child must always do what the child wanted to do. He propagated that children should express their ideas and that adults should not only listen to them, but discuss with them all the subjects including religion and sex. In Rousseau's words, "In the first place, you should be well aware that it is rarely up to you to suggest to him what he ought to learn. It is up to him to desire it, to seek it, to find it. It is up to you to put it within his reach, skilfully to give birth to this desire and to furnish him with the means of satisfying it"[21]. This became the principle of his idea of it being the child-centred. For 18th century mind-set, such idea was unorthodox for some and progressive for others.

French Scholars and academicians were among the first who found it attractive and soon it became popular in France. In other countries, it impressed personalities like Johann Pestalozzi, Leo Tolstoy, and John Dewey and they individually put it into practice. For example, Pestalozzi was one of the first fellow Swiss who practised it in his school for the poor children of his employees on his own estate [22].

Similarly, the Russian novelist Tolstoy, founded such a school on his own estate with principle that knowledge should be applied in a way to abolish grades and class distinction among the learners and the students should learn from experience without correction [23].

Friedrich Froebel, a German who was instructed by Pestalozzi, is said to have invented the Kindergarten Schools based on Rousseau's ideology. He taught many including Elizabeth Peabody who founded one of the early such schools in America. She, along with other like-minded colleagues became instrumental introducing Rousseau's ideas of education in the United States [24].

Romanticism

Another important thread sprang out of Rousseau's philosophy was Romanticism and its three elements namely; adoration of nature; interest in self-revelation; and longing for freedom. The first reached to extreme in environmentalism, the second in narcissism, and the third built rebellious mindset among students in the 1960s and early 1970s which included sexual revolution during that period.

The term Romanticism defied reasonable definition as it was described a virtue which went against rationalism on one hand, and theology on the other. According to its understanding, to go into romantic mode, one has to learn how to get preoccupied intuitively with his surroundings against the accepted day-to-day natural laws linked with ethics and morality. That meant, at times, it would put a person against the social customs and even legislated laws of the day. In a way, this teaching was akin to Mala'mati Sufis whose teaching defied normal traditional teachings on ethics and morality [25].

Rousseau, all his life went through such defying experiences leaving enormous effect on his personality. For example, once while sitting in a boat in Switzerland, he found himself inseparable from the surrounding nature. Describing the experience, he wrote, "if there is a state where the soul finds a setting solid enough on which to rest in its entirety, and gathers there all its being, without needing to recall the past, nor to rush towards the future, where time means nothing to it, where the present endures forever, without, nevertheless, noticing its duration and without any trace of anticipation, without any other feeling of deprivation nor of joy, of pleasure nor of pain, of desire nor of fear, than that alone of our existence, and that this feeling alone can fill it completely; as long as this state lasts, the one who finds himself in it can call himself happy, not with an imperfect happiness, poor and relative, such as one finds in the pleasures of life, but with sufficient happiness, perfect and full, which leaves in the soul no void that it feels the need to fill. Such is the state where I find myself often on the Ile St. Pierre, in my solitary musings, whether lying in my boat that I let drift at the water's whim, seated on the banks of the agitated lake, or elsewhere, at the edge of a beautiful river or a creek murmuring over the gravel" [26].

Such a state is known to Sufis as 'Fana' (Absorption). The only difference is that Rousseau's non-separation from 'nature' is called non-separation from 'divinity' in Sufism. In other words, Rousseau found himself absorbed in the surrounding nature and Sufis find themselves absorbed in divinity. An equivalent example can be seen in Sufism when Mansur Hallaj of 8th Century AD experienced an identical state of 'fana' and he uttered 'Annul Haque' (I am the Truth). It created a stir amongst the powerful Muslim clergy pressurising the then Caliph to arrest him on charges of heresy. Hallaj was arrested, prosecuted and sentenced to death by stoning. He accepted death with a smiling face [27]. A century later when another theosophist/ jurist turned Sufi, Al-Ghazali was asked about the incidence, he did not discredit the truth content of Hallaj's state however he held that his execution was justified since he had revealed the divine secret in public. In a way he was saying that Hallaj was right but he should have not uttered it in public [28].

One can see that Rousseau was at liberty to say about his experience of diffusing in 'nature' without causing any stir in society as opposed to what Hallaj had to face because of theologians' intervention. These two examples give a clear picture as to how two identical experiences be treated differently because of ill-understood knowledge of theology, philosophy and spirituality (in this case Sufism). A philosopher expressed his experience openly and became a quotable piece. A spiritualist (Sufi) mentioned it in public and was executed by the fellow theologians. It is this fine point which theologians and philosophers in the 21st century should keep in mind when discussing societal matters. To understand why theologians are so touchy and philosophers are so casual about divinity, the spiritualists can bridge the gap by adding them in relevant discourses. Because of this non-participation the followers of three Abrahamic theologies are put on warpath by the traditionalist theologians supported by self-centred philosophers after 9/11. In simple words, spiritualists can play vital role to make the world a liveable place and avoid the third world war.

In 1763 Rousseau wrote again, 'One would say that my heart and my spirit do not belong to the same individual. Feelings, strong but not clear, fill my soul; but instead of enlightening me, they burn and astonish me. I feel all and I see nothing' [29]. This is another example of similarity found between Rousseau and Sufis on relationship between 'soul' (called 'Nafs' in Sufism), 'heart' (called 'Qulb' in Sufism), and 'spirit' (called 'Ruh' in Sufism). The Sufis pass through these experiences during their spiritual ascent on the path they call '*Marateb-e-Insani*' (human ranks). This will be discussed later in appropriate chapter.

In the Romantic view of Rousseau, human consciousness exists at the crossroads of two incomprehensible worlds: the external realm of nature; and the internal realm of the mind. Again, this concept is close to the Sufi notion of having two paths; an external and internal taken from Quranic verses of '*Ilm*' (knowledge) and '*Amal*' (deed) respectively [30].

The core of this romantic philosophy can be described as, 'The ideas that everything natural is good, that existing society is unnatural and vicious, and that the bond between man and nature must be re-established' [31], Sufis understand this philosophy because they take 'nature' as part and parcel of 'divinity'. So when Rousseau talks of re-establishing bond between man and 'nature', Sufis take it as re-establishing bond between man and divinity without losing touch with reality of living peacefully with others whether they are non-believers, philosophers, theologians or theosophists.

Collectivism

The third philosophy of Rousseau was 'collectivism', a political philosophy that spiralled around paradoxes of inequalities. In his opinion, man in the 18th century was ravaged by the inequalities in the society. According to him, those inequalities could be corrected through three basic changes; first by establishing law and accepting the right of property; second, institutionalising magistracy; and third, transforming legitimate power into absolute power. Rousseau dilated up on it by stating, 'the first gave rise to the distinction of rich and poor, the second to that of the weak and powerful, and the third to that of master and slave, which is the ultimate degree of inequality and the one to which the others all lead, until new changes dissolve the government completely, or bring it back to legitimacy' [32].

His philosophy reached schools via the neo-Marxist critical theorists born in Germany, matured in France, and prospered in U.S. universities. It primarily targeted a social class which came out of deprivation and were motivated by profit as part of bourgeois class. Rousseau detested them because he felt that they were goaded by their egos and not compassion. He believed it was the main reason of inequality which shattered his visualisation of a utopian society wherein there would be no private ownership of property. It was this philosophy which was adopted by Marx and refined by Lenin into the Soviet system. The philosophy provided the basis for the collectivist movements which, "began in Europe in the 19th century and which produced such horrors throughout the whole world in the 20th century, all the way down through Cambodia"[33A]. These movements could not have come to power if Rousseau's ideas were not planted in the educated classes and then spread to the people at large [33 B].

He countered the inequality through a universal message that, 'Equal educational opportunity is necessary if all citizens in a republic are able to preserve their rights and to serve their country' [34]. The principle of equal educational opportunity ere applicable not only in government schools but also in private schools. Statistics presented by Ellis and Fouts shows that 12% of students attended private schools and 1% home schools in United States followed Rousseau's ideas [35].

Nationalism

Jean-Jacques Rousseau had the ability to impose his will on others. He proposed a national system of education much of which followed the principle of subjugating personal interests over communal. It also meant that education must shape the minds of the learners and mould them till they are patriotic by inclination, instinct and necessity, thus instilling the feelings of nationalism. On nationalism, he said 'A child should see his fatherland when he first opens his eyes, and till death he should see nothing else. The true republican sucks in with his mother's milk the love of his country, hat is of law and liberty. This love makes up his life; he only sees his fatherland, and only lives for his fatherland; his country lost, he lives no more; if not dead, he is worse' [36].

Rousseau's thirst for freedom became motivation to a series of revolutions all over the western world toppling monarchies and totalitarian regimes. The schools wrested out of the control of churches paving the way for nationalism that was not visible up until then.

2. Nietzsche School of thought [37].

The pioneer of the second school of thought, Friedrich Nietzsche was born on October 15, 1844 in Röcken, Prussia. He took up theology at the University of Bonn but soon abandoned it and opted for philosophy at the University of Leipzig. On nomination by his professor, Ritschl, he was appointed professor of classical philology at the University of Basel, in Switzerland, where he started teaching the subject in 1869. Ten years later in 1879, his poor health forced him to resign from the post. In 1889, he suffered a nervous breakdown in Turin, which ended his academic career. He was fostered by his mother and later by his sister Elisabeth Forster Nietzsche till his death on August 25, 1900, in Weimar.

His teachings primarily, concentrated on education and culture with strong observation that education had abandoned the humanist outlook in exchange for the scientific. As a result, the education was made to produce profitable men who were trained how to make money rather than build mature personalities. This trend ignored a balance between financial gains and moral values. He called it "unnatural methods of education" [38].

According to him education and culture are inseparable. As culture reflects psyche of community and community is made of individuals, he stressed on individual development as part of 'formation of the self'. He was against education which was forced upon individuals restricting their self-esteem. He thought that education at junior and high school level (gymnasium) were character builders and nothing was done at that important level. He found that, that level was reflected later at technical and university levels. Therefore, he insisted that renovation in education should begin in the gymnasium by imparting discipline as part of character building and obedience as part of habit. This approach apparently clashed with what Rousseau taught who stressed on free exchanges between teacher and student with possible interference both in discipline and obedience.

It is interesting to note that Nietzsche teaching on this subject is pretty close to Sufi teaching which gives tremendous importance to student teacher relationship built on discipline and obedience. On theology, Nietzsche blamed customs related to religion and those feelings forced him to target traditional Christian teachings.

Nietzsche remained non hostile to technical education but did not spare university teaching. On that he said, 'as the professor speaks, the student listens and writes and during that instant, he is connected to the umbilical cord of the university. It is up to him what he wants to hear he does not need to believe what he hears; he can cover his ears when he pleases' [39]. He called it "academic liberty". According to him on one side was the autonomous mouth on the other the autonomous ears, and at the back of these two was the state. Such liberty reminded the student that the state was 'his final objective, the end and the essence of these proceedings of speech and hearing' [40].

He believed that the state and business persons were responsible for the poverty of culture as they slowed down and even blocked the maturation of individuals as a result of students being indecisive in decision-makings. In this way, they lost the urge or even the will to pursue their dreams. Here comes a fine line of paradox in his teachings. On one hand he wanted to control the students mind through discipline and obedience at the gymnasium, (the founding block of character building), and on the other hand he was expecting them to grow as free-minded mature individuals. This paradox is solved by the Sufis, who while advocating similar discipline and obedience to their disciples at primary level of education do not let them loose self-confidence by guiding them to understand the philosophically acceptable yet divine way of working for humanity.

On poverty of culture, Nietzsche, found three tendencies that caused it; first, maximum amplification of culture; second, maximum reduction of culture; and third, journalistic culture. According to him, the third acted like a confluence point for the first two, forming an 'un-culture'. In that way, the third became the main stream of thinking and fashion, and he found aversion for it as it manipulated the other two.

His most misunderstood idea was his belief in individualism. He believed that group morality is a slave morality, and in that context he, on one hand, supported the concept of 'master race' coming out of individuals, and on other hand, opposed German nationalism and racism. The Nazis twisted his ideas of 'master race' into racial and social doctrine. He also challenged theologies especially Christianity, which according to him, adversely affected individual and cultural health, and propagated belief in life, creativity, power, and the realities of the world we live in, rather than those situated in a world beyond.

In that context, he gave a clear edge to life over knowledge claiming that the principle of "life" is more pressing than knowledge and that the quest for knowledge should serve the interests of life. Centuries earlier, Sufis talked about such a relationship in a slightly different way. They saw the ingredients of life in noble deeds (Aml-e-Saleh) which they extracted from Quranic verses, then put them parallel with knowledge (Ilm) making the two paths ('noble deeds' and 'knowledge') as components of Sufism [41]. These two paths are also termed as the 'internal' and the 'external' paths in Sufism which Rousseau called as 'internal and external realms' in a slightly different context.

As Nietzsche progressed in his thought maturity, he embarked on a new understanding of moral behaviour in 1883, when he emphasized on 'feeling of power' as opposed to its pleasure. He realised that pleasure could be deceptive depending on the state of mind we are in. He saw a link between 'feeling of power' and the strength of 'will' we carry within. According to him, "will" was not an inner emptiness, feeling of deficiency, or constant drive for satisfaction, but was a source of energy that strengthened one's aims towards expressing and discharging his faculties.

This notion was very close to the concept of 'contentment of soul' (Nafs Mutmaina) in Sufism which separates pleasure found at the lowest level of ego from contentment found at the highest level of pride. Nietzsche rightly did not see that drive in theology. In his piece, 'God is dead', he tried to divert public attention away from escapist, pain-relieving heavenly world and focused on inherent freedom in the existing world. He was pretty close to the original teaching of Buddha who tried to bypass concept of godhead. But, had Nietzsche explored the Sufi's path he would have understood that 'feeling of power' and 'strength of will' if used to achieve humility actually lead a soul towards a state of fine vibrations of 'fana'. The same sate, Rousseau went through on the boat in a lake in Switzerland a few decades earlier. Sufis in this state, understand divinity because they 'feel' it as they become part of it. In the case of Nietzsche, it might have stopped him 'killing God'.

Although, at some stage, he tried to touch the subject when he wanted to find out how people reacted to the doctrine of eternal recurrence according to which human is reborn again and again, to replay life's experiences exactly as before in every pleasurable and painful sequence of detail. He found the doctrine challenging as he saw it psychologically healthy myth, provided it was adopted therapeutically to help people become strong. He associated the doctrine with concept of "superhuman" (übermenschlich) which acted as a bridge for downtrodden deprived common men to overcome their mental miseries linked to their psychological and physical impoverishment in existing life [42].

As opposed to such meek people, he believed in the concept of 'higher human beings' and considered himself as one of them along with Goethe and Beethoven [43]. According to him to be counted as a 'higher human being' a person has to have the following five characteristics in various combinations;

1. Tends to be solitary,
2. Pursues a "unifying project,"
3. Is healthy,
4. Is life-affirming,
5. Practices self-reverence.

In explaining some of these characteristics, he mentioned that 'the higher man' remains solitary, secretive, standing alone and having to live independently. As a result, such a 'superhuman', constantly contradicts the great majority not through words but through deeds. But when Nietzsche said that the 'higher man lacked congeniality and good-naturedness seen in contemporary popular culture', and that 'self-loathing, self-doubt, and self-laceration are the norm among human beings.' he seemed to be contradicting himself [44].

This type of seemingly contradiction, which might not be contradictory, is seen in a section of Sufism called 'Mala'amati'[45], the followers of which tend to do things that go against the prevailing norms of society. They, by their deliberate actions, try to discredit themselves and bring themselves down in the eyes of the public. According to 'Mala'amatis', it is one way of controlling or even crushing their 'ego'. Keeping that in mind, one of the great Muslim philosophers and spiritualists of Indian subcontinent, Allama Iqbal, divided ego into three types; i), selfish, which is personal, ii), selfless, which is linked with community or nation; iii), and divine, which is cosmic [46]. It seems Nietzsche while expressing various 'characteristics' highlighted features of 'type one' ego at times, and 'type two' at others, making his utterances appeared contradictory, which in reality were not.

On morality, Nietzsche did not accept the notion that a universal morality is applied equally on all human beings. He believed that different moralities were applied according to social order in the society which differed for the plebeians and the nobles. In this way, they were made suitable for the role of the subordinates at one end, and for the role of the leaders at the other. He called it servant morality versus master morality. The effects of such morality is visible in Indian subcontinent where, for centuries, the society went through political orders that constantly induced slave mentality at all levels of social groups.

Nietzsche advocated valuations be linked to self-confidence, self-reinforcement, self-governance, creativity and commanding attitude, as opposed to reactive meek attitudes that sprang mechanically when a subordinate faced the more powerful. He put the blame on the Christian theologians who painted the lopsided morality with holiness and goodness and often applied it as revenge and hate. According to him, they also used guilt or 'bad conscience' as tool to propagate religious teachings on moral grounds [47]. Obviously he was talking about the theological aspect of religion from philosophical point of view unaware of its third ingredient-the spirituality.

He expressed his disgust how feelings of guilt, or "bad conscience," sprang from unhealthy Christian morality linking them with natural inclinations of men. He criticised priests who, in his opinion, were weak and shepherd even weaker people playing upon their guilt. It is interesting to find acute similarity between Nietzsche's aversion for traditional custodians of Christianity (the priests) and Sufis' dislike for fundamentalist Muslim Mullahs [48].

On socio-economic side, Nietzsche blamed business relationships between creditors and debtors which inflicted pain on the latter in contractual deals as part of Western culture. Writing in the section of "Why I Am a Destiny" in Ecce Homo he claimed that he was a destiny because he regarded his anti-moral truths had an annihilating power that could wipe out the morality born of sickness which had been reigning the Western culture for the last two thousand years [49].

On politics, two positions came out of Nietzsche political philosophy; first, his commitment to aristocratic forms of social ordering-"Aristocratic Politics View"[50]; second, his non-political philosophy- the "Anti-Politics View"[51]. Some, like Shaw [52] talk about a third position, stating that Nietzsche was sceptical and that according to him with the demise of theology, it would be possible to achieve an effective normative consensus in society at large that was untainted by the exercise of state power itself. While others, like Leiter [53 contested and questioned whether he was even interested in political philosophy? So like in other fields, Nietzsche left apparent contradictions in political philosophy.

Despite all the apparent contradictions, Nietzsche's thoughts left deep influence on those thinkers who found themselves on the periphery of established social fashion and practices in 20th century especially in Continental Europe. During 1930's, parts of his thoughts were twisted by the Nazis and Italian Fascists, partly due to Elisabeth Förster-Nietzsche's association with Adolf Hitler and Benito Mussolini. As a result, they selectively assembled, various passages from his writings to justify war, aggression and domination on nationalistic and racial grounds.

His teachings became especially influential in French philosophical circles during 1960's, providing his emphasis on inner power as the real motivator to challenge established authority and launch effective social review. In English speaking world, his ideas were kept away from serious philosophical consideration until the landmark works by scholars like Walter Kaufmann's [54], and Arthur C. Danto's [55], which paved the way for more open-minded discussions. In this way, his thought influenced variety of professionals such as painters, dancers, musicians, playwrights, poets, novelists, psychologists, sociologists, historians, and philosophers in 20th century.

Thus we find philosophy which budded in Greece was taken up by philosophers like Rousseau and Nietzsche in Europe and they spread it all over the world leaving its shadows on politics, religions, social behaviour, at individual, communal and national level.

Turning to China, we find three schools influenced Chinese society and the societies surrounding this vast country. The schools were 1) Confucianism, 2) Legalism, 3) Taoism):

1. Confucianism [56].

Kung Fu Tzu, who became the founder of the Confucianism, was born in 551 BC, in the district Tsow of province Lu in China. He was brought up as an orphan in poverty. All his life he struggled hard to get into administrative post (politics). To achieve this goal, he left his native town many times. This roaming, exposed him to meet different people, see different social customs and observe different administrative systems, which made him a gradual achiever of wisdom. When the time came for him to get what he always desired, he was too old. So he decided to teach what he learned all his life. Soon he became `the First Teacher'.

He died in 479 BC at age of 73, after spending the last years of his life compiling and editing his erudition - the classics. It became the fruit of his wisdom which took the Chinese society by storm. His intelligence faced two views; the realistic view based on strict administration, and Mohism (after Mo Tzu) based on love. He inclined towards the former leaving his doctrine devoid of spirituality.

He came up with the philosophy of;

1. Jen- the goodness;
2. Chum Tzu- the gentleman;
3. LI- the propriety;
4. Te- the government by virtue;
5. Wern- the art of peace;
6. Shu- the reciprocity.

His philosophy of 'Shu' became popular as 'Five Cardinal Relationships' also known as 'Wu Lun'. Those relationships were:

1. Kindness in the father, befitting piety in the son;
2. Gentleness in the eldest brother, humbleness in the younger;
3. Righteous behaviour in the husband, obedience in the wife;
4. Humane consideration in elders, difference in juniors;
5. Benevolence in rulers, loyalty in ministers and subjects.

In these relationships, the family was given preference to individuals. In the family, the father was considered an undisputed head while the eldest son had specific obligations toward the family and was expected to respect and care for the parents [57]. The bonding was so strong that it would make a person accept suicide rather than deviate from family loyalty [58 A].

Confucius, though himself was aware of theology, did not dilate upon the subject. Once he said `Before we are able to do our duty by the living, how can we do it by the spirits of the dead'. Again he said `Absorption in the study of the supernatural is most harmful'.

His idea of a superior man was a person whose mind was perfectly clear about names and duties and who acted with kind uprightness and good taste. He contained his struggle to improve the statehood on administrative plane.

In his last days of life, he said something which puts light on his insight about a path that could reflect spirituality, though he never confessed that he was a spiritualist. "At fifteen I set my heart on learning, at thirty I stood firm, at forty I had no doubts, at fifty I understood the way of heaven, at sixty I obeyed it, at seventy I could follow my own desires and do no wrong" [58B]. Negating `wrongs' from `desires' removes paradox in his statement and this can only be the saying of a wise man who found the path of reality through doubtless knowledge. This is a typical saying of a Sufi when he talks of various stations on the path of spirituality. This will be discussed in a later chapter.

Confucius' teachings played an important role in building the social life of Chinese society through, mercy, social order, and fulfilment of responsibilities.

2. Legalism [59]

The term means 'school of law' and was invented in the Han dynasty but took philosophic currents during the Warring States Period [60]. It is based on the principle that humans are evil and need to be controlled using laws in order to prevent chaos. This concept is pretty close to 'Nafs Amara' in Sufism. To make Legalism operational, meant to strengthen the political power of the ruler for implementing the prevailing rules. Legalism did not address higher questions like the nature and purpose of life. Its known proponent Han Fei Zi (非子) believed that a ruler should use the following three tools to govern his subjects:

1. Fa (法; literally "law"): The law code must be clearly written and made public so that people should know that law is equal for all and it should reward those who obey it and punish those who break it. Most importantly, the system of law run the state, not the ruler; thus when the law is enforced with success even a weak ruler becomes strong. Again, this concept is pretty close to the governance Sufis believe in.

2. Shu (术; literally "tactic"): Special tactics even secretive are employed by the ruler to make sure others don't take over control of the state. In this way, no one can fathom the ruler's motives and thus he does not know which behaviour might

help him to go forward except following the way prescribed by the law.

3. Shi (势; literally "power"): It is the position of the ruler not the ruler that holds the power. It also means that the ruler should detach self from the chair of position he holds to analyse the trends, the contexts and the facts as a real ruler.

This philosophy in coming decades dominated the political morality of Chinese society as governing force mingled with centuries old traditions. It spread to the Korean peninsula and Japan in the following centuries [61].

3. Taoism, [62]

Taoism is based on spirituality with overlying philosophy described in simple but effective way. It's originator is considered to be Li Erh. His historical existence is not clear but it is said that he was born around 604 BC in the `Ch U Jen' in the country of `KU' in the kingdom of Ch'U. He was named Lao Tzu, meaning the old boy, because of his white hair at birth. It is legendary that his mother conceived him from a shooting star and then kept him in her womb for eighty-two years, so when born, he could speak and had wisdom of an old man. He lived most of his life as palace secretary in the court of Chou at Loyang.

At the age of 160 years he decided to go to Tibet on the back of water buffalo. At the border he was stopped by the keeper of Hauku Pass named Hin Hsi, and asked him to leave his wisdom behind. He went into a solitary confinement for three days and came back with a book called `Tao Te Ching, containing 5000 characters. This book became the bible of Taoism.

Taoism revolves on three principles;

1. First, it is the way of ultimate universal reality which is rhythmic, divine and serene.

2. Second, it has the power to enter the flesh and assume the essence and likeness of dust.

3. Third, it refers to the way man should organize his life to coordinate himself with the universe harmoniously.

The Tao Te Ching is highly mystical and symbolic book filled with philosophical synchronicity. As a result, its readers take various meanings from its contents according to their logical perception. For example, the very first word `Tao' carries different meanings such as 'the way', 'the path', 'the word', 'the reason', 'the virtue', 'the road', 'the channel', or 'the way to go'.

'Te' on the other hand is an old Chinese concept which means 'power', 'force', 'energy' or 'virtue'. It is believed that every object in the universe has got `Te'. It is 'Te' which gives that object shape and makes it the way it is.

Lao Tzu said 'Tao' produces thing, 'Te' maintains it. So 'Te' is what an individual thing receives from 'Tao'. The total spontaneity of all things is 'Tao'. The spontaneity that individual thing receives from 'Tao' is 'Te'.

'Tao' is a balance between the opposites. It is the return of a phase to its origin which is the state of preexistence with the faculties of existence. Taoist does not struggle to assert himself aggressively. He believes in old saying `Be humble and you shall remain entire'. The entirety of Taoism projects in;

- power with quietude;
- production without possession;
- action without self-assertion;
- development without domination.

According to Taoism 'He who has ego has no Tao', or 'They who know, do not speak and those who speak do not know.' Comparing with Socrates who once said, 'All I know is that I know nothing', Lao Tze put the same thing in different way by saying, "The wise man is one who, knows, what he does not know." or 'The further one goes, the less one knows' [63].

Taoism believes in `wu wei' [64], meaning doing nothing or inaction. It does not mean physical inactivity. Instead, it points at noninterference in universal 'Tao' and individual 'Te' which restrain one from anger, ambition and meddlesome actions thus making him humble, kind, and sincere. The former are `Yangs'- the positive acts, and latter are `Yins' - the negative acts. A sober balance between Yang and Yin ripens love.

In this respect Taoism downgrades reasoning as reasoning involves one in discrimination of particulars which ignites egoism. The real knowing is passive and receptive. It stresses on negation of pomp and extravagance regarding them as pointless assertions, and emphasizing on modesty.

Taoism creates concord, peace, uniformity and simplicity in the minds of the people. It brings tranquility and equitable balance in their personalities. It can be compared with the smooth, calm and dulcet flow of water which fills the uneven, rugged surface of the earth.

In the following centuries, Taoism divided into three groups;

- Philosophical. Though Taoism is full of philosophical thoughts but yet the main components of philosophy-the active reasoning and the fiery discourses, are missing in their actual forms. More formal philosophy entered its door later with coming of Chuang Tzu, the philosopher.
- Magical. There is no mention of magic in original Taoism. It appeared later in its history, such as `Tao Te Ching' states 'a person who knows the secrets of Tao becomes immune to the attack of armed men and wild animals'. Or, 'he who attains Tao is everlasting'. These and similar statements became referral phrases for Chineses magic enthusiasts creating cults and sects from first century AD. The important among them were `Wu Tou Mi Tao' (the five pecks of rice way) founded by Chang Tao Ling [65] and the `Yellow Turbans' founded by Chang- Chueh [66] In the fourth century AD, Ko Hung

produced a pill of immortality [67]. With appearance of magic, mysticism and philosophy in Taoism, the concept changed into a religion. This concept attracted not just the common man of the society, but it got its acceptance by the elite as well.

- Mystical. When the Chinese emperor Chen Tsung needed moral support in his declining days of monarchy, he turned to Taoism. The mixing of the state with Taoism brought amalgamation of old Chinese gods with 'Tao' and 'Te' introducing mysticism in the religion. Impressed by the status of Buddha in Buddhism, Lao Tzu was given the divine title of Emperor of Mysterious Origin. Later, the Taoist gods and spirits were brought together into pantheon. Still later, the concept of paradise and hell was added to the religion. The Emperor was given a deitic eminence and he became the highest deity, bringing hierarchy in divinity. Three deities became very important; the Jade Emperor, Lao Tzu and Ling Pao. They were called 'the Three Purities', thus forming the official Taoist Trinity [68].

Thus, Taoism as spirituality started with basic fundamentals of humbleness, kindness, and equitable balance, was joined later by philosophy and theology changing into a religion. Having said that, Taoists do not recognize omnipotent or eternal deities though they believe in a vast pantheon of gods and goddesses which are considered as divine emanations of celestial energy. Taoism has no centralized authority and different sects have different headquarters but the White Cloud Temple in Beijing is a key administrative training center for priests [69].

So here we are seeing the history of mankind evolved in theological and philosophical scripts strengthening a base for religions on one hand and restructuring societies on the other. One through knowledge of intuition, the other through philosophical knowledge. We understand that one knowledge deals with the world of the unseen, the other with the world around us (world of the seen).

We also understand that one knowledge is unscientific, the other is scientific making the two knowledges and so the two worlds wide apart. At the same time, the modern human mental acumen is in need of a solution to bring the followers of the two closer for the greater global harmony and peace.

It is here that the history of mankind and spirituality comes in which is the final chapter of the book.

REFERENCES

1. (Spirituality: a new dimension, P.12)
2. (Ancient Greek philosophy)
3. (Article from PHILOSOPHY PATHWAYS Issue 130)
4. (Leonard Trelawny Hobhouse Facts)
5. (Ferdinand Canning Scott Schiller - Wikipedia, the free encyclopedia)
6. (Immanuel Hermann Fichte Quotes - Search Quotes)
7. (What is an Ontology? - Stanford Knowledge Systems Laboratory)
8. (Epistemology - Wikipedia, the free encyclopedia)
9. (Main Divisions of Philosophy - Philosophy Lander.edu)
10. (Aesthetics [Internet Encyclopedia of Philosophy)
11 (Ethics - Importance Of Philosophyef)
12. (Metaphysics - By Branch / Doctrine - The Basics of Philosophy)
13. (10 Best Socrates Quotes – HubPages)
14. (Essay | Plato's Concept of Philosopher-kings | BookRags.com)
15. (Plato (Stanford Encyclopedia of Philosophy)
16. (Aristotle)
17. (1905 French law on the Separation of the Churches and the State)
18A (Pan-Islamism and Iqbal) [18B], Juda ho Deen Syasat say to reh jate hay Changayze! - Gupshup
19. (PDF: A Bibliography of Alexander the Great by Waldemar Heckel)
20. (Mary K. Novello, Ed.D.; Washington Institute Foundation; Paper presented at the British Educational Research Association Conference, University of Sussex, at Brighton, 2-5 September, 1999.)
21. (1762/1979, p. 179....Rousseau, J.-J. (1979). Emile or on education (A. Bloom, Trans.). New York: Basic Books. (Original work published 1762).
22. (Johann Heinrich Pestalozzi - Wikipedia, the free encyclopedia)
23. (Leo Tolstoy - Wikipedia, the free encyclopedia)
24. (Friedrich Froebel created Kindergarten and designed the Froebel)
25. (Malamatiyya - Wikipedia, the free encyclopedia)
26. (Rousseau, 1775/1918, p. 724, translated by M. Novello.....Rousseau, J.-J. (1918). L' de Saint-Pierre. In Ch.-M. Des Granges (Ed.), Morceaux choisis des auteurs fran哲s (pp. 721-724). Paris: Librairie A. Hatier. (Original work published 1775)
27. (Husayn ibn Mansur al-Hallaj)
28. (Fahad Faruqui: Mansur Hallaj: The Sufi's Willful Erosion Of Self)

29. (Rousseau, 1788/1918, p. 712, translated by M. Novello)...Rousseau, J.-J. (1918). Son esprit et sa conversation [Spirit and conversation]. In Ch.-M. Des Granges (Ed.), Morceaux choisis des auteurs fran哲 s (pp. 712-715]. Paris: Librairie A. Hatier. (Original work published 1788)

30. (Spirituality-a new dimension P.27)

31. (Mulhern, 1959, p. 417 and p. 421.....Mulhern, J. (1959). A history of education: A social interpretation. (2nd ed.). New York: Ronald Press.)

32. (Rousseau, J.-J. (1975). Discourse on the origin and basis of inequality among men. In L. Bair (Trans.), The essential Rousseau (pp. 125-201). New York: Penguin. (Original work published 1755)

33A.. (For All the Wrong Reasons: The Story Behind Government Schools Walsh). 33B.(For all the wrong reasons: the story behind government schools - Page 65)

34. (Good, H.G. (1956). A history of American education. New York: Macmillan. p. 8)

35. (Ellis, A.K. & Fouts, J.T. (1994). Research on school restructuring. Princeton Junction, NJ: Eye on Education. p.132)

36. (Rousseau, J.-J. (1964). Extract from the treatise on the government of Poland. In R.L. Archer (Ed.), Jean-Jacques Rousseau: His educational theories selected from Emile, Julie and other writings (pp. 64-69). New York: Barron's Educational Series. (Original work published 1772)

37. (Rosa Maria Dias *Universidade Estadual do Rio de Janeiro – Brazil*)

38. (Nietzsche and Education · The Encyclopaedia of Educational)

39. (NIETZSCHE, 1975:152...NIETZSCHE, F – "Sur l'avenir de nos établissements d'enseignement". In: Écrits posthumes,1870–1873. Translated by Jean-Louis Backes, Michel Haar e Marc B. de Launay. Paris, Gallimard, 1975.)

40. (NIETZSCHE, 1979:152)

41. (In conjunction with taqwa, there exists ilm and amal || Imam Reza)

42. (Übermensch - Wikipedia, the free encyclopedia)

43. (Leiter (2002. Nietzsche on Morality, London: Routledge: 116-122).

44. (auf-eigne-Faust-leben-müssen) (BGE 212)

45. (Sufi Doctrines: the Path of Blame - The Chishti Order)

46. (Iqbal's Concept of Khudi (Ego) (G. Sabir) - Allama Iqbal)

47. (Zur Genealogie der Moral, Eine Streitschrift, 1887)

48. (Allama Iqbal on Takfiri Illiterate Mullah & Maulvies" Dr.Tahir ul)

49. (Der Antichrist. Fluch auf das Christentum, September 1888 [published 1895)

50. (Detwiler 1990....Detwiler, Bruce, 1990. Nietzsche and the Politics of Aristocratic Radicalism, Chicago: University of Chicago Press)

51. (Hunt 1985....Hunt, Lester, 1985. "Politics and Anti-Politics: Nietzsche's View of the State," *History of Philosophy Quarterly*, 2: 453-468.)

52. (2007.....Shaw, Tamsin, 2007. *Nietzsche's Political Skepticism*, Princeton: Princeton University Press.)

53. (2009. "Review of Shaw (2007)", *Notre Dame Philosophical Reviews*, 2009.01.21) Leiter, Brian and Neil Sinhababu (eds.), 2007. *Nietzsche and Morality*, Oxford: Oxford University Press)

54. (*Nietzsche: Philosopher, Psychologist, Antichrist* (1950)

55. (*Nietzsche as Philosopher* (1965)

56. (China Confucianism: Life of Confucius, Influences, Development)

57. (Ref, McLaughlin & Braun, 1998)

58A... (Additional references for the section: Lassiter, 1995; Tseng & Wu, 1985)[51^ "Confucianism and Confucian texts". Comparative-religion.com. http://www.comparative-religion.com/confucianism/. Retrieved 2009-04-18.) (58B...The Religions of China – home)

59. (Legalism (Chinese philosophy) - Wikipedia, the free encyclopedia)

60. (The Warring States Period of Ancient China - Ancient / Classical)

61. ("Chinese Legalism: Documentary Materials and Ancient Totalitarianism".Worldfuturefund.org. http://www.worldfuturefund. org/wffmaster/Reading/China/China%20Legalism.htm.)

62, History of Taoism - Wikipedia, the free encyclopedia

63. Tao Te Ching Quotes by Lao Tzu – Goodreads].

64. Wu Wei: the Action of Non-Action - Taoism - About.com]

65. A History of Chinese Civilization - Page 156 - Google Books]

66, Chang Chueh – Encyclopedia.com].

67, The Idea of Immortality in Chinese Thought And Its Influence].

68, The Three Purities - Taoism – About.com]

69. [49^ Miller, James. Daoism: A Short Introduction (Oxford: Oneworld Publications, 2003). ISBN 1-85168-315-1]

CHAPTER NINE

Mankind and Spirituality

———— ❖ ————

Spirituality is a vast field wherein, on one hand, an atheist can make a path for himself, on the other, it becomes an important component of organized religion. The history of religion [1] tells us that religions became organized when its three ingredients, 'theology' [2] 'philosophy' [3] and 'spirituality' [4] linked up in a triangle [5]. In making of this triangle, 'theology' appeared first, followed by 'philosophy' and then 'spirituality'. During the linkage, two major problems sprang up;

1. First, 'theology' being the oldest ingredient was given preference by its followers. They detested the other two late comers.
2. Second, the detest distorted the triangle which otherwise should have been equiangular.

A question may be asked as to how did the arbitrary triangle appear. And most importantly, how did the three ingredients of theology, philosophy and spirituality affected each other adversely or otherwise in this triangle. It seems 'theology' was like a straight line which lead humans in a simplistic way to an unknown world of godhead. People followed the line without asking questions. The first angle was formed when some followers of theology started asking inquisitive questions from its fellow theologians. That was the beginning of early philosophy. Philosophy was akin to a second line running parallel to theology. As human mental aptitude was under the influence of theology, the second line started converging on the first line making the first angle of religion.

With appearance of primitive philosophy in religions as a result of the merger of the two lines, envy was instilled amongst the custodians of theology creating turbulence in the smooth flow of religious understanding. While this turbulence was going on, a third line of spirituality appeared on horizon in the following millenniums which started converging on the first two lines and ultimately meeting them completing the triangle of religion. Spirituality got similar response from the other two which carries till the present day as part of 'organized religion' [6]. In this way theology, philosophy and spirituality which were running on separate lines converged into each other making a triangle and becoming pivotal ingredients of organized religions.

Depending on the mental aptitude of its followers, each component went through different phase of evolution. Thus theology created 'mythologies', philosophy introduced 'analytic systems', and spirituality presented 'paranormal phenomenons'. This uneven growth twisted the corresponding angles as time advanced. For example, at the peak of philosophical growth in Greece in the first millennium BC, philosophy was given preference side lining theology. While in the same period in India, Buddha was preaching spirituality downsizing theology. When asked about God, Buddha immediately brushed it aside advising his disciples to concentrate on spiritual aspect of self-improvement. In that very millennium, Confucius in China focused his attention on philosophy of life ignoring theological or spiritual aspects. Even today, opinions are divided whether to call Hunaism of Polynesia, a system, a spirituality or a religion.

So these ingredients instead of balancing each other and making an equiangular triangle distorted its shape. Such distortions meant envious built up between theologians, philosophers and spiritualists of the same religion on one hand, and conflicts with the followers of other religions on the other hand. In this way, the organized religions spread discontent, dislike and enmity among fellow humans. Major burden of blame for all this lies on shoulders of the custodians of theology but the followers of philosophy and spirituality cannot escape the responsibility either.

For example, spirituality and philosophy are two components of religion which should complement each other because both teach how to quash ego; spirituality through meditative techniques and philosophy through logical discourses. One without the other is like sugar without its sweetness. But yet when we study the history, we find clashes between the followers of the two which was made worse when the disgruntled custodians of theology joined the duel making religion a warring field. This was despite the fact that the custodians of the three entered religious folds to uplift societies through the rituals of theology, the reformation of philosophy and the fraternity of spirituality.

In previous two chapters I discussed the role theology and philosophy played in shaping up the history of the mankind. In this chapter I will take up spirituality and its role in making that history.

The origin of spirituality, like its other two sisters, theology and philosophy, is marked with confusion. Even the definition in dictionary hides its actuality, as its validity is determined only through communication with the spirits of the dead. For example, the dictionary defines it as: "(1) spiritual character, quality, or nature; religious devotion or piety; (2) the rights, jurisdiction, tithes, etc. belonging to the church or to an ecclesiastic; (3) the fact or state of being incorporeal" [7]. Houston Baker calls it "spirit work", which involves prophecy, healing, discernment. [8]

Part of this definition is right when it mentions things like 'spiritual character, quality, piety or rights' but when it links it with the church or religion, it restricts its sphere. Because an atheist can walk on the path of spirituality. Some of these definitions strengthen the concept that departed spirits communicate with the living especially through mediums to heal patients, give prophecies and talk to the dead etc. This might partly be true but it is not the essence of spirituality. It looks like these definitions have taken a lead from 30,000 years old history of mankind when primitive humans started communicating with the spirits of the dead through dreams and visions.

What such definitions lack is that spirituality is not just contacting the souls (erroneously called spirits) of the dead. But it is a path which has got many stations and at some stations, the seeker might communicate with the souls (erroneously called spirits). One should remember that such stations are located at various levels on the spiritual path to reach the ultimate goal of reality. Before a seeker reaches there, he has to pass these stations where he learns how to become a good human being by disciplining himself through meditative practices making him humble, tolerant and kind.

It means, a spiritualist must have humane qualities and be seen to portray them. The link with soul is a late phenomenon. In this context, spirituality can be defined as "a doctrine based on noble human acts, achieved through prescribed meditative methodologies which put a seeker on a path that leads to the knowledge of Soul, Spirit, and God and how to approach them."

This definition of spirituality brings five aspects upfront;

- First, it makes noble deeds and humanity as fundamental requirement;
- Second, it hints at the knowledge of the unseen and contacts with souls/spirits as late occurrence;
- Third, it separates spiritualists from charlatans by establishing precondition of human values;
- Fourth, addition of human values to spirituality, removes sectarian hate propagated by the traditionalist theologians whose words about god, spirit and soul do not match their worldly deeds;
- Fifth, it opens the path for an atheist to walk on it as an initiate spiritualist.

The history of mankind tells us that long before the establishment of societies, humans lived in caves. As discussed earlier the early humans of prehistoric times believed that an unknown entity lived in their skulls, which became active when they were asleep. What puzzled them the most was that in their sleep they met people who were already dead and were more powerful than they were alive. Not even that, they found the dead had control over time. They dreamt that the dead would do things in a blink of an eye which would normally take them lifetime to complete. It was the same story with time travel. They saw them moving from place to place in no time. They linked all these powers with the entity that seemed to reside in their skulls. [9] With passage of time, these events imprinted three impressions in their memory which turned into convictions:

1. First, the entity which allegedly lived in the skull was much more powerful than humans could ever imagine.
2. Second, life did not end with the death of an individual but continued in some unknown form.
3. Third, a person became extremely powerful after death.

The powerful entity became known as the 'spirit' in the following millenniums. The prehistoric humans lived by their instincts. One of the instincts was the fear of death which generated awe and reverence towards the dead. It also made them explore methods through which they could make the dead happy and find ways to make themselves as powerful as the dead. The former resulted in rituals for the dead and the latter in eating their brains.

Rituals for the dead, over the centuries, took shape in burial ceremonies, including offering various services and sacrificial rites. The custom of eating human brains was extended to eating the brains of animals in later centuries to improve their inner strength. To protect themselves from the spirits of the dead, people started collecting the skulls of the dead after eating their brains. Whether people killed their fellow beings to eat their brains, or severed the skulls of the dead, cannot be ascertained.

As time passed, the cave-dweller found that sometimes he would experience a dreamlike experience while wide awake. It was more of a vision than dream. This not only strengthened the belief in the 'spirits' but also opened the window of possibility to approach their residing place where, up until then, only the dead could reach. This was the first human experience of 'spirituality'; an experience perceived for no obvious reasons and without any prior preparations. Such an experience made a base for the 'original or nascent spirituality' in which a person could communicate with the spirits of the dead without falling asleep. It was a new dimension to budding spirituality.

The cave-dweller, after experiencing the new phenomenon of 'vision', started looking for ways to discover the abode of spirits of the dead so as to acquire their powers. With the advent of communal life and interaction between individuals, some people claimed to be able to reach the spirits through their own will. Whether they could actually do so would never be known, but one thing became apparent that those claiming to possess such power would act differently to influence people.

This new dimension of spirituality opened the gate of magic for the charlatans. Thus we find spirituality and magic started to run parallel in the field of beliefs. Magic needed acts, so a good magician had to be a good actor to deliver goods. The spiritualist, on the other hand, did not rely on acting. For a magician, spirituality was acting, while for a spiritualist it was reality. This holds true up to the present day.

With passage of time, the magician gained a larger audience than the spiritualist. People flocked around the magician. Through tricks, he would impress people by telling them about the unknown powers, sooth-saying, impending disasters, and so on. The spiritualist, by nature, tended to remain obscure. He, having no control over his powers to reach the world of the spirits, would unwittingly get in touch with them. There were no techniques, practices or systems to prepare him and reach them at will. All he knew was that something would happen to him and he would reach out to the unknown. This was the total shape of 'original or nascent spirituality' in prehistoric times.

Gradually, people realized that not everything the magicians did or said about or on behalf of the spirits was true. They saw many failed results. As there was a very thin line between magic and spirituality, people measured them with the same yardstick. Such failed results created doubts in their mind about the position they held on the 'spirits'. Thus, we find prehistoric people turning away from the 'spirit' and looking towards a new and more powerful entity.

This was the beginning of concept of the 'godhead', which was to nurture later in the tenets of religions. In this way, spirituality of the 'spirit' and theology of the 'godhead' evolved in religious field. In the process, belief in 'spirit' mixed up with belief in the 'godhead'. This mixing can still be seen in certain religions of present day.

The Palaeolithic, Mesolithic and Neolithic eras came and gone. During all this time, human thinking, psychic abilities and mental grasp progressed with linear acceleration. The solitary cave-life of a hunter evolved into communal way of living as agriculture and so the societies progressed. As part of evolution, religion also progressed, keeping pace with human imagination. The theology of 'godhead' changed to multiple gods having a variety of duties and powers.

Around 1900 BC in Mesopotamia, Abraham appeared on the scene. He challenged the concept of multiple godhead and promoted the notion of one god, laying the foundation of three major prophetic religions of Judaism, Christianity and Islam. While, elsewhere the concept of multiple godhead continued unabated.

Spirituality, on the other hand, remained unaltered until 5000 BC when a new concept of 'inner power' appeared in human thinking. This entity became more apparent in Egypt around 3000 BC, when it was believed to live in abdomen. It became known as 'Ba' [10]. The Egyptians could only explain it in terms of its resemblance to worldly things. This was the entire perception about its form. There was no knowledge of its powers, its energizing properties and ways of approaching it. It is said that this idea might have come to Egypt from Saharan peoples after the migration of eleven tribes, when that part of the world became desert as a result of global climatic changes.

The notion of 'inner power' spread to ancient Greko-Roman, Indian and Polynesian religions as 'Psuche', [11] 'Mana' [12] and 'Unipihili' [13] respectively. In Rome at one stage in history, it entered the realm of godhead and became its strength. In Mesopotamian religions, it became 'Farvashi' in Zoroastrianism, [14] 'Nephesh' in

Judaism [15], 'Soul' in Christianity [16] and 'Nafs' in Islam [17]. In China it became 'Te' in Taoism. [18]

This inner power was going to play essential role in evolution of spirituality. For example, in India, in second millennium BC, Hinduism saw successive changes in theology, especially in its concept of the changing scenario of godhead, from monotheism to polytheism and vice versa, and from generalized gods to personalized gods and vice versa. These changes made Hindus broad minded and tolerant. So when philosophy appeared on the scene, it was accepted readily. But, it was different story with spirituality.

At the end of second millennium BC, Hinduism gave birth to Brahmanism which introduced caste system to help Brahman. When spirituality surfaced a few centuries later, it clashed with Brahman's caste system. As opposed to Brahmanic approach, the philosophical Hindu theologians accepted spirituality in a unique manner. They attached it to Hinduism without integrating it with religion. This clever link created a platform for movements such as Hari Krishna and Hari Rama in subsequent centuries. Today, Ashrams all over the world are spreading spirituality in the name of Hinduism where the followers of different religions join Hindus for spiritual uplift without leaving their religions. They practice Raja Yoga [19] and its eight limbs to get Shanti (inner peace) by activating inner self.

Had spirituality entered officially the fold of Hinduism, this religion would have come so close to the last Mesopotamian religion of Islam that all it needed was acceptance of prophet-hood, and a natural union between these two great religions would have become imminent. It is very unfortunate to see that recently the die-hard Hindu theologians, forgetting the philosophical merger and spiritual affinity of past, have lost a grip over tolerance, which had been the mainstay of this religion, and started spreading hate in India.

The preacher of another offshoot of Hinduism, Buddha in the 5th century BC, seeing the discriminatory attitude of Brahman, based Buddhism on a new version of spirituality. He was the first preacher who preached that the way one could achieve enlightenment (Nirvana) was through good deeds. He used meditations for self-discipline and linked it to nurturing human values and bringing sobriety, tolerance, and love to personality paving the way to enlightenment. He stressed on strengthening 'inner self' and used it to refine deeds rather than craving for an 'outer power' for help through prayers and rituals. In a way, he set aside the concept of godhead. No wonder when he was asked about the godhead he replied to concentrate on inner self.

At this time in history, we find Spirituality evolving itself in two different forms:

- The old model in which a spiritualist would reach out to the world of the spirits, in uncontrolled, non-methodical and unknowing manner;
- A new form, in which a spiritualist would use certain known and specific methods to energize his 'inner power' (Mana) and instil noble qualities in his personality and then reach to the unknown world of the spirits.

Thus the new ingredient of becoming a good human turned out to be a pivotal step in evolution of spirituality. With addition of this ingredient, not only did true spirituality emerge, but it also drew a clear distinction between a spiritualist and a charlatan. Anyone claiming to be a spiritualist without having noble qualities of honesty, humility, selflessness, tolerance, patience, kindness and love could not be considered a spiritualist—a magician yes, but a spiritualist no.

Two centuries later, spirituality propagated by Buddha shifted to China, and took a new shape in the form of Taoism in the society of traditional multiple godhead. In doing so, the inner power 'Mana' changed to 'Te' that created a harmonious balance between 'Yin' (dark) and 'Yang' (bright) which in turn affected human deeds through the inner power of 'Te' as taught by Lao Tze [20]

In Mesopotamia, from times of Abraham around 1900 BC, theology and its associated rituals had progressed gradually over centuries but bulk of religion was empty in spirituality [21]. For example, Israel changed El (the god) to Eloah after the excursion of his grandson, Jacob [22]. Later, in the 13th century BC, Eloah was changed to Yehweh as divine unity by Moses putting a base for Judaism [23]

Socially, the followers of Abrahamic religion during all those centuries, suffered a despicable humiliation by the hands of Pharaohs. They became the victims of a polarized pagan society of Egypt. A society, in which the Pharaohs were gods, rulers, law-givers and the custodians of religion. And the believers were slaves, put in dungeons where they lived a degrading and humiliating life. They desperately needed a religious leader of Abraham's stature to save them from the cruel hands of Pharaohs. In the end they found one such leader. His name was Moses. Though he lived as prince in the palace of arrogant Pharaoh Manses but humbleness and human nature filled his personality. It pained him when he saw his fellow humans in wretched condition living a noxious life. He could not bear it when, one day, he saw a soldier killing an innocent labourer. In anger, he killed the soldier with his own hands.

This was rebirth of those very rebellious feelings which his forefather Abraham had against the unjust system seven hundred years earlier. The incidence was the start of revival of Abrahamic religion. Moses prepared himself to fight his adoptive Pharaoh father with the tool most fashionable at that time - the magic. Magic up until then had important place in religion. He proved that in the name of God and fought magic with miracles like turning his stick into anaconda, converting magical snakes into ropes, making his bare hand shine or breaking the flow of river etc [24]

He used those powers and helped his fellow men in mass migration to Palestine reviving the religion of Abraham. In Palestine, he upgraded the religion by introducing Ten Commandments and called it Judaism.

Spirituality in Judaism

As the mental acumen of mankind was not developed enough to appreciate the depth of divine unity and its link with spirituality, Moses concentrated only on codes of theology.

In the following centuries up-gradation continued on scholastic aspects in written and oral laws during the axial age. For example:

- In 1000-1009 century BC, David united Judah and Israel, making Judaism stronger politically [25]
- In 945 BC, Solomon built the Temple in Jerusalem and created a hub for future Judaism making the city the focus of Zion [26]. The affairs of the Temple were organized by the Elders of Zion, headed by a prophet of the time. This brought uniformity in the religion but exposed Jerusalem politically to external threats. In the following centuries attacks by pagans split the country into Judah and Israel and destroyed the walls of Jerusalem.
- In 457 BC, a Babylonian Jew Ezra came to the city to build the wall but got himself involved in scholarly work and 12 years later came up with the Pentateuch as written law [27]. He was supported by another Babylonian Jew, Nehemiah, who concentrated on building the wall which he did in 52 days [28]
- In the 4th century BC, another author, Malachi, appeared on the scene who took bold steps by altering the old laws and made them more appealing. His discourses became known as the Chronicles (Some historians link them to Ezra) [29]
- In the 3rd century BC Judah fell to Greece exposing Judaism to liberal Greek paganism which not only brought nudity but also mercenaries, greedy merchants and of course scholars and philosophers. In the following years the Hebrew Bible was translated to Greek and public libraries appeared for the first time in Jerusalem. Scholars like Ben Sira, influenced by Greek education introduced the school, master and disciple

relationship to Judaism exposing it to philosophy as part of religious evolution [30]

During all this period when Judaism was bombarded by scholastic themes, it remained dry in the field of spirituality. It was in the 2rd century BC when a group of ascetic Pietists infiltrated the religion. The group believed that the mysteries of God could be deciphered by those who knew the codes, and those secrets could be received through certain mystic methods and practices [31]

A few decades later, another spiritual group, the Essene, appeared on the scene. Literally the name meant 'the pious ones'. They believed in secrecy and piety towards God, which, according to them, could lead one to asceticism and thus to holiness. This was a splinter group of disgruntled Jews with affiliation to Peitist movement. They left Jerusalem and settled in caves near Qumran along the River Jordan.

Thus spirituality entered the fold of Judaism twice in three centuries. During this entry, it sprinkled the religion but the sprinkling was not strong enough to leave a durable impression. Metaphorically speaking, the spiritual coins were put in the theocratic bank of Judaism with minimum spiritual return. As a result, spirituality remained well behind theology in Judaism until the birth of Jesus of Nazareth in Bethlehem, around 8 BC. Even then it did not gather momentum because the movement parted its way in following decades and turned into a new religion – The Christianity.

By this time Judaism was divided in three Sectarian Groups;

- The Essenes; they were the spiritualists. According to Dead Sea Scrolls, seventy-three years after crucifixion of Jesus, Roman soldiers invaded Qumran killing all Essenes except two women and five children who somehow escaped the massacre. It brought an end to spiritual rise in Judaism [32]
- The Zedukins known also as the Sadducee. They believed in the Pentateuch, ignored the Oral Laws of Moses, were impressed by Greek knowledge, and accepted the changing concept of the religion. The Greek influence made them social

elitists who would look down upon other groups. Generally speaking, they were the moderates [33]

- The Penushins also known as the Pharisees. They belonged to the poor strata of society. They believed in the Pentateuch and the Oral Laws, and were committed to the Rituals of religion. Basically they were hard core traditionalists [34]

In centuries that followed, we find Rabbi Akiva and the Sanhedrin Rabbi - Judah the Prince, wrote the oral traditions of Moses and called it the Mishna, meaning Repetition [35]. It consisted of six orders:

- Zera'im ("Seeds"), dealing with prayer and blessings, tithes and agricultural laws (11 tractates)
- Mo'ed ("Festival"), pertaining to the laws of the Sabbath and the Festivals (12 tractates)
- Nashim ("Women"), concerning marriage and divorce, some forms of oaths and the laws of the Nazirite (7 tractates)
- Nazikin ("Damages"), dealing with civil and criminal law, the functioning of the courts and oaths (10 tractates)
- Kodashim ("Holy things"), regarding sacrificial rites, the temple, and the dietary (11 tractates) and
- Tehorot ("Purities"), pertaining to the laws of purity and impurity, including the impurity of the dead, the laws of food purity and bodily purity (12 tractates).

Others wrote commentary on the Mishna, calling it Gemara, [36] meaning completion. They combined the Pentateuch, Mishna and Gemara, and produced the Talmud. [37]

The scholarly work went ahead producing books of Judith, Tobit, Job, Jonah, Ecclesiastes, etc. Similarly, a few worked on apocalyptic literature, describing cosmic forces, supernatural powers, super-human beings, time beyond history, etc. The books included in this group were the Book of Enoch, Daniel, Jubilees, the testaments of the twelve patriarchs, the Dead Sea Scrolls, the Apocalypse of Alaraham, and so on.

After the destruction of the Temple by Titus in the 1st century AD and dispersion of the Jews, the clergy shifted from Jerusalem to Yahne. [38] There, a Pharisee cleric, Zakkai, and a Sadducee priest, Shammi, opened parallel schools and changed the title of High Priest to Rabbi. One school became traditional, the other philosophical; one ritualistic, the other reformist. The spiritualists never made it to the scholastic stage. Both schools believed that spirituality would split the religion, and those Jews who inclined towards spiritualism were branded as Christian heretics. Thus Judaism remained spiritually barren for a long time.

In the 8th century AD, a spiritual group called Karaites surfaced. They introduced poetry in Judaism taken from the Islamic lyrical literature of Spain. Thus they not only opened a window of understanding between the two great Mesopotamian religions, but they also reintroduced spirituality to Judaism [39]

In the 9th century AD, an Italian Jew, Kalonyums, who had strong spiritual inclinations, migrated to Germany. In the following centuries three rabbis of his clan, Rabbi Samuel, Rabbi Judah and Rabbi Elizar, taught spirituality that resembled the asceticism of Christianity. [40] Their concept of soul was called Shekhinah, which meant radiance of god. As usual, this doctrine was not taken well by the traditionalist Rabbis [41]

From the 9th century AD onwards, Islam and Judaism accommodated each other politically, and culturally but theologically they stayed apart. As a result, some non-Muslims branded Islam a carbon copy of Judaism. Christianity, on the other hand, based its policies on loathing Judaism and Islam.

In the 13th century AD, a Spanish Cabalist, Abulafia introduced a technique similar to Yoga or Sufism, to gain inner awareness and union with godhead. He did not get an encouraging response from the traditionalist Rabbis [42]

In the 16th century AD another spiritualist, Isaac Luria appeared on the scene who believed in cosmic disarray due to a divine catastrophe which, he said, could only be corrected through the re-adjustment of Israel by a Messiah [43]

In 17th century an ascetic spiritualist Rabbi Judah Loew from Prague revived Cabala doctrine promoting the concept of Ensuf according to which one could reach asceticism and thus holiness by deciphering the truth through mystical practices. His notion was fairly close to the Sufi concept of godhead [44].

Ensuf manifests itself in ten Sephiroths: [45]

1. Kether Elyon, as a supreme crown
2. Hokhmah, as wisdom
3. Binah, as intelligence
4. Hesod, as love or mercy
5. Din, as power
6. Rakhmin, as compassion (this is also called Tefereth, as Beauty)
7. Netsakh, as lasting endurance
8. Hod, as majesty
9. Yesod, as foundation
10. Malkuth, as kingdom (also called Shekinah)

According to Cabala spirituality god becomes 'He' in the first three Sephiroths and 'I' in the next six. Diagrammatically these Sephiroths are presented as an Inverted Tree. In this tree, Din is represented as a stern warning and it is depicted as the left hand of the godhead. Hesod is represented as mercy and depicted as the right hand. The balance between these two keeps a person in tranquillity. If there is breakage in the left arm the person gets astray and becomes evil.

As we will see later, the concept of tree known as 'Marateb-e-Elahi (Divine Ranks) is also seen in Sufism.

In 1626, Shabbetai Zevi from Smyrna in Asia Minor appeared on the scene. He started his spiritual movement when he was 18 and very quickly spread like wild fire. He was joined later by Nathan of Gaza, who became his prophet. But, as usual, upon experiencing the spiritual vacuum in Judaism, he turned to Islam on 15 September 1666 in Constantinople [46]

In the 16th century a group of mystics appeared in Poland among Cabalist and Rabbinic Jews. A Cabalist Jew was born among them. His was name was Israel Baal Shem Tov, later became known as 'Besht'. He would go into ecstasies and practice faith healing. He had powers of ESP and could read the future and talked about past. He was an ascetic and would dance in ecstasy and immerse himself in a ritual bath prior to healing sessions. He believed that the master of the universe got delectation in the happiness of his people.

He would chant;

- "Dance - God watches you,
- Sing - God hears you,
- Be joyous - God loves His people to be happy" [47]

His movement became known as Hasidism. His concept of Shakinah was filled with spirituality and pretty close to Sufism. Though this spiritual movement had no military aims and was based on love and happiness, a few Hasidim in the early 19th century carried out intrigues against Napoleon, because he was planning to destroy Jewish ghettos. Besht died in 1760 as a Jew, though rabbinic Jews never accepted him with open arms and always charged his mission [48]

In the 17th century, Spinoza went through similar mental turmoil. He became atheist after he was excommunicated searching to satisfy his soul [49]

It was the same story with the ascetic Jacob Frank from southern Poland in the mid-18th century. Impressed by Zevi, he started the Frankist Movement. He became Christian after he was excommunicated and branded as a heretic [50]

Again, in the last century, Martin Buber's doctrine of an 'I-It' and 'I-Thou' relationship with the godhead took him away from Judaism towards Christianity [51].

Reading the Judaic history, it becomes apparent that in the first ten centuries spirituality remained invisible. Then, in the next twenty centuries it appeared in pockets such as Pietist, Essene, Cabalist, Besht and Hasidism movements. The traditionalist Jews relentlessly opposed these movements. Their followers were punished and excommunicated. If we consider the original three sects of Essene, Sadducee and Pharisee of Judaism as three angles of a triangle, we find that the spiritual angle was never given a chance to increase.

In the last two centuries, people such as Theodore Hertz and his colleagues of the late 19th century made an intelligent move by giving political dimension to the three sects as three angles and fashioned them into two overlapping triangles as part of renewed Zionism. They refashioned Judaism by readjusting the original three sects according to global politics. So they;

- Brought the Essenes-based spiritual Cabalist into the fold of politics.
- Gradually reduced the influence of die-hard traditionalist Pharisee
- Rapidly strengthened the hands of Sadducee.

Their policy worked wonders. Within a few decades they managed to create a country for the Jews at the location the Jews always dreamed of. Bringing spirituality within the fold and reducing the role of traditionalists was a clever move.

In recent years the custodians of Judaism have been playing wise role by reforming religion vis-a-vis global politics especially in North America. They worked closely with the like-minded Christians and brought them together as Neo-Con Zionists on the platform of Judeo-Christian philosophy. This bond got strengthened after 9/11 especially against Islam.

The role of spiritual Cabalists seems awkward because Cabala is pretty close to Sufism in many ways. Keeping those commonalities in mind, it will be good for global peace if the politically powerful Cabalists take a progressive step and shake hands with Sufis on the principles of Ensuf. After all, the chief of Cabala is considered to be one of the most powerful politico-spiritual figures in north America.

In this way, they would help humanity by demolishing the hate wall erected by the traditionalists and the Neo-Con Zionists.

This brings us to the second prophetic Abrahamic religion of Christianity and spirituality therein.

Spirituality in Christianity

Christianity went through its own history not very different from Judaism as far as spirituality was concern. According to the Dead Sea Scrolls [52], a group of Essenes Jews who believed in mystical experiences, seeing the moral corruption and social degradation of society in Jerusalem, decided to move to the mountains along the River Jordan and live a holy life in caves near Qumran. Over the years, they attracted those Jews who were disillusioned by the declining religious zeal and increasing Roman interference in Judaism.

In the 1st century BC, Zachariah, the high priest of Jews in Jerusalem, took a vow that if he were blessed with a son he would send him to the Essenes for his upbringing. When John was born to Zachariah's wife Elizabeth, cousin of Mary, he fulfilled the promise and sent his son to the mountains. The Essenes way of life brought a profound change in John's personality. He correlated external purification of body with internal cleansing of soul. To symbolize this link, he started immersing Jews in water initiating the ritual of Baptism. Soon he became known as John the Baptist. The news of this innovation quickly spread and Jews started flocking from all corners. People coming from Jerusalem would inform him about the poor conditions and deplorable life the Jews were going through. In describing their miseries, they would talk about their;

- social wretchedness,
- religious degradation,
- moral corruption,
- ethnic persecution at the hands of the Romans,
- and most importantly, their inability to do anything when the Romans took over the most sacred place of Judaism-the Temple- and placed Golden Eagle on its top.

These and similar disturbing news would make John the Baptist desolate and angry. He would often plan ways to avert such a decline. It was during that time when Jesus was born to Mary around 8 BC in Bethlehem and Herod was killing all Jewish male new-borns. To avoid having being killed Jesus along with Mary were taken to Egypt where a colony of Essenes had already settled. After the death of Herod a few years later, they returned to Qumran and started living the Essenes way of life. John the Baptist baptised Jesus and made him his trusted partner [53].

The Essenes life changed Jesus. He absorbed love and tolerance into his mild, gentle and friendly personality as part of his spiritual growth. Meanwhile, John, started recruiting zealots among his followers in anticipation of a power struggle against the Romans. The Romans, realizing John's intentions captured and beheaded him in order to stop the movement.

After John's beheading, responsibility fell on the shoulders of the 30-year-old Jesus. He accepted the onerous role and went into solitary confinement for forty days to attain further spiritual heights and inner strength. After re-emerging from the solitude as a stronger and spiritual being he took the leadership role to complete the unfinished mission of John. In doing so he brought a few changes, such as:

- He stopped baptising the Jews.
- He started preaching spiritual message of divine unity through love, peace and tolerance.
- He appointed twelve disciples, representing the twelve tribes of Israel, who further enlisted seventy patriots to serve under them.
- He made militancy the last option against pagans to achieve his goals.

After spreading his message of love and tolerance for three years, Jesus became the symbol of hope for the downtrodden Jews. They called him the Messiah. Basing his movement on spirituality, he met their expectations by;

- lifting their emotional psyche;
- healing their physical ailments;
- strengthening their religious faith.

His sermons became enlightening experience for many Jews but an obvious threat to the Romans. Thus, Jesus, a Messiah for the Jews, soon became a thorn in the side of the Romans. His gentle, captivating and love-preaching movement became a forceful, detestable, and humiliating challenge to the administrative pagan elites.

Fearing an attack, the Romans placed strict security around the Temple and started using financial intrigues, oppressive techniques and psychological plots to split Jews and fail Jesus in his mission. But Jesus, with the help of his disciples and zealots, took over the Temple against all odds. He started cleansing the sacred place and delivering a new spiritual version of Judaism. A few days later, after reinforcing the forces and bribing a good number of Jews, the Romans broke into the Temple.

In confusion Jesus went underground only to be traced later when his perfidious disciple, Judas was bribed for 30 pieces of silver. A few days earlier, at the last supper with his apostles, Jesus had predicted such a betrayal.

What happened afterwards became the pivotal tenet of Christian Faith. According to Dead Sea Scrolls the soldiers captured Judas who resembled Jesus and after a speedy trial magistrate Pontius Pilate, a sympathizer of Jesus, sent him to the Cross [54]. Centuries later, for this act of 'Justice' Pontius Pilate and his wife were awarded posthumous sainthood by the Arius Church [55].

After the crucifixion/resurrection of Jesus, antithetical faith-based versions took root about:

5. The actuality of his being,
6. The nature of his teachings,
7. The authenticity of the Gospels,
8. The validity of the writers of the scriptures.

The varied interpretations resulted in sharp divisions amongst the followers of Jesus. Jesus by then had become the Christ, a title taken from the Greek word 'Christos' meaning 'the anointed'.

Immediately after his crucifixion, his devotees were Jews communing and preaching in synagogues. For a while they were called the Nazarene. Later they were labelled the Christians, a title given by the upper-class Jews and Romans to denigrate the converts who dressed in rags and preached morality. Jesus did not leave behind a written scripture as he did not write what he preached. The writings started to appear after his crucifixion. The chief writers of the scriptures were Peter, Mark, Paul, Luke, Barnabas, Matthew, John, Mathias, Andrew and Thomas.

Among all the disciples, Paul and Barnabas played crucial roles in shaping future Christianity.

1. Paul (Saul) [56] was originally a Roman. He studied Greek philosophy and lived in Jerusalem. He never met Jesus and was a staunch enemy and known persecutor of the Nazarene. At some stage, he started seeing visions of Jesus in dreams and receiving revelations. Being a classmate and friend of Barnabas-a disciple who met Jesus-he started to know more about the life of Jesus Christ. Soon he became his staunch follower.

2. Barnabas [57] was born in Cyprus to a Jewish family. He was a dedicated Unitarian and a tough adversary of Greek philosophy. He was a close friend, committed supporter, and original disciple of Jesus but apparently never understood his spiritual personality. He introduced Paul to the Jewish community as friend but parted ways with him years later after differences appeared between them on the divinity of Jesus.

Their teachings and writings split Christianity in two divergent denominations based on the question of divinity of Jesus that put a foundation of the Trinitarian and Unitarian churches. The former became the kernel of separation theory resulting in the Holy Trinity, and the latter the core of fusion theory of Unitarianism.

Paul, himself a spiritualist, misconceived the realm of spirituality by confusing Jesus' spiritual emanation from God as God's temporal separation from God, thus making God the Father and Jesus his Son. This created duality in Pauline theology. It was a typical case where a spiritualist, sometimes, in spiritual flow misconstrues revelations and confuses part with total. The spiritualist Paul in his quest for truth mingled Greek philosophy with notion of spirit and created the concept of the Holy Spirit, thus changing duality into Trinity. This novel idea attracted both Greeks and Romans who flocked to Pauline Christianity in Europe. Thus the original Article of Faith, which stated:

'I believe in God, the Almighty' changed in sequence to:

- 'God the father' and later to:
- 'God the Father, Jesus the Son' as duality and still later to:
- 'God the Father, Jesus the Son and the Holy Spirit' as trinity, while still later simply to:
- 'The Father, the Son, and the Holy Ghost'.

To make it more attractive to the morally corrupt pagan society, Paul, who by that time had pronounced himself the Divine Authority, introduced the doctrines of redemption and atonement.

In contrast to the changing theology of Trinitarian church, the Unitarian church remained confined to Unitarian theology, keeping Jesus separate from divine unity and thus ignoring his spiritual oneness with God. So, the Trinitarian Church in search of spirituality addled the notion of theology, and the Unitarian church in upholding theology neglected spirituality.

In other words, one group of churches highlighted spiritual Christianity and promoted Jesus Christ as God or Son of God. The other group of churches propagated a non-spiritual Christianity portraying Jesus something like Messiah and not God.

In the following centuries, the pagan Roman emperor, Constantine, killed his son Crispus out of jealousy and then murdered his wife to cover up the first crime. After his redemption was rejected by the priests of Jupiter in Rome, he left the capital and settled in Byzantium renaming it Constantinople. To reward his needy ego and wash his guilt for the crimes he committed, he found Pauline theology attractive as it had articles of redemption, atonement and Trinity. In 325 AD, he called a meeting at Nicaea to counteract his iniquity, bring administrative control over divergent churches and help his favourite sanctuary [58].

The meeting was attended by the representatives of various churches, which, by then, were preaching over three hundred gospels. Conspicuous were the representatives of Pauline Church, and noticeably absent were representatives of its arch rival, Arius, a strong supporter of the Unitarian Church. Constantine chaired the meeting. At the end of a heated and inconclusive debate over the divinity of Jesus and the authenticity of the Gospels, he ordered to leave all the Gospels under the table for the night. And the gospel found on the table the next day would be accepted as the genuine and official Christian Gospel. The hall was locked for the night. Only the emperor knew where the keys were hidden. The next day, when the door was opened they found the gospel of Athanasius, the Pauline representative from Alexandria, on the table.

Thus, the pagan emperor succeeded in enforcing his choice of gospels over other gospels and made the Pauline Church official tenet which was renamed later the Roman Catholic Church. The Gospels by Mark, Matthew, Luke and John became the official scriptures of the Bible. The rest of the gospels were burnt, destroyed or made apocryphal. Years later, these gospels were re-synthesized, selecting 50% of the writings from Mark, 75% from Matthew, 66% from Luke and 96% from John, giving a new shape to the Bible in the form of The New Testament.

The other decisions tabled and accepted by the Council at Nicaea were:

- The Roman sun-god day, the Sunday, was made the Sabbath day for the Christians.
- December 25th being the traditional birthday of the sun-god, was made the official birthday of Jesus Christ.
- Cross being the sign of the sun-god became the symbol of Christianity.
- The sacred festival of the goddess of fertility at Easter was made the Christian Easter.

Constantine converted to Christianity in 336 AD and died a year later as a Christian, but not before reverting from Pauline to Unitarian faith, having been impressed by Arius of the Apostolic Church. After his death his successor, Constantius, became a strong supporter of Unitarian Theology, giving administrative strength to that church. This change of heart of the emperor, from one church to another, reduced the power of the Pauline Church in the East. Thus we find that the Unitarian Church expanded aggressively in North Africa and western Asia—the regions influenced by Constantinople—while the Pauline Church-Catholicism grew stronger in Europe.

In centuries that followed, Christianity absorbed Greek and Roman philosophies into its spiritual fold resulting in appearance of three major schools of thought based on the doctrine of Trinity.

- First, the St. Augustine school of the 4th century, which states that the doctrine could not be proved but could be illustrated [59].
- Second, the St. Victor school of the 12th century, which states that the doctrine could be both proved and illustrated [60].
- Third, the 14th-century school, which states that the doctrine could neither be proved nor illustrated, but it should be accepted unquestioningly [61].

Further subdivisions in these schools divided Christianity into additional groups. Against this background, we find the rise of theosophists, spiritualists, and thinkers in the following centuries such as;

- Kierkegaard, who based his spirituality on distinction between objective (outward) and subjective (inward) knowledge [62],
- St Benedict, who based divinity on poverty, chastity and meekness [63],
- Augustine, who was the pioneer of St Augustine School of thought, differentiated good from evil, and revealed that the latter could be conquered by the former through spiritual development [64].
- There were other thinkers and theosophists in the first five centuries of Christianity.

After studying the life of Jesus and the turbulent growth of Christianity afterwards, one might think that the spirituality of Jesus was misjudged by the Pauline Church and neglected by the Unitarian Church. This can be true. The custodians of Pauline Church recognized Jesus Christ having a divine personality with embodiment of godhead added a spiritual dimension to the prophetic religion of Abraham. While the followers of Unitarian Apostolic Church accepted him as Messiah and concentrated on theosophical dimension of the religion.

The simple fact was that Jesus had a spiritual personality and wanted to give spiritual dimension to Judaism as continuity of Abrahamic Faith. But the custodians of various churches portrayed him according to their understanding creating doubts in the followers and sowing the seeds of discontent within Christianity.

This misunderstanding created hate among Christians towards other religions and towards reformist Christians who were labelled as heretics. As a result of such hate over one million Christians were killed in the first few centuries of Christianity. It is a great pity to see that spirituality which entered Christianity as its main ingredient was lost in its evolution for a long time. With advancement of thought process and improvement in sense of realization, one can see that in the second half of the 20th century, a lot of Christian churches in the West have moved in the right direction by allowing Christians to have mystical experiences through sermons, chants, meditations, and even drugs. This is especially the case in North America, where materialistic and over-worked Christians look for a spiritual refuge.

There is vast spiritual depth in Christianity and if followed in its true spirit, it can play enormous role as essential component of Abrahamic Faith to bring peace in the world. A world which is gradually captured by the wildly spreading greedy corporations helped by politically motivated traditionalist theologians.

This brings us to the third component of Abrahamic religion Islam which emerged in 6th century AD.

Spirituality in Islam

The last Abrahamic religion was passed on through Abraham's son Ishmael and reached the bare and rugged land of Arabia by his great, great...great grandson Muhammad. He added the pillar of 'submission' to the already existing pillars of previous monotheistic religions creating a balance between theology, philosophy and spirituality.

1. Theology through continuity of monotheism of Abraham;
2. Philosophy through the in-depth theosophic knowledge of the Quran';
3. Spirituality through his equitable words and deeds.

Such a unique combination brought the following balancing innovations:

- First, the role of the prophet came to an end as the theological notion of godhead reached its zenith.
- Second, to keep the divine continuity intact, prophet-hood (Risalat) changed to sainthood (Walayat)
- Third, Imam Ali, the cousin of Prophet Muhammad was made the first Wali (Saint) at Ghadeer-e-Khum when the prophet gave a sermon after performing his last Hajj. Thus he became the nucleus of Islamic spirituality also known as Sufism.
- Fourth, spirituality (Sufism) received an important position in the last Abrahamic religion of Islam.
- Fifth, 'Wali' (the saint) became the guiding player in Sufism acting as the leader. He followed the Quranic teachings and Sunnah (life style) of prophet Muhammad.
- Sixth, 'Wali' (saint) as the custodian of faith kept the continuity of divine understanding to improve human psyche.
- Seventh, 'Wali' (saint) started meditative techniques (Tariqa) by repeating certain specific words from Quran as part of

'Dhikr' thus converting non-Islamic spirituality (Asceticism) to Islamic spirituality (Sufism).

Thus Imam Ali, the Wali, under the guidance and shadow of Muhammad, supported spirituality through the enlightening and thought-provoking verses of the Quran. The Prophet called him "the gate to the city of knowledge" [65]. This change gave a wider dimension to Abraham's religion by approaching it through total submission seen later in Sufism. Imam Ali's mentor, Prophet Muhammad foresaw the future of mankind in spirituality.

Generally, Muslims at that time unknowingly absorbed themselves in spiritual practices, by showing humbleness, mutual love, obedience and fraternity. The methodology used for spirituality was none other than the five fundamentals of Islam: Kalma, Salah, Soam (Roza), Zakat and Hajj. The first as the initiator and the rest as the maintainers and enhancers of spirituality.

This fact was never perceived by the traditionalist Muslims right from the beginning during the lifetime of Muhammad and up until the present day. They considered the five pillars as ritual obligation ignoring their spiritual weight. They failed to realize that the enormous spiritual linkage of these pillars were the fundamental requirement in growth of Islamic society if performed as worship and not as mere rituals. They didn't understand that such a relationship could bring a harmonious balance in understanding of theology and perception of spirituality.

Also, the place of philosophy was not appreciated well at that time, because there was no need for it to be perceived. Muhammad was revealing it through gradual revelation of the Quran and through his discourses.

After his death, the Prophet left behind the Quran as his ultimate miracle with its logical and intuitive knowledge. Imam Ali took the duty of interpreting both knowledges. After Ali's death, his descendants amongst Shias, and the Sufi dervishes (saints) amongst Sunnis, took upon the duty. Thus 'Imam' amongst Shia and 'Wali or Dervish' among Sufis became the spiritual and corporal leaders respectively. We should keep in mind that Sufis were (and still are) from the Sunni sect.

To interpret Quranic knowledge, two centuries later, schools mushroomed in the Islamic world, some of which mingled Greek philosophy to explain its verses. The philosophical approach in theology in these schools resulted in challenging each other thus opening confrontational gates. Such confrontations led to sectarian hate which trickled down to the present day. The in-fights were exploited by the opponents of Islam both within the Muslim community and from outside. The Muslims who steered such in-fights were from a group called KhariJees. Again, they are conspicuously visible in Muslim world of today's global politics.

Though spirituality (Sufism) received an official blessing in the verses of Quran and the living style of Muhammad, it had its own share of opposition from the Muslim traditionalists after his death. The resistance still exists till present time.

Against this background, the Islamic history can be divided in four periods [66].

These period have the following distinctions;

1. They cannot be measured in context of time for their duration.
2. They do not correspond to any specific caliphate, dynasty or kingship.
3. They overlap each other.
4. They are linked to the changing roles of the rulers, aristocrats, theologians, scholars, and spiritualists.

In this way;

a) The first period is characterized by parity,
b) The second by dichotomy,
c) The third by trio-partisan,
d) The fourth by conciliation. This period goes on till the present day.

a) The first period of Parity

This period bracketed a society which was built on the basic theological tenets of Abraham with additional evolutionary changes introduced by prophet Muhammad according to the divine messages he received and the humanity-filled life-style he followed. Thus Quran and the living style of Muhammad became the driving force during the first period. Prophet Muhammad introduced the Quran as a continuity of previous divine scriptures and as a complete code of conduct placating deeds with theological knowledge in the most appealing fashion.

At societal level, he put forward Tawheed (unity), Salah (prayers), Soam (fasting), Zakat (alms) and Hajj (pilgrimage) as five fundamentals to unify Muslims at theological, corporeal and spiritual planes. This was a period of parity, where the chief executive was monotheistic in Abrahamic theology; knowledgeable in Quranic philosophy; and had insight of spirituality.

The people were conventional Muslims bound by the five fundamentals. Most importantly, there was no gap between the chief executive and the public. Prophet Muhammad made himself available to everyone and would treat them equally according to their positions and status. He would solve individual and communal predicaments of the Muslims. Thus minimum grievances existed between the fellow Muslims while he was alive.

After his death, the Quran and his life-style (Sunnah) became the linchpin for each Muslim to follow Islamic way of life. This also became the principle for decision-makers. With exception of a few variables, the basic principle of unified statehood and system of justice became the art of governance during this part of the first period. The traditional approach of the first Caliph, Abu Bakar; the militant approach of the second Caliph, Omar; the soft approach of the third Caliph, Osman; and the philosophical approach of the fourth Caliph, Ali, contributed to building up an Islamic society.

During the caliphate of Ali, the deposed governor of Damascus, Muawiyya who according to some Islamic scholars had leaning towards KhariJee group, created a dent in the progress and cleared the way for the second period of dichotomy. He rebelled against Ali - the caliph. After martyrdom of Ali, his son Imam Hassan took over the caliphate but soon gave it to Muawiyya through an agreement. The agreement was flouted by Muawiyya later.

After becoming the caliph, Muawiyya disengaged himself from the norms of the first period. He changed the governance style by creating a gap between caliph and the public opening the door to the second period.

b) The second period of dichotomy.

With passage of time as the second period reached to the Abbasid caliphate, the gap between the caliph and the public had reached to irreparable dimension. In the process, it was filled by the aristocrats (Darbaris) on one side and the traditionalist theologians (Mullahs) at the other. The former group became the eyes and the ears of the rulers at the royal courts, and the latter a link between the caliphs and the public at the mosques. Both these groups played intriguing role on their part. The aristocrats were successful in changing the caliphate into Persian and Turkic-style dynasties, where Wazirs and Raisul-Ummara respectively played decisive part in running governments. The theologians on other hand, used their position as religious custodians in mosque supported and propagated the caliph's changing image from pragmatic Islam to ritualistic Islam.

With passing time, the Muslim psyche was changed with expansion of dynasties and mingling of the new societies. Thus, a book by Abu Ishaq was added as decision-making tool in the early 7th century AD when the Persian-style Qazi (judge) took over the courts and started giving Rai (edict). In the second half of that century during the Abbasid dynasty the caliph created a parallel judicial court, the Muzalim, making the Qazi more powerful by awarding him the authority of Qiyas. This arrangement paved the way for the creation of the third period of trio-partition.

c) The third period of trio-partisan

Three events in this period played important role in shaping Islamic society in the coming centuries;

1. First, with the introduction of Qiyas [67], reasoning was introduced which led to appearance of Juristic schools (Fiqhi Madrasa) combining theology with philosophy [68].
2. Second, the caliph of the time decided to compile Ahadith in 8th century AD.
3. Third the caliph on the advice of his Wazir decided to register the schools.

Soon, from the original two schools at Kufa and Medina they multiplied rapidly in private homes in Persia and in the mosques in the Arab world. These schools concentrated on selective groups of intellectuals. Its scholars started making discussions and discourses which were beyond the grasp of ordinary Muslims. Similarly, compilation of Ahadith and registration of schools by caliph added fuel to fire. So the already divided society of the second period was left disillusioned by the schools in the third period. In this period the caliphs slipped faster towards secularism, the theologians grew stronger in mosques and the theosophist scholars consolidated steadily in the schools making a trio-partisan Muslim society.

As a result of this trio-partisanship, this period can be identified with following events and their reflections:

• First, with registration of the schools, their initial rapid growth started to decline. In the end only four major schools were left on the registry. They were, Hanafi, Shafi, Maliki, and Hambali schools from the Sunni sect. These schools yielded a bag of positive and negative results both in short and long terms.

- Second, the Ja'afari school of Shia sect did not register for its own reasons. By the time it joined the other four schools at Al-Azhar University on July 11, 1959, the split in Islam had already taken deep roots.
- Third, the increasing competition between the schools uplifted the philosophy at the expense of theology, which became obvious between Al Ashari and Al Mutazali sub-schools of thoughts in Sunni sect.
- Fourth, the ban on Ijthehad (the drawing of religious conclusions in light of the teachings of the Quran and Sunnah of prophet), Ijma (consensus) and Bida'a (innovation) by some schools in the 9th century AD had a negative impact on the future of an otherwise progressive Islam.
- Fifth, the collection, compilation and proliferation of doubtful Ahadith had negative consequences on credibility of Islamic history during those few crucial decades. That dis-credibility fell adversary on Muslim society in coming centuries.
- Sixth, the debates/discourses between the schools led to ideological differences, juristic dislikes, verbal conflicts, and finally physical confrontations. Compilation of selective Ahadith by these schools multiplied conflicts in the Muslim society.
- Seventh, militant groups were created by some of the schools increasing the scope of conflicts with rival schools.
- Eighth, with advancement in theo-philosophy schisms grew faster. As a result, the in-fights increased and turmoil flourished creating a scenario in which; the caliphs wasted the nobility of Islamic governance; the aristocrats piled up personal favours; the traditionalists played in the hands of conniving Muslims and non-Muslims; the schools lost their original aims; and the public drowned slowly in a sea of confusion.

It was against this background that the fourth and the final period of conciliation appeared on the horizon.

d) The fourth period of conciliation.

The hallmark of this period was Islamic spirituality also known as Sufism. [69] Sufism received an unannounced official blessing at the birth of Islam and remained dormant for a few centuries. The reasons for its dormancy could be two-fold:

- First, the early Sufis were inward-looking and ascetics, so they isolated themselves from the rest of the society;
- Second, they went to the non-Muslim regions, where they started preaching Islam.

Either way, it took them five centuries to emerge as a movement in 11th century AD. The movement itself was obscure and some might not even call it a movement, but it did appear in response to:

1. the dynastic approach of the rulers;
2. the diversifying approach of the schools;
3. the aggressive approach of Safavi and Ismaili of Shia sects;
4. the ultra-conservative approach of the Sunni traditionalists.

The Sufis saw Muslim society taking a nosedive in moral values and class discrimination. To put the Muslims on the conciliatory mode, they started educating them in Sufi schools (Khanqahs) parallel to juristic (Madrisa) schools.

Their schools ran on principles of love, obedience, tolerance, and selfless service. In this way, they wanted to remove hate, distrust and animosity among Muslims and to build respect and tolerance towards non-Muslims. Unlike juristic schools no certificates (Ijaza) were given at the end of the courses. Also there were no syllabus, regular classes or fixed schedules for the training. It was a completely different approach to learning, using guided techniques to self-assessment and inner vision at individual level between student and teacher. The teacher was not just a degree holder scholar. He was a Dervish (guide, mentor) and a Sufi, full of wisdom.

So Sufism became the hallmark of the fourth period of conciliation. Whilst studying the history of Sufism, we learn that it went through four phases of developmental approaches;

- First, the asceticism, which was influenced by Christian spirituality. It laid its principles on getting closer to God through ascetic practices by becoming isolated from family, friends, and community living like a Christian monk [70].
- Second, the mysticism, which was based on the principles of nearness to God through esoteric knowledge (Irfan) meaning by seeing the unseen in this life rather than waiting for it in the next life. Among the Sufis known for Irfan was Mulla Sadra from 17th century [71].
- Third, the theosophical, which principled on nearness to God through ecstasy (Wajad)[72]. 'Wajad' manifested itself in different forms, such as tears, sighs, laughter or dance. Through 'Wajad' the seeker gets divine union with the desired ones. It has three aspects:

1. The devotee visualizes the desired one after his heart fills with love, admiration and gratitude.
2. Union with the beauty of the character of the ideal rather than its shape or form.
3. Union with the divine beloved, who is beyond any restriction of name, virtue or merit. This is a state of blissful joy and may intermingle with the phase of Irfan. The chief Sufi in this group was Al-Thisiri

- Fourth, the pantheism, which was based on extreme closeness to God. The important Sufis in this group were: Bistami, who placed his doctrine of Fana, (absorption) with the like of nirvana of Buddhism [73]; Hallaj, whose 'Unnal-haque' ('I am the Truth') cost him his life [74]; and Al-Arabi, who propagated the concept of 'Hama oost' (everything is He) in Sufism [75].

With time, Sufism divided in different orders. These divisions were arbitrary, as they all shared identical aims. The differences laid in their approaches and meditative practices. Not a single Sufi instructed his pupils to create an order in his name after his death. They were created by the followers to show their love, respect and gratitude. Another reason may have been to immortalize their services and names. The orders were not meant to compete with one another or to set up any rivalry among each other as the various traditionalist juristic schools did. Sufis were dervishes. No matter which order they followed, their aims and objectives remained identical.

In this way, the Sufi movement of conciliation developed in a peaceful manner, which was its norm. It gathered some momentum from the 13th century onwards, slowed down in later centuries, and geared up again in the 20th century. The reason for this uneven pace was the intermittent opposition of forces mentioned earlier especially the die-hard traditionalists. It revived in late 20th century and its revival was twofold;

- First, there was re-awakening of original Islam among Muslim intellectuals, scholars, and philosophers.
- Second, it corresponded to the universal trends in spirituality seen in Christian churches, Hindu temples, Jewish synagogues, and eastern sanctuaries.

Interestingly, the second half of the 20th century saw a remarkable surge in human thinking. Most of the progressive societies in developed countries based their politics on basic human rights, tolerance and mutual respect. These were the same qualities required in spirituality at communal level.

It is in this respect, that in the fourth period of conciliation, the Sufis realized that they could play an important role building bridges between other religions especially the Abrahamic faiths by linking Sufism with their respective spiritualties.

At the same time, they also realized that in 20th century, studies in human subconscious highlighted extrasensory phenomena in parapsychology which were similar to the paranormal experiences in Sufism.

Take for example hypnosis or self-hypnosis in parapsychology. It plays an essential role in creating altered state. Similar state is created by "Dhikr' in Sufism. Both use different techniques but create identical states and provide identical results in changing personalities. As a result, the western parapsychology borrowed techniques of self-hypnosis from the spiritual schools of the east and vice-versa. The results were used by both sides to uplift human psyche for the good of humanity. This association exposed eastern spirituality such as Sufism to the western science for the benefit of both. It opened new channels of understanding between parapsychologists and Sufis paving the way for new understanding between parapsychology and Sufism. In this way a new dimension was opened up in the fourth period.

While scrutinies were going on in 20th century to find identities between parapsychology and Sufism, a few Sufis started to find similarities between newly surfaced quantum physics and Sufism.

For example; Sufis believe in existence of the two worlds; 'the world of the seen'; and 'the world of the unseen'. The quantum physicists also talk of the two worlds; 'the macro world'; and 'the micro world'.

The knowledge to understand 'the world of the unseen' of Sufism is different from the knowledge to understand 'the world of the seen'. Similarly, the knowledge to understand 'the micro world' of quantum physics is different from the knowledge to understand 'the macro world'.

In both cases the knowledge of the unknown is based on irrationality while the knowledge of the known is based on logic.

One is linked with intuition, the other with reasoning. So, both in Sufism and quantum physics, the calculations and understanding about the happenings in unseen (micro) worlds do not necessarily coincide with the calculations and understanding of the world of the 'seen' (macro world).

For example, in the macro world of physics, one plus one equals to two. But not so in the micro world, where 'one' behaves as 'one' at one place and 'many' at other place without being divided. Furthermore, 'one' appears as a 'particle' at one place and a 'wave' at another place. The Sufis also find similar disparities in the world of the unseen of religion.

The science books and spiritual scriptures are full of such examples. Going into the details of a few, we find that Werner Heisenberg [76] while studying electrons in the first quarter of the 20th century, faced a difficult situation when he observed that he could not find a definite position and a definite motion of a particle at the same time. If he measured one, he could not measure the other as at that precise moment it lost its existence for the purpose of measuring its position, and vice versa. This made quantum scientists bewildered as to how can an existing particle becomes non-existing, or philosophically speaking how can a particle as a 'thing' be called a 'thing' with no existence? According to Stephen Hawking's logic, as Kitty Ferguson put it, "what we cannot measure cannot happen" [77]. But yet, it was happening.

To make the situation more puzzling for the physicists, it was observed in the micro world that the movement of a particle was predictable, but when it changed from particle to wave, its character changed and it became interchangeable and at a certain point indistinguishable from one another and unpredictable. This became a constant feature of particle-wave relationship and the 'Indeterminism Theory' rests on this principle [78].

Einstein, who was a strong proponent of cause and effect theory, observing this bizarre behaviour once in desperation said, "God does not play dice". To which Stephen Hawking replied, 'not only that

God does play dice, but that he sometimes confuses us by throwing them where they can't be seen" [79].

Such observations by the quantum physicists do not surprise the Sufis and the spiritualists who understand the working of the 'unseen' or the 'micro' world.

In 1927 Heisenberg, while working on the uncertainty principle, found that an observer could alter the course of an observed particle-wave by the mere act of observation [80]. The Kahuna of Polynesia spirituality - the Hunaism - has been doing this practice for centuries [81].

Again, in an experiment, Einstein observed that if a particle is exploded into two sub-particles A & B, and then allowed to move in opposite directions without hindrance, each resulting sub-particle, according to action and reaction theory, will have two components: a clockwise and an anti-clockwise. If at any stage a specific motion is measured in one sub-particle, the opposite motion in the other sub-particle stays, while the similar motion in that sub-particle disappears, no matter how far away the two sub-particles are[82]. Commenting on this Paul Davies said, "It seems baffling to say the least, how fragment B can possibly know for which of its two ghosts fragment A has opted" [83]. Bohr considered the sub-particles A & B as one, though for all practical purposes they were two and light years apart [84].

Again the Sufis don't get baffled by such phenomenons because they understand the working of the 'micro' or the 'unseen' world and quoting of similar relation between the two epiphanies of godhead for over thousand years. This will be discussed later.

David Balm, a leading quantum theorist, put emphasis on undivided wholeness [85], which again points toward Wahdat of Sufism.

Writing in her book 'The Probability of the Impossible' about an experiment she conducted, Dr. Thelma Moss of UCLA was surprised when she found a single particle going into two slits of a shield simultaneously without splitting into two [86]. Again, in another experiment, when an electron was scattered to the left and right of the observer, it stayed as ghost particles on both sides. But when it was observed on one side, the other side collapsed. What caused this collapse is not known.

These and other similar experiments led physicists to believe that a particle can be observed in more than one place simultaneously without it getting divided and the resulting ghost particles mysteriously stay in touch without any apparent linkage. This bizarre unity of multiples and their freakish linkages had been a constant feature in the micro world of quantum physics.

The Sufis are however not surprised when they hear scientists talk of bizarre movements of particles or sub-particles as they have been observing and talking about such occurrences for centuries. They link this with intuitional knowledge the Sufis receive while passing through the paths of 'Ilm' (knowledge) and 'Amal' (Action) which will be discussed later.

It is for this reason, some of the quantum physicists and philosophers such as Paul Davies after observing such phenomenons saw similarities between science and spirituality. Paul Davies once said, "holistic science is rapidly developing into something of a cult, partly perhaps because it is in tune with oriental philosophy and mysticism." He further said, "many modern writers are finding close parallels between the concepts used in quantum theory and those of oriental mysticism such as Zen" [87].

Einstein's 'parent-and-daughter universe' theory and Stephen Hawking's 'wormhole and baby universe' theory strikingly resemble the concepts of Toh-Nahl and Nah-Uhal of Yaqui spirituality [88].

The Higg's Field of physics closely resembles the 'Aka' of Huna spirituality, which has been known to the Kahuna for thousands of years [89].

Yuval Ne'eman and Murray Gell-Mann, who were the first to discover the hidden symmetry in a collection of eight hadrons, called their new principle the 'eightfold way' after the Eightfold path of Buddhism [90].

The Big Bang and the Big Crunch theories suggest that the universe started as Singularity and will end in Singularity. That is what the Sufis have been saying for over thousand years.

The mathematical physicist Henri Poincaré came up with mathematical formula that the earth will be reconstituted after its disappearance along with all its inhabitants. This theory is known as the Poincaré Cycle [91]. Again, the Sufis have been saying about such happening for centuries.

John Wheeler, while working on Young's two-slit theory, came up with the theory that an observer can be made partially responsible for generating the reality of a remote past by bringing it nearer in present. In other words, we are participators in bringing about something of the universe from the distant past. If we have one explanation for what happened in past as if it's happening now, why should we need more? [92] This theory is not something new for Sufis and other spiritualists who understood it for thousands of years because they saw/still see past, present and future as one unit through the unique knowledge of intuition they had/have.

Heisenberg once said, "the common division of the world into subject and object; inner world and outer world; body and soul; is no longer adequate in the micro-world" [93]. It seems like he was describing the state of Nirvana of Buddhism, Toh-Nhal of Yaqui spirituality and 'Fana' of Sufism

St. Augustine (354—430 AD) said, "the world was made not in time but simultaneously with time" [94]. How close he was to the theory of Singularity.

According to Paul Davies, "a singularity is the nearest thing that science has found to a supernatural agent" [95].

Stephen Hawking once used the term God as the embodiment of the laws of physics. A Sufi concept of 'Hama az Oost' is pretty close to this notion. Stephen Hawking also said "what is it that breathes fire into the equations and makes a universe for them to describe" [96]. It is pretty close to the Sufi concept of 'Wahdiat'

The physicists say that waves are vibrations which are interchangeable and that one wave can affect the other wave.

Spiritualists say that vibrations created by intense concentration can affect the vibrations of another person positively as in healing, or negatively, as in a 'death prayer' seen in Hunaism [97].

The most fascinating similarity seen between quantum physics and Sufism is in the concepts of 'Singularity' and 'Ahdiat' respectively. Talking about 'Singularity', the quantum physicists say that its nature, shape, form, structure or type is not known. It is a state where time and space cease and billions of years are like a fraction of a blink of an eye. All known energies lose their pattern and nature. Measurements lose existence. The Sufis describe 'Ahdiat' exactly in identical manner which makes the two indistinguishable from each other.

These are some of the reasons which can bring the Sufis of the fourth period of Islamic history close to the science and make the 21st century as the century of conciliation. Such conciliation can be accelerated if the following three apparent similarities between Sufism and quantum physics are explored further.

1. First, similarities that exist in 'Singularity' and 'Ahdiat'.
2. Second, similarities in the working of the 'micro-world' of quantum physics and the 'unseen world' of Sufism.
3. Third, psychological convergence that exists in the aims of quantum physicists and Sufis.

The research from both side will come up with answers as to why similarities existed right from the time of 'Singularity' and continue till the present day. The physicists will find them in the books of quantum physics and the Sufis in the verses of the Quran. Though their methodologies are different but the results will be the same. The Physicists will discover them through knowledge of science; and the Sufis through knowledge of Quranic signs. One type of knowledge is hidden in the books of science; the other in the Book of revelation. One reveals itself through experimentation, additions and abstractions; the other through meditations. Despite all similarities the major difference between the two knowledges is that one is achieved from countless new emerging science books; the other is all there in one unchangeable book written 1400 years ago-the Quran.

The Sufis keep on insisting that they are not there to compete with scientists. They insist that Quran has never been a book of 'science'. They call it a book of 'signs' which has countless layers of understanding for the people of learning. They argue that it is because of this understanding that they found commonalities between 'Singularity' and 'Ahdiat'. They correlate the infinite energy which made 'particles' and 'sub-particles' of the micro-world of quantum, with an analogous energy that generated 'spirit' and 'soul' of the unseen world of Sufism and so on so forth. In this context, they talk about the 'godhead', 'spirit' and 'soul' in a manner which seems acceptable to the mental acumen of quantum physicist and for that matter to a modern man as the notions fall in the theories of quantum physics.

They make the knowledge of 'godhead', 'spirit' and 'soul' as the primary tool in conciliatory progress of the fourth period of Islamic history to change the societies constructively.

This brings me to talk about the working of 'godhead', spirit' and 'soul" in the world of the unseen of Sufism; as the physicists talk about the happening in the micro world of quantum physics. So let me take 'godhead', spirit' and 'soul one by one.

Godhead in Sufism

Religion and an unknown power have influenced mankind ever since the development of societies: the former as a divine system and the latter as the force behind that system. With passage of time, in the course of religious evolution, the power took three closely linked forms; the god, the spirit, and the soul. The Sufis make the understanding of these three attractive and easily acceptable by the custodians of other religions, scientists and parapsychologists.

Take, for example, the concept of god. To make its nature rationally perceivable, the Sufis portray god in 'three divine ranks' termed as 'Marateb-e-Elahi'. These three ranks are 'Ahdiat', 'Wahdat' and 'Wahdiat'.

According to them the notion of god evolved with evolution of religion as mental acumen of human progressed by projecting itself in three forms or ranks. By projecting three ranks of god, the Sufis distanced themselves from the traditionalist theologians who perceive god only in one unknown and indescribable form.

History tells us that with evolution of human acumen and religious beliefs, the third rank of god started to multiply like branches of a tree. The narrow-minded theologians mistook each as the first rank and began to claim them as such. They started to project their god superior to the gods of other. In the process, they spread hate amongst fellow humans at individual, communal, and regional levels with devastating results. As opposed to such narrow version, the Sufis simplified notion of god by understanding its ranks philosophically as mentioned in the Quran.

Thus, the theological concept of god living in an unknown place beyond the reach of human understanding was made approachable by the Sufis. This approach made Islam more appealing and tolerant countering the traditionalists who propagated it as religion of rigidity, intolerance and hate. The traditionalists, instead of facing them on theosophic turf turned against them, labelling them heretics. But the Sufis sticking to spiritual teachings faced them with compassion and tolerance, which according to their beliefs was actual Islamic way propagated by Prophet Muhammad. They also sent similar message to the custodians of other religions that the multiple gods they believed in were actually the 'ranks' or 'epiphanies' of one god.

They compared these ranks with a tree as similitude mentioned in Quran which states, *"Seest thou not how Allah coineth a similitude a goodly saying as a goodly tree, its root set firm, its branches stretching into Heaven, Giving its fruits at every season, by permission of its Lord, Allah coineth the similitude for mankind in order that they may reflect"* [98A]

To explain it further the Sufis compared the three 'ranks' of god with the root, the trunk and the branches of a tree, symbolizing; 'Ahdiat' (absolute unity) with the root; 'Wahdat' (plural unity) with the trunk; and 'Wahdiat' (multiple unities) with the branches. Thus; 'Ahdiat' also called 'Dhaat' (the Essence) became indescribable and non-comprehensible god; 'Wahdat' as an abstract and indescribable combination of Dhaat (the Essence) and Sifaat (the attributes); and 'Wahdiat' as describable combination of Dhaat (essence), Sifaat (attributes), Afaal (actions) and Ayaan (realities).

It is this understanding of god which gave Sufism an edge over other spiritualities.

They support their argument in the; light of Quran; sayings of Prophet Mohammed; and narrations of known Muslim theosophists. Giving the details of each rank they say;

1)....Ahdiat is the highest state of god; where there is unity with no otherness; where knowledge is inner and not manifested; where god is formless, limitless, and colourless; where it is, as it was, and will remain as it is. God in this state is the first, the last, the inward, the outward, the infinite, the absolute, and the indefinable. It has absolute power the strength of which is indescribable and immeasurable. It is absolute knower, and has absolute knowledge only known to itself. It is conscious of its own 'I-ness', which is internal with no abstraction, addition or deletion. It has internal ideas with no 'otherness' in it. This is the state of absolute and infinite 'I-ness'. Describing its indescribable nature, power and form it can easily be taken in similitude with 'Singularity.

Quran describes this state in Sura Akhlas by saying *"Allah is One; is the eternal refuge; is neither begets nor is born; nor is any equivalent to him"* [98B]. In another place God says in the Quran, *"I am One and no partner with Me,"* or, *"God was and there was naught besides Him"* and *"Allah is independent of all creatures"* [99]. He is 'Hu, the One who is hidden. The knowledge of His-self is with Him and no one else.'

The exact nature of 'Dhaat' (the Essence) cannot be conceptualized at this level because He/It has not revealed Himself/Itself to anyone in totality, as He/It is beyond totality. He/It is in the state of infinite unity with no isolations. Here, there is none but one with no boundaries. Here, when God says 'Kun' (be) it is 'Fayakun' (it is) without time or space between the command and action [100].

God, at this level, doesn't link itself to anyone/anything, in any form, shape or relation, because it is beyond any relationship, including a father and son relationship. To attach a son to god at this level is akin to creating a human image of god, while in this state godhead is beyond any image. That is why it is forbidden to understand 'Dhaat' (Essence) with our limited faculties. The Quran says, *"And He makes you cautious of Himself"* [101] and it says *"God keeps the knowledge of His-self hidden from you"* and *"They shall not encompass Him with their knowledge"* [102].

Keeping this state of godhead in mind, the Prophet Muhammad said, "I have not known Thee to the extent that Thy knowledge demands" and "I have not seen Thee to the extent to which I ought to have seen Thee." He further said, "Don't indulge in speculating on the nature of God lest ye may be destroyed" [103]. A hadith says, "One who understood God does not know Him" [104].

Then, this unknown, non-graspable, and indescribable entity called 'Ahdiat', 'Dhaat', Essence, God, Allah, Ishwar, or Reality, wanted to be known. According to a hadith quoted by Ibn-e-Arabi, 'I was a hidden treasure. I loved to be known' [105a]. Another Sufi said this, "Had we not existed, God would not have been known" [105b]. God is in absolute unity in state of 'Ahdiat', where every occurrence, phenomenon, action, and reaction is internal (Batin) with no otherness in the form of attributes. Quran, mentions, *"Praise and Glory be to Him: For He is above what they attribute to Him"* [106]. So to be known, there had to be 'other' in 'Ahdiat' and there was no place for 'otherness' in that state. Thus, god became 'Wahdat' by creating 'Attributes' (Sifaat) and adding them to its Essence (Dhaat) in abstract form.

This was akin to God uttering 'Kun' (Be) and like 'big bang' without creating space and time it was 'Fayakun' (It is) and wilfully evolved itself into the next 'rank' of 'Wahdat'. Figuratively speaking root of the tree came out as trunk.

2).....**Wahdat**, It is the state of god where there is 'Dhaat' (the Essence) along with limitless 'Sifaat' (attributes) and their countless variations but yet showing no details or individuality. All the 'Sifaat' and the 'Dhaat' are in 'Abstract Form'. It is like the trunk of a tree showing no details yet encompassing all its branches, leaves, fruits, seeds etc. Sufis call this level the 'first epiphany', the 'first limitation', 'Burzakh-e-Kubra', or the 'reality of Muhammad'. Quran refers to this level as, "Muqaman Mahmud" [107]. Rumi linked this title with the title given to Prophet when he said, "Mahmud ("the Praiseworthy One") is one of the titles of God, as well as Muhammad" [108].

Here the truth is manifested to itself in occult plurality and this plurality is bounded in unity. This is the level where the knower, the knowledge and the known meet in singleness. The oneness of 'Dhaat' (the Essence) does not hide the 'Sifaat' (the attributes) and vice versa. Thus, in this collective unity, the Quran uses the word 'We' instead of 'I' for god. *"We are nearer to him then his jugular vein"* [109] and *"And we delivered him and his people from great calamity"* [110] and *"Thus indeed do We reward those who do right"* [111] and so on so forth. It is the highest level for any human to reach. Sufis believe that the Prophet Muhammad reached this level during 'Miraj' (the ascent) [112].

According to Sufis, following the 'big bang' of 'Kun' and appearance of god as 'Wahdat', God still could not be known the way He wanted to be known, because though there were attributes but they were all in singleness with 'Dhaat' (the Essence) in an Abstract Form. There were no 'separations' and 'details'. So He created 'Afaal' (Actions); separated 'Ayaans' (realities); and introduced details of 'Sifaat' (attributes). As there was no place for 'separations' and 'details' in this state, so God wilfully evolved into the third state of 'Wahdiat'. Metaphorically talking, trunk of the tree changed into branches.

3).....**Wahdiat,** is like branches, leaves, flowers, fruits and seeds of a tree where its component parts can be described in details. God in this state, is perceived by his Sifaat (attributes), Afaal (actions) and Ayaans (realities) in elaborate details while keeping his Dhaat (essence) intact. His attributes come in different shapes and forms expounding upon their otherness. God is individualized, personalized and presented in his detailed similitude and illuminations.

For example, he appears in the rock of Tur, the stones of the Ka'aba, the Fire of Zoroastrians, the Ganges of the Hindus, the

Bu Tree of Buddhists, the Kami of Shinto, the Eagle of Native Americans and in the Granth of Sikhs.

According to Sufis, whichever way one looks, he can find god. He is there to be seen, to be perceived, to be found, and to be discovered. In this Form, he is the fragmentary godhead seen in various religions of the world. The Sufis call this level the 'second epiphany', the 'second limitation', or the 'reality of humanity'.

As mentioned, god in this form shows himself primarily in his attributes (Sifaat). Some of us call such appearances as his 'Dhaat' (essence) which is not right, because by doing so, 'Sifat' (attribute) is equated with 'Dhaat'(Essence). This can be bracketed as 'shirk' which is forbidden in Islam. It is also important to note at this point that 'Dhaat' (essence) can be called by any of his 'Sifat' (attribute) but not the other way around. For example, Lord (Rubb) is an attribute of God (Allah), so God can be called as Lord but Lord cannot always be called as God if such Lordship is linked to someone else than God. For example, in Quran parent are called Lord (Rubb) [113]. That does not make them god.

Another important point to note is that the enlightened people can have union with godhead at the level of 'Wahdiat' where god is in its 'attributes'. In that context the Christians are not wrong when they call Jesus Christ as Lord. But when they call him God then they equate a spirited but manly Lord with God which is not right.

There are 99 attributes ('Sifaat') of God (Allah) mentioned in the Quran. They are distinct from each other and identical to God (Dhaat), but still they are not like God (Dhaat). Such as:

1. They range second to God (Dhaat)
2. They depend on God (Dhaat)
3. They display diversity
4. They are hidden sometimes and manifest other-times.
5. Their manifestations may conflict with each other.
6. They have no self-consciousness.

The resultant manifestations of 99 attributes come out in multiple of multiples in the form of illuminations which are beyond numerical grasp. If we compare these numerical aggregations with the assemblages of our genes, we can get some idea of its multiplicity.

For example, there are only four basic elements, G, C, A and T, which make up the genes in our body. The different combinations of these four result in 100,000 chains of genes, with six billion character codes. Comparing the multiple of four with the multiples of 99 brings out non-graspable accumulations of godhead in the form of attributes (Sifaat) at the level of 'Wahdiat.'

Such is the depth and intensity of divine illuminations at this level which is the level of created-ness in internality of godhead. It is for this reason Quran sometimes refers to God as a second or third person such as 'He' or 'Him' or symbolizes itself with someone or something such as 'hand' or 'face' or 'shadow' and so on so forth.

The Quran says, *"Wherever thou turnest, there is the face of God"* [114] and *"Do you not see your Lord has lengthened His shadow"* [115] and *"He created man in the image of Rahman (graceful/merciful)"* and *"God presents Itself in different ways"* and *"The Hand of God is above their hands"* [116] and *"God truly surrounds everything"* [117] and *"I have breathed into it from my breath"* [118] . The Quran is full of such attributes, ie, 'Al-baith' (the causer), 'Al-Hafiz' (the watcher), 'Al-Khaliq' (the creator), 'Al-Massawir' (the painter) and so on.

The prophet said, "I saw my Lord in the form of a beardless youth" [119]. On another occasion he said, "Reflect upon the qualities of Allah but never think on His nature because you are unable to conceive Him." When asked about his relationship with God, the prophet said, "I am Ahmad without 'm'" [120]. 'Ahad' in Arabic means 'One'. He also said, "The first thing which God created was light of prophet" [121]. He further said, "The first thing God created was reason" [122] and so on so forth. This is the level where similitude of God (Dhaat) comes out in various shapes, forms and actions.

A Hadith says, "Do not ponder over His Dhaat (Essence) but ponder over His bounties. (Sifaat)" [123]. The grandson of the Prophet Muhammed, Imam Hussain, pointed at the second epiphany of

God, the 'Wahdiat', by saying, "You have made yourself known to everybody. Therefore, there is nobody who does not know You. You have made yourself known to me through everything and I see You in everything. Thus You are evident in everything". The Sufis reflected this in the notions of "Hama Oost"(Everything is Him) or "Hama Az Oost" (Everything is from Him). This notion is also mentioned in the Quranic verse which says, *'Say: 'Everything it from God'* [124].

How close is this concept with the 'Theory of Everything' presented by Stephen Hawkins [125] .

According to a Sufi, Shah Kamal Qadari, "A person is seen in the reflections, that is the Lord in the world. Reflection is seen in the person that is the world in the Lord" [126] . Jami another theosophist said, "The ayans (realities) are mirrors and God is manifest, or the light of God is a mirror and ayans (realities) are form" [127].

The great Muslim Sufi poet Rumi once stated, "You cannot visualize for yourself any path, beyond the utmost reaches of your vision. The utmost reaches possible for reason's quest can certainly not be God (who is beyond the grasp of reason)" [128]. A known Sufi, Junaid said, "Who is there in my garment except God. (of second epiphany)" [129]. Another Sufi, Bayazid once said, "Holy am I, how great is my glory" or "praise to Me for My Greatest Glory" [130]. Karkhi, yet another Sufi, said, "I am your Lord, obey me" This notion is explained by Shiekh Nazim in Sheikhnazim forum [131]. And it was that well-known Sufi Mansur Hallaj who was stoned to death by the traditionalists when he uttered, "Unnal Haq" (I am the Truth) [132]. When Shibli was asked to comment on Mansur's utterance, he said, that he was right but he should have not said it publicly.

Sufis give special attention to seven attributes and sub-attributes which are important in reforming our life. They call them the 'Primary attributes' or the 'Seven virtues'. According to them these attributes play important role in shaping human psyche and personality through a filtration process called 'Burzakh'. The attributes are; Existence (Wajud); Knowledge (Ilm); Light (Nur); Observance (Shahud), Hearing, Sight and Speech. Some Sufis include Breathing in the list.

According to Sufis, the filtration occurs when individuals go through the three realms of 'Nafs', (soul) 'Qulb' (mindfulness) and 'Ruh' (spirit). These realms are also called the 'human ranks' which will be discussed later.

Sufis also say that such a filtration had been part of a process throughout the evolution of universe, planet earth, and the life therein. For example;

- Divine 'existence' (Wajud) was/is transmitted from non-existence to existence and then onwards from non-life to 'life' in the process of evolution of universe and planet earth.
- Divine 'light' (Nur) was/is transmitted into 'will' at the level of spirit ('Ruh') in human spiritual development.
- Divine 'observance' (Shahud) changes into mental ecumenical 'power' at the levels of soul ('Nafs'), mindfulness ('Qulb') and spirit ('Ruh')
- Divine 'knowledge' (Ilm) splits into logical or visible and explainable knowledge ('Ilm-e-Safina'); and intuition or invisible and unexplainable knowledge ('Ilm-e-Sina')
- The 'Hearing', 'Sight', and 'Speech' remain unaltered although they are placed according to the age and mental development of a person. For example, a newborn baby can hear but cannot focus visually or speak verbally. The 'Hearing' becomes active in womb. 'Sight' starts focusing a few weeks after birth, while 'Speaking' capability comes a few months later. 'Breathing' is essential part of living which starts as the umbilical cord is cut and carries on throughout our life. It is given special place in spiritual growth by Sufis when simple breathing is changed into 'controlled Breathing'. Quran links 'Breathing' with special existence five times which will be discussed in forthcoming pages.

It is interesting to note that Quran put the three virtues of 'hearing', 'seeing' and 'speaking' in chronological order according to human development known only to the present-day embryologists.

For example, Quran states, *"Say it is He who created and made for you the faculties of hearing, seeing and understanding"* [133]. As understanding is bracketed primarily with speech and determinant speech is linked with wisdom Quran further says, *"We made his kingdom strong and gave him wisdom and decisive speech"* [134]. Keeping this chronology in mind, the Sufis utter the name of Allah as 'Adhan' (the prayer call) in the ears of a new-born to show that he/she can hear and may register God's name.

Talking further about the primary virtues when as a result of division of 'knowledge' into logical (visible or explainable) and intuitional (invisible or unexplainable) knowledges, two paths also emerged to accommodate such knowledges for humans to tread. Those paths are:

- The 'Path of act' (Amal). This is also called the 'Internal path'
- The 'Path of knowledge' (Ilm). This is also called the 'External path'

On 'Path of act' Quran says, *"Now no soul (Nafs) knows what delights of the eye are kept hidden for them as a reward for their good acts"* [135].

On 'Path of knowledge' Quran says, *"And gave them reasoned commandments and differed not until after the knowledge came into them"* [136].

The aim is to put humans on either of these paths for the betterment of societies they live in and in some cases to let some of them reach the zenith of the respective path they tread.

According to Sufis the seeker of intuition knowledge starts his journey on the 'path of act' (Amal) or 'the internal path' after learning how to control his 'breathing' and, how to rhythmically utter verses from the Quran as 'Dhikr'. He uses 'Shahud' (divine observance) as his 'power' and 'Nur' (divine light) as his 'will' to proceed on the path, sharing 'Wajud' (divine existence) as his part of 'life', until, he reaches the peak and captures the end-station of 'Faith'. Thus, he becomes a 'Faithful'

While the seeker of logic on the 'path of knowledge' (Ilm) or the 'external path' uses his 'power' and 'will' as part of life to reach its peak and captures the end-station of 'Wisdom' and thus becomes a 'Wiseman'. Before reaching this peak station, he, has to pass through the station of 'philosophy' which is full of 'reasoning' and 'doubts' making this path difficult to tread. [137]

It is for this reason, Sufis prefer 'the path of act' or 'the internal path' where they learn how to control their breathing and use it as facilitator in their spiritual growth. They find philosophy an obstacle in spiritual ascent on the 'path of knowledge'. Moreover, they believe that the two paths converge on one another at their respective end stations of 'Faith' and 'Wisdom'. So when a seeker reaches the zenith of 'Faith' on the 'path of act' or the 'internal path', he becomes aware of the intricacy of 'Wisdom'. Thus he achieves 'Wisdom' without going through the station of 'philosophy'. They give the example of Imam Ali who was the nucleus of Sufism and an iconic of 'Wisdom', yet he never studied philosophy.

The Sufis believe that the convergence point of the two paths is located at the junction of the worlds of the 'seen' and the 'unseen' in the realm of 'Ruh' (the spirit) which is also the meeting plane between 'human ranks' (Marateb-e-Insani) and 'divine ranks' (Marateb-e-Elahi) They also say that from here a single 'straight path' (Sirat-ul-Mustaqeem) opens up. This term is mentioned in the Quran and repeatedly uttered in Salat [138]. It is at this spot the enlightened Sufi goes into the state of 'Fana' (Absorption) which is equivalent to 'Nirvana' of Hinduism. But unlike 'Nirvana' which is linked with the departed soul, 'Fana', is a transitory state in the living. The Sufi comes out of 'Fana' and stays in the state of 'Baqa' as an elevated human being.

So, six things happen at this level;

1. First, the paths of 'the acts' and ' the knowledge' merge;
2. Second, the end stations of 'Faith' and 'Wisdom' on the paths of 'acts' and 'knowledge' respectively integrate;

3. Third, a single 'straight path' (Sirat-ul-Mustaqeem) emerges as a result of the merger of the 'two paths'
4. Fourth, a door between the two worlds of 'seen' and 'unseen' opens;
5. Fifth, 'the human' and 'the divine' ranks adjust;
6. Sixth, the enlightened Sufi goes in the state of 'Fana' (absorption) and comes back in the state of 'Baqa' as normal but elevated human.

This is the place where an atheist spiritualist becomes aware of the world of the 'unseen' and, with that, he realizes the presence of a divine power in the world of the 'seen'. It is this realization which made many atheist philosophers, academicians and scientists theist.

The Sufis, at this point, find a fine distinction between a philosopher and a dervish. Dervish considers philosophy as a station on the 'path of knowledge' somewhere at mid-point. According to him, it is at this station a philosopher starts creating 'reasons' to counter the created 'doubts' to reach shades of 'beliefs', finds forms of 'realities' and discovers various 'truths'. He stays in it forever as he is caught between 'reasons' and 'doubts' discussing logic as part of philosophy.

Every time his reasoning overcomes his doubts and he reaches to a level of 'belief', 'reality', or 'truth', he finds more doubts appearing in his mind and he starts looking for other reasons. This unending cycle does not let him out of logical search and the process goes on. He gets caught in it running between 'reasons' and 'doubts' based on cause and effect in search of 'beliefs', 'realities' and 'truths'. For him, the philosophy becomes an unending or open-ended knowledge and like a 'black hole' he is sucked into it moving up and down the ladder of 'beliefs', 'realities' and 'truths'. The great Sufi Inayat Khan spoke about such situation philosophically by saying that `Reasoning is a ladder. By this ladder one can rise and from this one may fall' [140].

In the end, the philosopher confesses what Socrates, the father of philosophy, once said, 'All I know is that I know nothing' [141].

It is for this reason a philosopher does not consider philosophy a station on the 'path of knowledge'.

While dervish considers philosophy as a station. He goes beyond it towards 'Wisdom' by adding intuition to logic leaving behind philosophical 'beliefs', 'realities' and 'truths'. For him the 'beliefs', 'realities', and 'truths' perceived by the philosophers are under the influence of doubts and so transitory. According to dervish at the end-station of 'Wisdom' 'beliefs', 'realities', and 'truths' become doubtless no matter whichever way they are attacked. In other words, the 'Wiseman' conquers doubts [139].

Quran distinguishes this point for the people of understanding, when it says *"And say we (now) believe there in but how can they reach (faith) from far off"* [142]. Those who understand the two 'paths' and the 'stations' located on those paths see how far off the 'faith' is from 'belief'. (One is on the 'path of act', the other on the 'path of knowledge'. One is the end station, the other a mid-station.)

The Sufis say that it is the fight between 'doubt' and 'reasoning' which binds philosophers to the station of philosophy. According to them, it is possible for the philosophers to come out of this cycle. They give the example of Mawlana Rumi and his encounter with Shams Tabrez saying that, like the Mawlana if the philosophers want to progress further, they have to open up their mind for;

1. Existence of a 'path of act';
2. Existence of a 'path of knowledge' and the separate stations of 'philosophy' (and so 'belief', 'realities', 'truths') and 'wisdom' on that path;
3. The role of a guide at some level during the passage through philosophy;
4. Existence of intuition knowledge which has link with an unknown power.

As mentioned earlier the seeker on the 'path of act' has to pass through three realms of 'Nafs' (soul); 'Qulb' (mindfulness. In layman term it is also called heart); and 'Ruh' (spirit). These will be discussed later. But for the time being, Sufis say it is in the realm of 'Ruh' (spirit) where the stations of 'Faith' and 'Wisdom' are located. And it is in this realm that 'Marateb-e-Insani' (human ranks) meet 'Marateb-e-Elahi (divine ranks) at the second epiphany of godhead-'the Wahdiat'- in the state of 'Fana' (absorption) which is equivalent to 'Nirvana' of Hinduism.

In support of their arguments the Sufis point to the verses of the Quran;

1) *'We will show them our signs in the world (path of knowledge-external path) and in their selves (Path of act–Internal path) until it becomes manifest into them that is the truth'* [143]

2) *'Say this is my way, I am inviting you towards God by the way of internal sight (Path of act-Internal path)* [144]

3) *'On the Earth are the signs for those of assured Faith.. As also in your own selves (Path of act or the Internal path).Will ye not see them?'* [145]

4) *'and do not follow [your own] desire, as it will lead you astray from the path of Allah." (Path of act or the Internal path)'*,[146A].

5) *'We made his kingdom strong and gave him wisdom and decisive speech (Path of knowledge-External path)'* [146B].

6) *'Is he who payeth adoration in the watches of the night, prostrate, and standing bewaring of the Hereafter and hoping for the mercy of his Lord (Path of act or Internal Path). Are those who are knowledgeable equal with those who know not (Path of knowledge or the External path). But only man of understanding will pay head'* [147] etc.

To recap the scenario so far, the Sufis believe there are two worlds; the 'world of the seen' and 'the world of the unseen'. These two run parallel and sometimes overlap each other. Three entities are essential part to understand the working of the 'world of the unseen'. They are godhead, spirit and soul. They play important role in both worlds. Godhead has three ranks, 'Ahdiat', 'Wahdat' and 'Wahdiat'. They are called 'Marateb-e-Elahi' (Divine Ranks) as discussed earlier.

The 'world of the seen' is the world around us which we observe and feel through our five senses. Knowledge and deeds play essential role in its working. Knowledge is pivotal part of the 'path of knowledge'. Deeds are crucial part of the 'path of act'. Logic as part of Philosophy plays major role on the 'path of knowledge'. The two paths pass through the three realms of 'Nafs' (soul), 'Qulb' (Mindfulness) and 'Ruh' (spirit). In the realm of 'Ruh' (spirit) six things happen:

- First, 'the path of knowledge' converges on the 'path of acts'.
- Second, the two paths unite to make a single 'straight path' (Sirat-ul-Mustaqeem').
- Third, the station of 'Wisdom' merges with station of 'Faith'.
- Fourth, the 'world of the seen' and the world of the unseen' meet as the door opens between the two.
- Fifth, at the opening of the door, 'human ranks' ('Marateb-e-Insani) converge at 'divine ranks' ('Marateb-e-Elahi').
- Sixth, the enlightened Sufi goes into state of 'absorption' ('Fana') after getting divine showers and absorbs in divinity following which he returns back as an elevated human ('Baqa').

In the process of spiritual ascent, I mentioned that Sufis talk of three divine and three human ranks. I talked about the divine ranks. I also said that to reach the state of 'Fana', the soul has to go through three human ranks to get enlightened. They are called 'Marateb-e-Insani'. In order of spiritual ascendency, they are called, 'Nafs' (the soul), 'Qulb' (the mindfulness), and 'Ruh' (the spirit). Sufis believe it is the role of these three ranks which make up the personalities of individuals. In that way they influence individuals and with that the communities and so the societies.

Let us take them one by one.

The concept of Nafs (Soul)

The word 'Nafs' comes from the Hebrew 'Nephesh'. The term is close to the Greek word 'PSYCHEE', which means 'soul' or life. It is considered as an integral part of 'self'. In the New Testament, the word 'soul' is used for 'conscience', while the Quran binds 'Nafs' with 'self'. The 'soul' of the New Testament can be bracketed with the 'Nafs' of the Quran, as both are intimately bonded with 'self'.

The Oxford Dictionary gives ten different definitions of 'soul'. The one that comes closest to 'Nafs' is 'conscience', which is intimately connected to 'self'. So whichever way one looks at 'Nafs', it is closely linked to 'self'.

There are seven major forms of 'Nafoos' (souls) taken from Quran out of which five pass through the realm of 'Nafs', one through 'Qulb' and one through 'Ruh' In other words, the soul of an individual passes through five stations in the realm of 'Nafs', and one each through the realms of 'Qulb' and 'Ruh' respectively before it is blessed with divine showers. It is also pertinent to mention that Sufis believe that all humans are born with their own 'Nafs' (souls). So it is taken as an entity. At the same time, they believe that during the journey of a soul, it goes through a realm they call 'Nafs' having its stations, meaning by, it is also considered as a sphere or a realm.

In this way, the soul (Nafs) as an entity passes through five stations in the realm of 'Nafs'. Sufis believe that during this passage, the soul as an entity is under the control of free will of man rendering man accountable for his actions-bad or good. He lets his soul ('Nafs') free to choose between evil and good. In doing so, man bears the consequences for the action of his soul (self). In the process of choosing between evil and good, the soul passes through the following five stations in this realm as the seeker goes forward on spiritual path;

- Nafs-e-Amara – in this station, the soul is prone to evil-hood [148]
- Nafs-e-Mulhema – in this station, the soul reveals both evil and good [149]

- Nafs-e-Lawama – in this station, the soul becomes self-accusing [150]
- Nafs-e-Hasiba - in this station, the soul becomes aware of accountability [151]
- Nafs-e-Mutmaina – In this station, the soul becomes contented [152]

1) Nafs-e-Amara:

At this level, the soul causes a person to do malicious things in the form of greed, jealousy, hatred, rage etc. This puts him in a state of egoistic selfishness where he makes no attempt to differentiate between evil and good. Consequently, he trades the hereafter in exchange for meagre worldly desires. When, at some point, he starts seeing things in their proper perspective and begins to distinguish them according to their merit, he finds himself in the next station of Nafs-e-Mulhema.

2) Nafs-e-Mulhema:

Here, the soul induces a sense of realization where a person sees wickedness in his deeds. The difference between 'Amara' and 'Mulhema' is that in the former, a person is blinded by negativity and sees no distinction between evil and good, while in the latter, he distinguishes between the two. He begins knocking on the door of self-reproach. Guilt starts to appear in the psyche and good deeds make their presence felt. However, some abhorrent qualities continue to contaminate him, causing an inner fight between guilt and lubricious desires. The growing sense of realization leads to censure his own wrongdoings and prepares him for entering the third station of Nafs-e-Lawama.

3) Nafs-e-Lawama:

In this phase, the desire to follow goodness is instilled in seeker's mind. He starts measuring good against evil. Whenever he commits an evil deed, he blames himself. The difference between 'Lawama' and 'Mulhema' is that at the level of 'Mulhema', the seeker separates evil from good but finds himself helpless to release himself from wrongdoing or to follow goodness, while at 'Lawama', he is vigilant and aware of his wicked deeds and wilfully strives to remove repugnant habits. This forms a basis for his improvement.

Theoretically, it seems an easy task but in practice it is shrouded with difficulty as it is closely linked to a broad range emotion, from joy to sadness. Joy is ignited by things like lust, lewdness, sensuality, and carnality. Sadness is heightened by grief, misery, dejection, hopelessness and fear. It is up to him to select one amongst many changeable directions, pick one amongst various options. Accordingly, after a difficult but conscious effort, he comes out of these dilemmas and moves forward towards the fourth station of Nafs-e-Hasiba.

4) Nafs-e-Hasiba

It is interesting to note that the Nafs at this level leans more on the 'path of knowledge' rather than the 'path of act'. For this reason, some Sufis give less importance to this station and not even mentions it as one of the stations. But others value it giving reference to the sayings of prophet "Read your book, which is enough for your soul for today as accountability from above" or "The best among you are those who learn the Qur'an and teach it". These sayings point to be from amongst the best in knowledge, actions and manners [153].

The grandson of Prophet Mohammad, Imam Hussain, quoted Nafs-e-Hasiba in his book "Mirat-ul-Aarifeen"[154] by saying that whoever reads the Quran, it is as if he received the knowledge of that which is going to happen or which will happen. On this occasion, he quoted another verse of the Quran which says, *"we will soon show them our signs in skies and within their souls so that the truth is revealed to them"* [155]. It seems that Nafs-e-Hasiba entertains the seekers by pointing at knowledge after they pass through the stations of negative Amara, self-awaking Mulhema, self-accusing, Lawama towards the final station of self-contenting Mutmaina.

During this journey towards fulfilment, the seeker learns specific techniques with an aim to help himself discard greed, jealousy, hatred and despondency, and absorb humility, patience, gratitude and justice. The journey gives a new dimension of awareness to the seeker while passing through the terrains of actions or knowledge or both, and he enters the final station of Nafs-e-Mutmaina.

5) Nafs-e-Mutmaina.

This is the station of perpetual contentment where the seeker has overcome his ego and expelled selfishness from his nature, rendering him selfless. He manages to suppress evil thoughts, retracts from evil deeds and concentrates on performing noble acts. This fills him with feelings of understanding, tolerance and love. As a result, he derives pleasure from things which he would have ignored in previous stations.

He feels pleased with his Lord because he believes that his Lord is pleased with him, strengthening his contentment. A few Sufis have given separate stations to these two states as Nafs-e-Radhiyah, and Nafs-e-Mardhiyyah respectively [156]. Others call it a part of total contentment and so count them as part of 'Nafs-e-Mutmaina'. Such contentment makes the seeker euphoric, brimming with goodness.

However, the soul is not yet complete in its essence as its vibrations are still rough. Therefore, the seeker keeps tilting towards Amara which tries to pull him back but he has to exercise control and resist entrapment. Also, the seeker has not yet explored the depth of 'true love' and its link with 'obedience'. The reason for this is that Sufism has located a separate sphere called the Qulb (mindfulness), for 'true love' and 'obedience' which is the next realm in spiritual ascent.

Quran refers to the 'Nafs' as singular some times and plural at others. This makes it changeable from time to time and place to place thus changing mindsets and habits as age advances. In other words, the soul accompanying a baby at the time of his birth is different from the soul at the time of his death. This delicate point is missed by many Muslim scholars, creating confusion about its understanding or differentiating it from the spirit (Ruh).

The various states of 'Nafs', its links with the person's free will and accountability, its changeable nature etc can be observed in various verses of Quranic verses; sayings of the prophet Muhammad; and narratives of certain theosophists.

For example, the Quran says;

- *"And there is a type of man who sells his soul to earn the pleasure of Allah"*[157]. This verse identifies soul as a separate entity in a person.
- *"Every soul shall have a taste of death"* [158]. It is interesting that Quran uses the word 'taste' rather than process of 'dying'. It is because soul, as part of godhead, does not die. It changes its shape (which it always does in this life) without dying and goes into another 'Realm'. So at the time of death, human body dies but the soul survives in a changed form. It is for this reason Quran uses the word 'taste of death'.
- *"Then shall every soul be paid what it earned"* [159], or,
- *"It (the soul) gets every good that it earns and it suffers every ill that it earns"* [160], or,
- *"Of men who have wronged their own souls, it is not Allah that hath wronged them, but they wronged themselves"* [161], or,
- *"O ye who believe, guard your souls"* [162].

All these verses mean that it is the soul of a human which is going to face the music in the end. That is why at the physical death of the person his soul moves on into the next realm of life.

These verses also indicate the soul's link with free will and the freedom of choice given to man in choosing between right and wrong and the consequences of his actions. Quran further says;

- *"Say it is He who created and made for you the faculties of hearing, seeing and understanding"* [163].

Again it says;

- *"We made his kingdom strong and gave him wisdom and decisive speech"* [164],

And again it says;

1. *"And gave them reasoned commandments and differed not until after the knowledge came into them"* [165].

These verses point towards the 'path of knowledge' at the station of 'Nafs-e-Hasiba'. These verses were mentioned earlier also when 'path of knowledge' was discussed in context of 'Primary attributes'.

Pointing at the 'Nafs-e-Amara' Quran mentions;

"and follow not the lusts for they will mislead them from the path of God" [166].

As mentioned earlier, the Quran refers to the Soul as singular as well as plural. For example, it says;

- *"every soul [used as a singular] will know what it hath made ready"* [167], and,
- *"when the souls [used as plural] are reunited"* [168].

Talking about the soul, the Prophet said, "the struggler is the one who strives against his Nafs in obedience to God, the Mighty and Majestic." or, "He who understood his Nafs, understood his God" [169]. He was actually hinting at the spiritual ascent of a seeker from negative 'Nafs Amara' to the positive 'Nafs Mutmaina' and onwards journey towards divine showering.

Describing the changing nature of 'Nafs,' once the Sufi, Sufyân al-Thawrî said, "I never dealt with anything stronger against me than my own Nafs; it was one time with me, and one time against me" [170].

Talking about controlling the Nafs, Yahyâ ibn Mu'âdh al-Râzî once said, "Fight against your Nafs with the four swords of training: eat little, sleep little, speak little, and be patient when people harm you ... Then the Nafs will walk the paths of obedience, like a fleeing horseman in the field of battle." He was giving one of the methodologies to the seeker as to how to walk on the Sufi path. By mentioning obedience, he was hinting at the path landing in 'Qulb' as obedience is given preference in 'Qulb'

Another Sufi, Bayazid Bistami said, "I reached God by two steps, one foot on my own Nafs and the other in the street of the beloved" [171]. Again, the Sufi is hinting at close relationship between 'Nafs' and 'Qulb' as the 'street (path) of beloved' falls in the realm of 'Qulb'

A saint once said, "Forgetfulness of God is the forgetfulness of Nafs" [172]

To summarize, the soul of a person is rebellious in nature and thus, out of control. God has given every man intellect and free will to control his evil soul and lead it through a gradual process of refinement and turns it into a contented soul. Once he does that, he finds himself a changed person. The evil in his nature is replaced with goodness and he becomes humble, tolerant, compassionate, and loving. In other words, he achieves long-lasting contentment.

With this frame of personality, the seeker, along with his 'contented soul', journeys on in his search, into the realm of 'Qulb' (mindfulness).

The concept of Qulb (mindfulness)

Qulb, literally meaning heart, is a reprocessing realm identified by Sufis as 'Burzakh'. It is placed between the realm of Nafs (soul) of desires and the realm of 'Ruh' (spirit) of solace. The two paths of 'acts and knowledge' pass through it as they did in the realm of 'Nafs'. Metaphysically, it alludes to a host of ideas such as: mindfulness of our thoughts; consciousness of our feelings; awareness of our will; and recognition of our acts in respect to their philosophical applications.

In that sense, Qulb is closely linked to our rational perceptions, but a sudden outburst of emotions makes it respond through palpitations of the anatomical heart. That is why people in general confuse Qulb with heart which is wrong. As mentioned earlier, Qulb is mindfulness while heart is an anatomical organ. This relationship creates two diverse opinions. First, Qulb is bracketed with emotional desires, which lie in the realm of Nafs. Second, it is linked to the logical mind. This duality between emotional outbursts and logical sobriety creates a perplexity about the nature of the Qulb.

According to Sufis, the Qulb holds both logic pertaining to beliefs and emotions related to actions. It acts as a conduit for the two paths of 'knowledge and act' through which the seekers pass forwards to achieve 'Wisdom' and 'Faith' respectively in the next realm of 'Ruh'

The seeker on the 'path of knowledge' advances as he scrutinizes the logic of 'beliefs' (Ilm-ul-Yaqeen) and 'realities' (Ain-ul-Yaqeen). The seeker on the 'path of acts' cleanses his actions through love and obedience. The Quran says *And the wandering Arabs say, We believe. Say Ye believe not but rather say we submit for the faith hath not yet entered into your Qulbs, yet, if ye obey Allah and His messenger, He will not withhold from you aught of your acts'* [173].

After distinguishing spiritual Qulb from anatomical heart, the Sufis divide Qulb in three layers. Each layer has two common and one specific ingredients. The common ingredients are 'reason' and 'doubt' which make logic as the base for all the layers. And the specific ingredients are 'thought', 'feeling' and 'will' which shape up the logic as the seeker passes through each layer. Thus basic effect on the seeker is logical shrouded by specific ingredient as he passes in individual layers. The three layers are;

1. Superficial: in this layer 'thought' plays essential role as it joins 'reason' and 'doubt';
2. Middle: in this layer 'feeling' plays pivotal role as it links with 'reason' and 'doubt';
3. Deep: in this layer, 'will' plays crucial role as it creates nexus with 'reason' and 'doubt'.

The existence of 'reason' and 'doubt' as part of logic makes Qulb a philosophical stage on the 'path of knowledge'. The addition of individual ingredients specific to each layer changes the nature of logic as the seeker moves from one layer to another on his way towards the stage of 'belief' and contentment. In support of this interpretation, the Sufis quote the Quran in which a conversation takes place between Abraham and God, which goes like this, *"My Lord, show me how Thou giveth life to dead. He said, dost thou not believe? Abraham said: Yea, but (1 ask) in order that my Qulb may be contented* [174].

Talking about the three layers one by one, the Sufis say that the 'superficial layer' represents the human mind and as knowledge attaches itself to 'thought' it either creates 'reason' or 'doubt' or both in this layer. In the process, the two become main rivals opening a gate for philosophical discourses in which philosophers swing to and fro in search of 'reality'. Prophet Muhammad spoke about this part of Qulb in a delicate manner when he said, that the 'Qulb is like a feather in the middle of a desert, hanging from a tree and blown to and fro by the wind'. Qulb in this quote is the human philosophical mind, the tree is a symbol of knowledge and the wind is uncertainty. This saying also points to a sense of vibration created by the 'wind'. Sufis refer to such vibrations from coarse to fine, confronting the seeker as he passes through these layers.

The Sufis say that 'thought' plays important role in this layer. According to them, it creates 'impression', 'form' and 'imagination'. For example, when a 'thought' reaches this layer, it leaves an 'impression'. Depending on whether it is mixed up with other 'thoughts' or not, it is reflected outward to others. In whichever way it reflects, this layer gives it a body which becomes 'form' or 'imagination'. It is relevant to note that when a 'thought' is reflected outwards without mixing with existing 'thoughts', it becomes 'information'. But when it is mixed with existing 'thoughts' prior to reflection, it becomes 'knowledge'.

Thus, 'thought', with the help of intellect and knowledge, assists 'reason' in exposing 'doubt' in the superficial layer. But because this layer is close to the realm of 'Nafs', it still carries the coarse vibrations of impulses and emotions. Therefore, reasoning stays weak and earthly, while 'doubt' remains dominant. Additionally, 'form' and 'imagination' in this layer have a close association with the impulses and emotions of 'Nafs', which is why they are usually uncontrolled. It is for these reasons Sufis strongly recommend seekers to have a guide in the realm of Qulb, who leads them through this layer.

The guide could be living or someone who has passed, provided he has the status of 'wali' or 'dervish'. The Quran says *Your wali (guide) is God, and His messenger and those who believe, who establish worship and pay poor due while they bow down*[175]. Sufis say that without a guide, a seeker (in this case a trainee philosopher) can lose track, get confused and ultimately fall astray. In this regards, the Quran says *That is because they believed, then disbelieved, therefore, their Qulbs are sealed so that they understand not*[176].

These are the people who become their own masters or guides and tread the path independently, as they were doing in the realm of Nafs. The Quran also says *Those are they whose Qulbs Allah hath sealed and they follow their own desires* [177] or *And keep thy Nafs content with those who call on their Lord morning and evening, seeking His face. And let not thine eyes pass beyond them, seeking the pomp and glitter of this life. Nor obey any whose Qulb we have permitted to neglect the remembrance of Us. One who follows his own desires is he whose case has gone beyond all bounds* [178].

The vibrations in this layer are still rough, albeit finer than they were in the realm of 'Nafs'. Such vibrations are parallel to what is known as 'Tamas' in Hindu spirituality.

One of the main differences between the realms of Nafs and Qulb is that in the Nafs, one starts on a negative note and moves towards a positive mark independently. While in the Qulb, he starts with a positive record and moves forward with the help of a knowledgeable guide. That is why the Qulb is likened to a clear mirror. Each time the seeker commits an iniquity, he puts a stain on it. Repetitive misdemeanour result in a completely blemished mirror. For such a taint, the prophet Muhammed said, 'There is a polish for everything that taketh away the rust, and the polish of the Qulb is the invocation of Allah'[179].

The guide, using his wisdom, helps the seeker overcome his doubts. He makes him understand the relationship between 'thought', 'reason' and 'doubt', their exposure to impulse from the nearby 'Nafs', as well as how to control them. Through support of the guide, 'reason' and 'doubt' become important tools in this transformation from 'impression' to 'form' and to 'imagination'. Sufis stress upon the presence of a guide immensely at this crucial philosophical stage. Without a guide, they say, a seeker goes astray in field of philosophy, running amok between 'reason' and 'doubt'.

It is also important to realize at this point that 'thought' is perceived by any of the five senses of the body and is reflected out as 'impression', 'form' or 'imagination' through the eyes, skin, speech and postures. In addition to reflection, the superficial layer of Qulb may also store 'thoughts' in various 'forms' and 'imaginations'.

'The middle layer' of Qulb has specific ingredient of 'feeling' in addition to 'reason' and 'doubt'. In the process of transformation, some uncontrolled 'forms' and 'imaginations' from the superficial layer, filter into this layer, making it have a combination of controlled and uncontrolled imaginations. In this way, it acts like a temporary storehouse for the subconscious. Because of constructive guidance in the superficial layer, 'doubt' in this layer becomes weak as the power of 'reason' becomes convincing and strong, changing the logical approach of the seeker. This change is coincided with finer vibrations this layer has because of its linkage with 'feelings'. These fine vibrations are akin to the vibrations of 'Rajas' in Hindu spirituality.

Because of these fine vibrations, the seeker starts seeing beyond earthly reasons. In other words, he sees reasons hidden behind the reasons. But despite having fine vibrations, seeing hidden reasons and elevation in logical approach, the seeker is still bombarded by new doubts.

The role of 'feeling' in this layer is very interesting as it is feminine in nature. Accordingly, it shapes the psyche of the seeker by making his character soft, delicate and amorous. Thus, 'feeling' awakens the heart to sensitivity and makes a person tender and open to the thoughts and feelings of others, which coincides with the type of vibrations this layer harbours.

The deep layer, which is also called the core has specific ingredient of 'will' in addition to having 'reason' and 'doubt'. According to Sufis, this layer is placed next to the realm of 'Ruh' (spirit), as opposed to the superficial layer which is placed next to 'Nafs' (soul). Just as the emotional outbursts of 'Nafs' influence the superficial layer, the combination of sobriety and reality of 'Ruh' affect the deep layer. This influence introduces finer vibrations into the 'will' which plays a vital role in this layer.

Thus, 'will' takes over the dominant role from 'reason' making 'doubt' disintegrate and sets aside the power of logic. This is because of the fine vibrations of 'will' which enables the seeker to see not only the 'reason' but its cause and the expected effect. This 'will' is completely different from the 'free will' we saw in the realm of 'Nafs'. That 'will' had rough vibrations. Vibrations of the third layer make the seeker aware of the totality of things. As a result, his 'doubts' vanish and he transcends the stage of reasoning. Such vibrations are known as 'Satva' in Hinduism. This is the point where logic ends and intuition begins. From here, the path enters the realm of 'Ruh' towards 'inspiration' and 'revelation'.

In this layer, the vibrant 'will' turns logic upside down. The question arises: what is 'will'? Sufis call it 'power in completeness', which pushes the seeker through stages of 'belief', giving him glimpses of 'realities' on his journey towards absolute truth. The Quran says *'Is not the time ripe for the Qulbs of those who believe to submit to Allah's reminder and to the truth which is revealed'* [180].

This type of 'will' is the actual force behind life. Its strength increases as the seeker advances through the shades of 'reality' towards 'totality'. According to Sufis, it controls 'thoughts', 'form' and 'imagination' and puts them in memory. In this way, it helps to hone and mature the seeker. Some spiritualists refer to it as divine power. As they perceive love to be divine, they bracket 'will' with 'love'. As mentioned earlier, this 'will' should not be confused with the free will of 'Nafs'

Some Sufis consider the power of 'will' as 'consciousness'. They say when in action, it is 'will', when at rest it is 'consciousness'. They compare this relationship with the relation-ship between the particle and wave of quantum physics which are identical but different in vibration. They describe this unique relationship by saying that 'consciousness' of 'will' makes it stronger, while ignorance of it makes it weaker. They say that characters are built on this relationship.

To recap so far, we find that 'Qulb' has three layers. Each layer has 'reason' and 'doubt' which create philosophical lineage. In addition, each layer has its own ability in shaping 'thought', 'feeling' and 'will', which affects corresponding reasoning and doubts of individual layers. This relationship is so complex that the seeker needs a guide to lead him through the difficult passage of philosophy. During the journey, the particular ability of each layer, with support of the guide, acts on 'reason' and 'doubt'.

It also exposes the seeker to 'beliefs' and 'realities' on their way toward 'actual truth'. In this process, 'doubt' gradually wither away and 'reason' is taken over by 'will' of the deep layer. Sufis link these changes with specific vibrations held by each layer.

This was the passage of a seeker (in this case the trainee philosopher) through the 'path of knowledge' in the realm of 'Qulb'.

But what about 'the path of act'?

That path also traverses through the same layers, in the same manner as the 'path of knowledge'. A guide is also needed on this path to steer the seeker on his journey towards the realm of 'Ruh'.

After passing independently, on his own volition, through the five stations in the realm of 'Nafs', the seeker becomes tolerant, humble and contented, infused with love. It is important to mention here, that there is no compulsion in having a guide in the realm of 'Nafs'. Sometimes seekers are lucky to have guides, in which case the journey through the stations of 'Nafs' becomes faster. But, generally the seeker goes through the stations independently.

While passing through the three layers of 'Qulb', the seeker, with the help of a guide, experiences the vibrations of each layer. As a result, three things happen to him;

- First, the love which he carried from the realm of 'Nafs' passes through fine vibrations of femininity of the 'middle layer', shaping it into 'motherly love'. He finds himself looking at others, as a mother would look upon her offspring.

- Second, he discovers the actuality of 'obedience' by separating it from fear. In this way, he takes away obedience from the fold of weakness linked to fear and makes it a symbol of quality linked to courage. With the help of a guide, he learns how to stay obedient in places and at occasions where obedience is required without getting fearful. On fearfulness, Rumi says, "Forget safety. Live where you fear to live. Destroy your reputation. Be notorious." Then he says "Ignore those that make you fearful and sad, that degrade you back towards disease and death" [181].

- Third, he bonds obedience with 'motherly love', which he learned in the 'middle layer', by mixing their vibrations and converting them into a new kind of love. The Sufis call it 'Ishq' (adore). It is the combination of 'Ishq' (adore) and 'obedience' which takes the seeker to the realm of 'Ruh'. He comes to know about the real validity, actual reality and tangible endurance of 'Ishq'. He feels its steady and sustainable flow through its fine vibrations.

Having no 'fear' and infused with 'Ishq', the seeker does things his intellect will not dare allow. The great Sufi philosopher of the Indian subcontinent, Iqbal, compared the two in one of his poems when he said;

'Be Khatar Kood Para Aatesh-e-Namrud Main Ishq'; 'Aqal hai Mahv-e-Tamash-e-Lab-e-Bam Abhi' (Without fear, adore jumped into the fire of Nimrod, while intellect watched it with amazement from the edge of height).

Vibrations being waves, the seeker reaches a peak at times, making him ecstatic. It was in such a state of abundance when the great Sufi Hallaj once stated, 'I saw my lord with eyes of my Qulb. I said Who are thou? He answered, Thou'[182]. On other hand, sometimes the reduced flow of vibrations brings him down. In such an event, he feels debased. In similar situation, a Sufi was heard saying 'I lost my God'. At another occasion, a mourning dervish was turned out thrice by Junaid from his Khanqah (cloister) when he said 'My God is dead'. It is in circumstances like these that a wise guide becomes crucial in the reformation process during the seeker's 'path of act' through the layers of 'Qulb'.

With help of a guide, the seeker sheds his 'doubts' in the 'realm of Qulb', surpasses his 'reason' and replaces it with 'will' (as we saw it on the path of knowledge), and changes his 'love' to 'Ishq' (adore) by linking it with 'obedience' on the 'path of act'. During this process, and the processes he went through earlier in the 'realm of Nafs', he purifies his soul. Some Sufis call such a soul 'Nafsi Saffiya' and put it on a separate station [183]. Others link it to the 'deep layer of Qulb'. They argue that such soul though purified and possessor of finer vibrations, still not complete in its essence. But, it is ready to enter the 'realm of Ruh'.

It is pertinent to note that the role of the guide ends in the realm of 'Qulb'. The seeker, along with his 'purified soul', enters the realm of 'Ruh' alone and he stays alone in his onward journey.

To recap, he started his journey alone in the realm of 'Nafs'. The journey began with negativity and his soul moved slowly towards positivity. On the route, the negativity and positivity kept sucking him back and forth until he succeeded to reach the fifth station of contentment (Mutmaina). From there he entered the realm of 'Qulb' as 'contented soul'. While in the realm of 'Qulb', he started with positivity and with help of a 'guide' he gradually crossed the layers towards finer vibrations. Along the way, if and when he lost his footing and slid down, the guide pulled him up. So his soul which entered the realm of 'Qulb' as a 'contented soul' was ready to enter the realm of 'Ruh' as 'purified soul'.

Now, he is left alone again in the realm of Ruh which is the third and final step of Marateb-e-Insani (human ranks).

As one could see this is the journey of the soul (Nafs)

The concept of Ruh (Spirit)

'Ruh' is taken from the Hebrew word 'Ruakh' which means spirit, soul or life, thus making spirit and soul as one entity. The Quran uses the word 'Nafs' for soul and 'Ruh' for spirit. At times soul (Nafs) is portrayed so closely to spirit (Ruh) that one has to use all his mental aptitude, according to his understanding, to distinguish one from the other. That is why, it is not surprising to see vast number of theosophists and theologians over the centuries presenting the two concepts as one for all illustrative interpretations. In doing so they translated 'Ruh' in plural as they translated 'Nafs' in plural. In this way over fourteen different types of 'Arwah' (spirits) are described by Muslim scholars, such as Ruhul Insani (human spirit), Ruhul Haiwani (animal spirit), Ruhul Nabathi (vegetable spirit), Ruhul Azam (exalted spirit) and so on and so forth.

In the Quran, the word 'Ruh' is altogether mentioned nineteen times; [184]

- Five times as God's breath;
- Four times as God's transmutation;
- Four times as God's command;
- Twice as an entity accompanying angels;
- Twice as an entity linked with the Quran;
- Once as an entity bracketed with Mary.
- Once as a person coming to Mary

In all these revelations, it has never been directly or indirectly referred to as 'Nafs' (soul). Although, at times it is brought into close relationship with 'Qulb' (heart), which is natural, keeping in mind the spiritual adjacency of realm of 'Qulb' with realm of 'Ruh' in 'Marateb-e-Insani' (Human ranks) mentioned earlier. Moreover, in all the nineteen revelations, 'Ruh' is always mentioned as singular in spite of its association with plurals. For example, the Quran says, *"the angels and the spirit [used as single] descend therein, by the permission of their Lord, with all decrees"* [185].

In contrast, 'Nafs' (soul) is reported in singular as well as in plural. For example, the Quran says, *"every soul [used as singular] will know what it hath made ready"* [186], and *"when the souls [used as plural] are reunited"* [187].

When a few Jews asked Prophet Muhammed about the nature of 'Ruh' he replied, "the Ruh (spirit) proceedeth at my Lord's command, but of knowledge only a little to you is given." This saying became a verse in the Quran [188].

Against these vague descriptions, various Ahadith and different scholars described it according to their understandings. For example;

- A hadith says "Ruh is God, nothing moves except by the command of God" [189].
- Imam Ali symbolized it with an entity having 7,000 mouths each with 7,000 tongues praising God without a break [190].
- Ibn Abbas believed it meant the Angel Gabriel [191].
- Mujahid said, it meant a 'being' of another world [192]

- Abu Bakr said, "Ruh has not come under the command of 'Kun' (Be)[193]
- Abu Bakr-i-Mukti said, "Ruh is the command of God and does not come under the category of commanded, like Angels, Jinns, animals, vegetable etc" [194].
- Abu Sayid Salmi quoted, "It is related that the spirits had knowledge of God, before the manifestation of the world" [195].

In this way, different authors, theosophists and scholars give different versions of 'Ruh'. Its closest analogy can be found in the concept of 'Aumakua' in Hunaism of Polynesia which controls 'Unipihili'-the lower self-through invisible channel called 'Aka'. The 'Unipihili' is equivalent to 'Nafs' in Sufism.

Sufis are somewhat clearer about the nature of 'Ruh' as compared to their counterpart theologians. It is because of the understanding they have about the three 'human ranks' and the two paths of 'knowledge' and 'acts' described earlier.

According to them, a seeker with its soul treading either the 'path of knowledge' or the 'path of acts' reaches the realm of 'Ruh' (spirit) after successfully passing through five reprocessing stations of 'Nafs' (soul) and three corresponding layers of 'Qulb' (mindfulness). In the process, the seeker overcomes his doubts from his philosophical knowledge and becomes a 'believer' with the help of a wise guide. Then, in the realm of 'Ruh' (spirit) his knowledge of 'belief' (Ilm-ul-Yaqeen) and 'realities' (Ain-ul-Yaqeen) which he brought from the realm of 'Qulb' gets refinement before reaching the ultimate station of 'Wisdom' (Haq-ul-Yaqeen) at the top end of 'path of knowledge'.

Similarly, a seeker with its soul on the 'path of acts' reaches this realm after passing through the same stations of 'Nafs' and same layers of 'Qulb'. At the level of Qulb he is exposed to the fine vibrations of love and obedience with help of his master dervish. After entering the realm of 'Ruh', he goes through further tuning without the help of a guide and reaches the ultimate station of 'Faith' on the 'path of act'.

Before he reaches the ultimate stations of 'Wisdom' and 'Faith' as the case may be, the seeker passes through three stages in the realm of Ruh. They are; 'Intuition'; 'Inspiration'; and 'Revelation'.

1. 'Intuition' is defined as immediate mental awareness about something without reasoning. It widens the range of knowledge where reasoning is not needed to pursue truth. A person with this capability should be taken seriously, because his knowledge begins where logic ends. For this reason, an intuitive man takes dreams seriously and accept them as reality. Dreams for him become tools of expression. Through dreams he can describe past and present events and predict the future. As he advances in this knowledge, dream intuition changes into vision intuition, wherein visions appear about past, present and future events. St Paul is a typical example in this context. Some people confuse intuition with instinct. The latter is influenced by motives of 'Nafs,' the former is independent of such motives and is powered by urges of 'Ruh.' After acquiring this knowledge, the seeker is ready to enter the stage of 'Inspiration'.

2. 'Inspiration' is defined as a creative influence or a stimulus. According to Sufi Inayat Khan it is; a word which is drawn in the form of lines; or composed in the form of notes; or written in the form of words; or painted in the form of colours; or spoken in the form of wisdom. In all circumstances, the source is the same but its manifestations are different. The streams of these manifestations flow through developed intuition. Thus, inspiration may come in three forms;

•   In the presence of someone who is inspiring;
•   In thinking about someone who is inspiring;
•   In the tranquil heart ('Qulb') when it communicates with the inspired heart ('Qulb') of another being.

In all these forms, the original source is divine which creates a sense of ecstasy bringing awareness in a higher being. Quran mentions the state of 'Inspiration' when God speaks to the prophet by telling him, *"Say thou: I am but a man like you: It is revealed to me by Inspiration, that your Allah is one Allah, so stand true to Him, and ask for His Forgiveness. And woe to those who join gods with Allah"* [196]

Some theosophists translate it as 'revelation' which is the next step in the realm of 'Ruh'. In any case at this level, the atheistic spirituality reaches its end. For onward journey, belief in higher being becomes mandatory. As Sufi Inayat Khan put it, an inspired person at this stage is like a tree laden with fruit that is waiting to ripen which happens with enlightenment through revelation.

3. 'Revelation' is defined as making known by unveiling the inner self. It is the final stage in the realm of 'Ruh' where the seeker is showered with inundation of 'Nur' (light). As a result, his soul enters the radiant vibrations of enlightenment. The Sufis call it the 'Divine Command' (Aamr-e-Elahi). The Quran says *"He sendeth forth the spirit (Ruh) at His own command on whomsoever of His servants He pleaseth"* [197].

It is this 'Command' which takes the seeker;

1. On the 'path of knowledge' completing his knowledge of 'belief' (Ilm-e-Yaqeen) and 'realities' (Ain-ul-Yaqeen) elevating him to 'Wisdom' (Haqul-ulYaqeen);

2. On the 'path of acts' sprinkling his adoring and obedient 'Qulb' with radiant vibrations and raising him to the station of 'Faith'. The Quran says *"On the Qulb (hearts) of these hath God graven the faith and with a spirit proceeding from Himself (Ruhun min-hu) hath He strengthened them"* [198].

So it is the 'Divine Command' which reunites the 'soul' of the seeker with the 'spirit' making the 'soul' complete and perfect as if it was in the womb of a mother. Such a soul is also called 'Nafs-e-Kamillah' (the complete soul) because it makes the seeker 'Insan-e-Kamil' (a perfect person) [199]. Some Sufis give such a soul a separate status. But other don't. They argue that after its reunion with the 'spirit', the 'soul' cannot have a separate and independent status as it is in union with 'Divinity'.

As mentioned earlier, in this realm six things happen;

- First, 'the path of knowledge' converge on 'the path of acts'.
- Second, the two paths unite to make a single 'straight path' (Sirat-ul-Mustaqeem').
- Third, the station of 'Wisdom' merges with station of 'Faith'.
- Fourth, a door between the 'world of the seen' and the 'world of the unseen' opens.
- Fifth, 'human ranks' ('Marateb-e-Insani) meet with 'divine ranks' ('Marateb-e-Elahi')
- Sixth, the seeker goes into state of 'absorption' ('Fana') after getting divine showers and gets absorbed in divinity. After dipping in 'Fana' he comes back in state of 'Baqa' as an enlightened Sufi.

It is for this reason the realm of 'Ruh' is also called the locus of 'Divine Enlightenment'. Because, the enlightened person becomes the master of visible (rational) and invisible (intuition) knowledge as he commands the knowledge of both the paths. From here on, he acquires the art of the finest vibrations of 'will', 'feelings', 'dreams' and 'visions' which are the essential alphabets of 'cosmic language' interpreted through his improved sixth sense. He shares this language with 'Nature' as he becomes part of it and feels its vibrations and understands its harmonious working.

At temporal level, he becomes, contented, tolerant, rational, understanding and humble. At spiritual level he floats into 'the world of the unseen' in state of 'Fana' and experiences extraordinary phenomenons which otherwise are bounded by time and space. For example, he can be seen at different places at one time. Or, he can know the answer to questions before they are asked. Or he can see the events before they occur etc etc. It is at this level; the seeker achieves the status of a 'Wali' or 'Dervish' (Saint). It is quoted that great Sufi Abu Yazid once prayed one Juma'a prayer in 24,000 different places. He told the religious authorities in one place: "I was praying in 12,000 different houses of worship today." They asked: "How?" He said, "By the power of the Lord Almighty. If you don't believe me, send people around to ask." They sat and waited until messengers returned saying that he was seen in many places [200].

Before going further, I want to compare 'Ruh' (spirit) with 'Nafs' (soul) as many Muslim theosophists and scholars take one for other.

'Ruh' (Spirit) *and* 'Nafs' (Soul)

Many Islamic theosophists do not differentiate between the Ruh (spirit) and the Nafs (soul). This becomes apparent from literature on the subject and from various translations of the Quran. As a result, many speak of the Ruh (spirit) in the singular as well as plural, which is a quality of the Nafs (soul). As a result, they mention Ruh in plural such as 'human spirits' (Arwah-e-Insani) or 'animal spirits' (Arwah-e-Haiwani). This is against Quranic interpretation as Quran always mentions 'Ruh' in singular form. It is like calling 'Allah' in plural which is shirk.

The New Testament separates the two in I-Thess V.23 when it states, "And I pray God, your whole spirit and soul and body be preserved blameless until the coming of our Lord Jesus Christ."

The Quran also distinguishes between the Ruh (spirit) and Nafs (soul) by mentioning them as two separate entities. If these two are one, as some of the theosophists believe, it begs the question, why they were mentioned separately in the Quran? Furthermore, there is a narration verified by all the schools of thought about a few Jews who went to the holy Prophet (pbuh) and questioned him about the nature of the Ruh (spirit). He asked for time. Two weeks later, he supplied them with a revelation, or the word of God, instead of his own response. This leads one to conclude that it was God's will to establish, through His divine revelation, that the concept of Ruh remains unchanged.

The Prophet's narrations were modified over the passage of time, as we can see them when we read various Ahadith, but the Quran remains unchanged. In the case of the Ruh and Nafs, neither the Quran nor the sayings of the Prophet imply that they are one. In fact, the Quran always distinguishes the Ruh (spirit) from the Nafs (soul).

History of religion also tells us that the concept of the Ruh (spirit) appeared well before the appearance of notion of the soul (Nafs). It also becomes apparent that the spirit and soul are not only two different entities, they even influence the human psyche in different ways as mentioned previously.

The following paragraphs compare and emphasize the differences between the 'Ruh' and 'Nafs':

- The 'Ruh' (spirit) is a positive power and never creates negativity. The 'Nafs' can be negative as well as positive.
- Both the 'Ruh' and 'Nafs' have intimate and inexplicable links with godhead. God refers to the 'Ruh' as His 'Ruh' [201] and the 'Nafs' as His 'Nafs'. According to the Quran, humans are created from a single 'Nafs' [202], while this is not stated implicitly regarding the 'Ruh'.
- Literature describes the 'Ruh' as 'uncreated' but is silent about the 'Nafs'.
- The 'Ruh' is mentioned 19 times in the Quran and always in the singular [203], however, the 'Nafs' is mentioned tens of times in Quran in singular as well as in plural [204].
- The Quran mentions the 'Ruh' in singular while working with a single 'Nafs' (soul) or multiple 'Nafoos' (souls). This makes the 'Ruh' non-multiplicative and the 'Nafs' multiplicative.

- Because of its indescribable existence and singularity, the 'Ruh' acts as singular in all matters, including humans, without being divided. The Quran says, *"Therein descend the angels and the spirit by the permission of their Lord for every matter"* [205]. The 'Nafs', goes through indescribable changes and becomes an integral part of matter, plants, animals, and man [206].

- The 'Ruh' fine-tunes the human psyche through revelation as Divine Command (Amr-e-Elahi) when the soul of a person reaches the realm of 'Ruh'. The Quran says, *"Thus have we sent the spirit to thee with a revelation, by our command"*. This command enlightens the human 'Nafs' (soul), not the other way around [207].

- Only selected people get this exposure to the 'Ruh'. The Quran says, *"Spirit is sent only to those people on whom God pleaseth"* [208]. However, all humans are exposed to the 'Nafs'. Therefore, only chosen 'Nafoos' (souls) gain enlightenment.

- The 'Ruh' is very close to 'Ahdiat' of godhead in its essence. But unlike 'Ahdiat', which does not take any form, the 'Ruh' can take the form of a person. The Quran states *"And we sent our spirit to her, Mary, and he took before her the form of a perfect man"* [209]. 'Nafs' is close to 'Wahdiat' of godhead in its core, and takes many forms, shapes and identities.

- The 'Ruh' is unchangeable, while 'Nafs' is mutable.

- The 'Ruh' is neither created nor does it create, hence, man is not created from 'Ruh', nor is it a part of man. 'Nafs', being created from a single soul, exists in every man.

- The 'Ruh' plays its role once in a man's life, when the 'Nafs' of a person, in spiritual ascent, reaches the realm of 'Ruh'. The Nafs starts playing its role right from the birth of a person, until the day he dies. That is why the 'Nafs' of a newborn is different from the 'Nafs' at the time of his death as an old man.

- The 'Ruh' cannot be projected in any form or shape by man. The 'Nafs' can be projected outside body, even to faraway places. This is what is known as an out-of-body-experience. The projected 'Nafs' is not bound by time or space, and it may or may not be seen by others in projected places.

- The 'Ruh' does not interfere in a man's ordinary routine life. Meanwhile, the 'Nafs' can bestow supernatural powers to the person it resides in. With this power, a person can become a healer, a soothsayer or a fortune teller.

After differentiating the spirit from the soul, and the way spirit influences soul, the question arises as to how does that influence mankind? Most importantly, can it play a role in creating harmony at individual, communal and societal levels?

To find answers to these questions we have to consider the following factors;

- The role of the soul and spirit in corporal and spiritual growth of individuals and how to identify commonalities between spirituality and parapsychology.
- The commonalities between godhead as perceived by Sufis and 'singularity' as described by scientists and how those commonalities can bring religion and science together.
- In light of the commonalities between Science, Parapsychology and Sufism, what role can scientists, parapsychologists and Sufis play towards developing a better society in the 21st century.

1. The role of soul and spirit.

To understand the role of soul and spirit in man's life, one has to understand the nature of the link between the two. This link is described appropriately by the Yaqui spirituality of Mexico. Though some do not confer upon it the status of spirituality, its functions and messages are brimming with spiritual fervour. That spirituality propagates two powers or spheres called Toh-Nahl and Nah-Uhal, akin to soul and spirit respectively. The two are merged with each other as a single bubble similar to the covering that encases the foetus in a womb. At birth, with the cutting of the umbilical cord, the two gets separated, leaving man with Toh-Nahl, which becomes an integral part of his self. Having no 'Nah-Uhal' and sticking to Toh-Nahl his personality becomes incomplete filled with large ego for the rest of his life. Nah-Uhal stays as an outer power or sphere, waiting to get linked again with Toh-Nahl.

According to Yaqui spirituality, the connection between the two can be established in two ways:

- First, during the present life, with the help of two guides in different stages of self-development specific to that spirituality. When the union between Toh-Nahl (equivalent to soul or Nafs) and Nah-Uhal (equivalent to spirit or Ruh) is restored, the person becomes spiritually complete and turns from a normal human being into a Brujo (equivalent to saint, dervish or wali).
- Second, after death. (equivalent to Nirvana)

Sufis also subscribe to an almost identical belief. They say that the Quran as a powerful book of knowledge and spirituality identifies four important senses as tools to help man link his soul (Nafs) with spirit (Ruh). These tools or senses are hearing, sight, speech and breathing. They connect 'hearing', 'sight' and 'speech' to a knowledge termed as 'Ilm-e-Safina'. The seeker needs it when treading the path of knowledge or the 'external path'. And they connect breathing to a knowledge they term as 'Ilm-e-Sina', which is needed when the seeker walks on the path of act or the 'internal path'.

It is for this reason Quran places enormous importance on breathing and links it five times with the spirit (Ruh) [210], twice with Mary [211], and three times with Adam [212]. Linking breathing; with the Ruh, which has unidentifiable qualities; with Mary who gave birth although she was a virgin; and with Adam who was created without parents, adds a spiritual dimension to its use in everyday life.

Taking hints from the Quran, Sufis pay special attention to control breathing which is an important part of 'Dhikr' and Dhikr itself is an essential tool in meditation. It is responsible for putting the seeker on the 'internal path' or 'path of acts'. This is also one of the reasons why Sufis prefer the 'path of acts' over the 'path of knowledge' – the 'external path'. They say that the path of knowledge harbours philosophy and philosophy thrives on doubts, while doubts in turn create hurdles in spiritual progress. According to them, 'control breathing' combined with continuous repetition (Dhikr) of Quranic verses play a major role in meditation. 'Dhikr' clears the mind of controlled and uncontrolled thoughts and prepares a fertile field for suggestions.

It is interesting that self-hypnosis, which is an important component of parapsychology, acts on similar principles. It also prepares a person for suggestions. Thus 'Dhikr' and self-hypnosis initiate meditative and paranormal states respectively. Both are identical in creating altered states. Both play an identical role in inculcating self-discipline. Parapsychologists use hypnosis primarily to treat patients with ailments linked with psychological problems. Sufis use 'Dhikr' for ailments linked with spiritual disturbances. If these two were made a study project, one would find a lot of commonalities between Sufism and parapsychology.

The Sufis go one step further by training the seeker how to control his ego while instilling self-discipline. This is an essential step on the path of acts or 'internal path' for the onward journey towards spiritual fulfilment. That fulfilment is relevant in re-establishing the link between soul and spirit which was lost at the time of birth. A seeker works on his soul and makes it worthy of creating that linkage while passing through the three realms of 'Marateb-e-Insani' (human ranks) on the path of act or the internal path. Parapsychologists don't go that far.

Sufis aim to reconnect the seeker's soul (Nafs) with the spirit (Ruh) as they were in the womb. It is pertinent to mention here that some historical personalities were born without the separation of the two. The Sufis cite the example of Jesus Christ who they believe was born without dislocation of his soul from spirit. That made his birth unique. He was born enlightened, performing supernatural acts from the time of his birth. His birth confirms the validity of the Yaqui notion of 'Toh-Nahl' and 'Nah-Uhal' or the corresponding Sufi concept of 'Nafs' and 'Ruh'. This phenomenon also holds true in cases of other spiritual personalities in history such as Maha Vira and Lao Tze. According to the Sufis, such births are exceptional and unusual.

They say, under usual circumstances, the stage of reunion comes very late in spiritual development. Normally, at the time of birth, the soul (Nafs) is set free from the influence of the spirit (Ruh) and is controlled instead by the free will of man in the realm of 'Nafs'. Such a soul is influenced by worldly desires and is closely associated with ego. Thus, depending on the surroundings, desires steer the soul towards negativity or positivity. If it is driven towards negativity, it changes the personality of man accordingly and he becomes evil. But if it is driven towards positivity, the person embarks upon a journey of goodness which he constantly refines while passing through three spheres of 'Marateb-e-Insani' (human ranks). One should remember that during this struggle, the soul of a person is refined by the free will in the realm of 'Nafs', by a mentor in the second realm of 'Qulb', and by divine shower in the third realm of 'Ruh'. In the final realm of 'Ruh', with the divine shower, his soul is coupled with spirit.

Sufis perceive a fine distinction at this level. They say, it is the spirit (Ruh) and not the soul (Nafs) which decides on this linkage alluded to in the Quran as 'divine command' (Amr-e-Elahi). Also, it is the spirit (Ruh) which influences the soul (Nafs) and not the other way around. After the linkage, the soul (Nafs) goes into the finest vibrations of the spirit (Ruh), rendering the person enlightened. Such an enlightened person develops enormous powers, acquiring control over space and time. He tastes divinity through divine absorption of 'Fana', as his enlightened soul (Nafs) merges with 'Wahdiat' of godhead. The union is called 'Walayat' (sainthood). It is the highest achievement in Sufism, elevating the seeker to 'Wali' and 'Dervish'. This aspect is missing in parapsychology.

Thus the path of act or the 'internal path' in Sufism works in two ways;

- First, the journey itself makes the seeker a good human being. It makes him realize human values and strengthens his belief in fraternal bonds between mankind, irrespective of caste, creed and religion.
- Second, reaching its peak, the seeker achieves faith, making him a 'Wali' or 'Dervish' (Saint)

Either way, the purpose is solved by turning a man who was inclined to evil, into a good human being or even a 'Dervish'. As 'Dervish' he gets engaged in spreading the message of peace, tolerance and love in communities.

Similarly, if a parapsychologists take one extra step and use hypnosis to change the personalities of their patients to become good human beings, they will be doing exactly what the Sufis do. They could join Sufis in a unique experiment of using both hypnosis and 'dhikr' in the reformation of communities. And two divergent groups, with different followers would work together to eliminate the pain created in communities by hate, dislike and enmity. It would most certainly improve societies which have taken the wrong track after 9/11.

2) Godhead and its equivalence in science.

The question arises, can the concept of Godhead in religion help bring science and religion together for the betterment of societies? As we all know, Islam became a most debated subject in the political arena after 9/11. Circumstance brought Islam to confront not only its two other sisters of Abrahamic faith, but it pitched it against the whole world. The attacks of 9/11, whether by design or chance, linked

Islam to terrorism. Traditionalists from Judaism and Christianity joined hands with Zionists, Neo-Cons and started a political war against Islam. They targeted a section of Islam which is run on a narrow but strict code based on 1400 years old Arab tribal culture. Unfortunately, the powerful global media tried to put the blame on Muslims in general rather than on small section of Islam. It also happened that the followers of that section control the world oil, making them very powerful economically. They showed that power in 1971 after Arab-Israel war of 'Yom Kippur'.

The custodians of that sect accept a concept of godhead which according to them made Islam simple to follow. They call it 'Wahabism' or 'Tawhidi Islam' (Unitarianism). Influenced by Arab tribal culture, that sect spreads hate, discontent and enmity, not only amongst their brethren Muslims but against all other religions, especially Judaism and Christianity. The Neo-Cons in the United States took political advantage of this by making the defence establishment strong through global conflicts.

They ignored the fact that there is an equally important sect of Sufism in Islam which believes in the spiritual aspect of godhead. In population they are more than 'Wahabis', but they are not powerful economically and are primarily apolitical. Their concept of godhead is slightly different from the one 'Wahabis' have. They give importance to human values of fraternity, tolerance, and love. They believe in existing commonalities, not only between other religions, but also between science and Islam. It is the way they understand godhead which makes the difference.

According to them the concept of godhead portrayed in divine attributes confuses people in two ways;

1. First, people take each attribute as an independent god and worship it as such.
2. Second, they guard their gods jealously close to their chests and consider them superior to the gods of others.

The Sufis argue that if people could realize that there is only 'one impersonal god' common to all humanity with its multitude shades of attributes, they would not feel threatened by the gods of others. Even a non-believer like Stephen Hawking speaks of an 'impersonal God' in a non-confrontational, philosophical and interesting manner. He interestingly links such an 'impersonal god' with 'laws of physics' when he says "We shouldn't be surprised that conditions in the universe are suitable for life, but this is not evidence that the universe was designed to allow for life. We could call order by the name of God, but it would be an impersonal God. There's not much personal about the laws of physics" [213].

The main reason for this non-cohesion may be the envious nature of narrow-minded traditionalists who, over the centuries, stirred the mind of the public by propagating the concept of godhead the way they perceive it. In doing so, they concentrated on values of theology, ignoring the role of philosophy or importance of spirituality in religions. Within Islam, 'Wahabis' are said to follow such trends.

Pointing at such a dubious stand of the traditionalists, a Sufi poet once said:

Na Tera Khuda Koi Aur Hai
Na Mera Khuda Koi Aur Hai
Ye Jo Rastey Hain Juda Juda
Ye Mua'mela Koi Aur Hai

'Your god is not different from my god. My god is not different from your god. The reason that we have taken separate paths has different connotation'

Keeping this perception in mind, the Sufis not only find similarities between the gods of different religions but they also find commonalities between 'Ahdiat' perceived by them and 'Singularity' described by the physicists. For example, the physicists tell us that 'Singularity' exploded with a bang, starting the creation of the universe. In the process it went through the phases of 'SUT' and

'GUT' making the base for the 'Theory of Everything' (TOE) put forward by the physicists.

The Sufis say that God, in 'Ahdiat' decided to be known. According to a hadith, "I was a hidden treasure, I loved to be known, so I created the creation." [214]. In doing so, God uttered, 'Kun Fayakun', literally meaning 'be and it is', going successively through the two epiphanies of 'Wahdat' and 'Wahdiat'. This also became the basis of 'Hama Oost' (everything is Him) or 'Hama Az Oost' (everything is from Him) belief of Sufism.

The Sufis argue that this was followed by the controlled stepwise creation of the universe and its ingredients, including life-forms as we understand them today. As part of these life-forms, god created man in an evolutionary process repeatedly mentioned in the Quran. The stage-wise process of human creation corresponded with the evolutionary activities of the universe and earth. The Quran mentions man having to pass through different stages of evolutionary creation such as 'dust', 'sounding clay', 'sticky clay' and 'water' as the universe and earth went into corresponding evolution. Finally, it gives minute details of human embryological development, which came to light scientifically only two centuries ago [215].

The Sufis say that god differentiated man from other life-forms by giving him two types of faculties.

- First, a power to think, add, subtract and synthesize coherently.
- Second, a power to think non-coherently.

Both these require different types of knowledge. One is based on logic, the other on intuition. Today, we see humans amongst the first group, such as logicians and scientists who believe in 'singularity' and its explosion with the 'big bang'.

At the same time, we find people amongst the second group, such as Sufis, who believe in 'Ahdiat' and its transformation with a big bang of 'Kun Fayakun'. Scientists theorize that 'singularity' went through phases of 'SUT' and 'GUT' as part of the creation of the universe. The Sufis believe that 'Ahdiat' went through 'Wahdat' and Wahdiat' as a part of the creation of the universe. Scientists call this the 'Theory of Everything' (TOE). Sufis call it 'Hama Oost' (Everything is Him)

If we look at it minutely, both groups are talking about the same process but in different languages. It is like looking at a signboard on a roadside displaying the same directions in two different languages.

Taking it further, we find that the logical minds from the first group use presumptions to base their theories about the happenings in the initial phases of creation such as 'SUT' or 'GUT' phases and even much later during the evolution of planet earth. For them, the history of the universe, and for that matter of the earth, is unknown beyond a certain point. Yet they presumptuously calculate all the happenings during the period of the unknown and present them as credible theories.

Not just that, the physicists from the same group, in the early 20th century, noted certain occurrences in quantum mechanics, which do not follow the rules of conventional physics. They call it the micro or the quantum world of the atom. In logical terms, that part of the quantum world and the irrational happenings within it, became unexplainable or 'unknown' to them. Yet, they accept them without scientifically proving them. In this way, peace prevails in the field of science.

When it comes to the Sufis from the second group, we find them facing similar disputes with traditionalists in their beliefs about godhead and its working. But unlike the scientists, the traditionalists not just reject Sufis, they despise them for their beliefs. As a result, we don't see peace in religion and instead find resentment and hate brewing in religion.

Therefore, the Sufis, have problems on two counts;

- On one hand, they have to convince die-hard traditionalists about the nature of godhead and its animations.
- On the other hand, they have to convince the scientists that there may not be gross dissimilarities between science and religion.

Furthermore, the Sufis face frustration when they see quantum physicists readily persuade the general public about an unknown world of 'Singularity', with an infinite power exploding and turning into enormous energies of 'SUT', and 'GUT' phases, paving the way for the evolution of the universe. But they cannot convince the same public to agree on an unknown world of 'Ahdiat', with infinite power animating its energy into two 'epiphanies' of 'Wahdat' and Wahdiat' and starting an evolutionary process in the same universe in a more or less identical manner.

In other words, both quantum physicists and Sufis talk of identical transformation of infinite energy from a single source- 'singularity' as defined by scientists and 'Ahdiat' as perceived by the Sufis. But people accept one group and not the other, which is what leads to frustration among Sufis

Then there is another cause for frustration. Scientists use mathematical equations for their theories, which are beyond the grasp of ordinary people. The Sufis use spiritual techniques for their beliefs which are also beyond the perception of ordinary people. But a vast number of people accept what the scientists theorize about, even things which have no logical basis. However, they reject similar non-logical comments when they come from Sufis. Such indifferent attitude baffles them, which is unfortunate, since both groups have identical intentions. Scientists try to improve the physical well-being of mankind and the Sufis work towards improving spiritual well-being. Both fall in the definition of World Health Organization (WHO) and are essential for human health at individual and community levels.

However, some differences do appear in the understanding of 'singularity' and 'Ahdiat' by scientists and Sufis respectively. For example, scientists cannot find a cause for the initiation of the Big Bang. Also, they do not know what happened in the initial phases and how the transformation of 'singularity' progressed. They presume that immediately after the Big Bang, the unknown energies of 'SUT' and 'GUT' were transformed into four 'known energies' and one 'unknown energy'. The known energies are categorized as 'gravity', 'strong nuclear', 'weak nuclear' and 'electro-magnetic'; while the unknown energy as the 'dark energy'.

The Sufis on the other hand, are comparatively clearer about the transformation of the infinite divine energy of 'Ahdiat' to 'Wahdat'; 'Wahdiat' in its early stages; and the spirit and soul at a later stage.

They also speak of an 'unknown divine energy' akin to the 'dark energy' that deals with the working of the universe.

Moreover, the scientists theorize that 'Singularity' exploded for no apparent reason, while Sufis believe that 'Ahdiat' changed for a reason. According to them, 'God wanted to be known', making it a valuable reason for creation. Furthermore, the scientists say that the 13.7 billion years old 'Singularity' plays no role in present-day happenings, while Sufis believe that God runs the universe and the lives of His creation. They say when God decided to be known, He wanted to create man in His own image of 'second epiphany'.

That image, according to Sufis, represents the spiritual aspect of humans, not the physical. So it is God who works through humans in the realm of 'Nafs', where man is given 'free choice' to choose between good and evil, to reform or destroy the world. It is God who works in the realm of 'Qulb' through guides, guiding mankind on the paths they chose for themselves in the realm of 'Nafs'. And finally it is God who works through 'Divine Command' (*Amr-e-Elahi*) in the realm of 'Ruh', on selected people and takes them to the zeniths of their spiritual careers. So it can be concluded that God works in mysterious ways, be that at subatomic, atomic or physical level.

When it comes to God working at a subatomic level, quantum physicists are not far behind the thinking of the Sufis. They also believe in an energy working at the quantum level, the nature of which is 'unknown'. The only difference is that being scientists, they don't call it the work of God. In a nutshell, if studied in detail, one can find a lot of similarities in certain aspects of quantum physics, parapsychology, and Sufism.

This brings us to the third and final point as to what role scientists, parapsychologists and Sufis can play towards developing a better human society in 21st century.

• The role of Science, Parapsychology and Sufism in 21st century.

The above discussion concludes that scientists (especially quantum physicists) and Sufis seem to be on the same page about the beginning of the universe. They are not far off on the end of planet earth. They also have identical aims to help humanity. It is the grey areas scattered between the two groups which is cloudy because of the different approaches they pursue. A scientist depends on experiments based on logical knowledge of experimentation, addition, and subtraction. A Sufi depends on unexplainable experiences based on the illogical knowledge of intuition. And this is the stumbling block between scientists and Sufis.

We find that in a scientific experiment, a physicist becomes a mere observer when a particle changes into a wave and joins other waves to become indistinguishable from each other. The Sufi on the other hand, joins the particle as its soul in the journey and becomes indistinguishable from other divine souls in the process of 'Fana' at the finest vibrations of 'Wahdiat'. Metaphorically, it is the same journey which the particle takes on its way to change into a wave before mixing up with other waves. The scientist can only observe the particle part of the journey, while a Sufi becomes a participant all the way in the journey.

If there was a scientific way for a scientist to join a particle in its journey towards a wave, he would have felt the experimentation rather than simply observing it. The Sufis go through this process and feel the working of godhead at sub-atomic level. So a scientist becomes an observer and and a Sufi a participant. This is the grey area which creates a gap between the two.

Ignoring the gap in the procedural techniques between the two, it is the commonalities which should be used as a platform for the uplift of societies. Uplifting of societies comes with uplifting of humanity. The differences in methodologies should not stop them++ from working together in this innovative task as the end goal is worth achieving. A successful experiment was conducted in the medical field in New York on similar grounds between a group of medical doctors, psychologists and priests. They worked in unison and treated patients successfully using three completely different methods. Why can't this type of unity work between scientists, parapsychologists, and Sufis?

Some might give three reasons for it;

- First, the procedural differences between the three are given more importance than the core similarities.
- Second, the hard-core religious traditionalists are creating misunderstanding between the scientists and the Sufis through their sermons and actions.
- Third, a few atheistic scientists and philosophers who are averse to religion are taking advantage of this rift and widen the gap between the two groups.

As a result, those Sufis, quantum physicists or parapsychologists who want to work together on the subject are swept away by the tsunami of opposition. They are not given a chance to sit across the table and seriously discuss as to why such similarities exist between religion, quantum science and parapsychology and how can those similarities be used for the betterment of global societies.

In the battle between religious and non-religious forces, Islam has become the main target after 9/11. In that context, great responsibility lies on the shoulders of the Sufis. Despite the tough challenges they face, they can reduce the gap in the following four stages;

1. Stage one - they can make traditionalist theologians realize that if convention and quantum physicists, with all diversities of quantum mechanics, can accept each other's' theories for the sake of scientific progress, why can't they (traditionalists) sit with the Sufis and come up with an amicable solution for the sake of theosophical advancement. The internet has provided them with unlimited access to a vast ocean of knowledge. All they need to do is to find a place where they can come together and have brain storming sessions. The best place for the purpose can be the centuries-old Al-Azhar University in Cairo which has the offices of the five major theosophical schools of Islam.

2. Stage two - they can identify quantum physicists with similar thoughts through the internet and arrange meetings with them on the commonalities that exist between these two diverse subjects and make them as primary talking points to open a window of discussion between science and religion.

3. Stage three - they can apply the same formula and principle on likeminded parapsychologists.

4. Stage four - after an understanding has developed between likeminded scientists, parapsychologists and the Sufis, the forum can be expanded to include hard-core Islamic traditionalists. Gentle persuasion through mature discussion and discourse will positively affect the egoistic mind-set of the traditionalists to look at science, parapsychology and religion with an open, welcoming mind.

In this way, a window of respect can be opened towards dissimilar ideologies, reverence for other religions and tolerance for different systems and science. Such an integration of knowledge will help various religions, spiritualties and science to come close and plant a tree of solace under the shadows of which humanity will prosper in a peaceful coexistence.

Working on the philosophy of coexistence, the rigid religious custodians will look at science as the spiritual theosophists do.

Similarly, the rigid scientists will start looking at religions as spiritual scientists. We have example of such scientists, like Paul Davies and others. Later on or at the same time, the parapsychologists will also join them in such understanding.

After all, the language of physics is mathematics, which is based on simplicity, harmony and symmetry. This language introduces mathematician to the reality of the micro world of quantum physics. Similarly, the language of the Sufism is love, which is also based on simplicity, harmony and symmetry. This language introduces Sufis to the reality of the unseen world of religions. According to the science writer Kitty Ferguson, 'Reality is something whose existence is the same, whether we are observing it or not, waiting to be discovered and studied' [216]. It is the reality which can create atmosphere of peaceful coexistence.

Creating that atmosphere cannot be that difficult. Some of the Sufis give importance to the 21st century because it is in this century that the Mayan Calender comes to an end in its corporeal phase and is replaced with a spiritual one. For that matter, the Sufis label it the century of spirituality. They believe that spirituality in this century will be nurtured through mass awareness and shape the global human psyche positively. According to them, before that stage approaches, the world will go through religious, social, and political crises when the hard-core traditional theologians from the three Abrahamic religions try to create an atmosphere ripe for Armageddon. But the spiritualists, especially the Sufis will prevail and stop the bloodshed.

They will play upon the modern human psyche by highlighting the most important virtue of spirituality – human values. Using these virtues as harmonizing tools, they will pursue a conciliatory role between various religions, spiritualties, science, and political systems to counter those who want to destroy the world through war games. With the help of social media, they will spread their Sufi message as to how man's soul (Nafs) can be linked with spirit (Ruh) through good deeds, thus bringing serenity at individual levels. Through mass awareness, they can convince people that spirituality is not a cult, but a way of living in peace. No single individual, religion or system can lay an exclusive claim on spirituality. Its doors are open to anyone, irrespective of race, creed, gender, profession or religion. It is this quality which refines the human psyche at an individual level. They know that individuals make the community and communities make societies. By turning individuals into good humans, they can reshape global societies with the help of like-minded scientists and parapsychologists. Modern technology is there to help spread ideas that can change mental psyche of the masses within months as opposed to the years it would have taken in past.

When the number of such individuals reaches critical mass, a change in communities will become imminent. That will be the greatest achievement as communities will start transforming, one by one, all over the world, reshaping global societies. This will become a spiritual surge of 21st century. The Sufis know such changes will prevent world wars as it will create compatibility in human relationships. They believe it has become imperative for the spiritualists of the world to come forward and play their role in spreading harmony and peace in the turmoil-ridden post 9/11 global society.

A similar idea was proposed by Agha Murtaza Pooya, a theosophist, scholar and a political figure from Pakistan. He discussed it with another world renowned Sufi scholar Allama Dr. Tahir-ul-Qadri from Pakistan. Agha suggested opening of centres in major cities of the world calling it 'Bait-e-Abrahim' (The House of Abraham). The aim of 'Bait-e-Ibrahim' was to widely disseminate the following ideas and aims and how to implement them through tasks;

- Religion is not a negative influence on society, provided its custodians understand its theological, philosophical and spiritual aspects.

Task: 'Bait-e-Ibrahim' will set up Intra-faith lectures, sessions, workshops and seminars for the purpose.

- Religion can have a positive impact on society, provided its custodians understand other religions.

Task: 'Bait-e-Ibrahim' will arrange Inter-faith lectures, sessions, seminars and workshops to create such impact.

- Science, psychology and religions can work together without antagonising each other, provided its custodians find a common ground.

Task: 'Bait-e-Ibrahim' will encourage independent sessions, programs, and workshops to find those common grounds and how to work on them once identified.

- Spirituality is a unique subject, not understood by the custodians of religion and the public at large.

Task: 'Bait-e-Ibrahim' will promote special sessions on the subject of spirituality to make public aware as to how spirituality can help religious and non-religious groups in uplifting individual psyches and with that, the psyche of communities.

- Quantum physicists from science, parapsychologists from psychology, can play their role to involve non-religious groups in activities pertaining to social uplift programs in communities.

Task: 'Bait-e-Ibrahim' will hold Seminars and lectures in participation of quantum physicists and parapsychologists to encourage non-religious groups to create understandings between divergent minds on the subject.

- The spiritualists from Abrahamic faiths can play their role by involving the custodians of other religions in the spiritual uplift of communities.

Task: Bait-e-Ibrahim' will arrange programs regarding this to involve major players in discussions.

Working on these principles, 'Bait-e-Abrahim' (The House of Abraham) will become the hub of activities all over the world, providing information and facilitating the implementation of all such activities. In this way, they will spread and share message of; Salvation; Peace; Justice; Security; and Prosperity.

With these aims and Terms Of Reference (TOR), 'Bait-e-Ibrahim' will not only help people to become tolerant, humane and loving, but also help stop wars instigated by hard-core traditionalists of various religions in connivance with war mongers. It is a demanding job which involves a lot of hard work, technical skills, manpower and of course, vast financial backing. As they say 'where there is a will there is a way'. It is hoped that someday, a few dedicated enthusiasts will join hands and lay the foundation of 'Bait-e-Ibrahim' (House of Abraham) for a prosperous future wherein people will live in harmony without fear of being killed in the name of God, religion or ideology.

Otherwise, as Stephen Hawking drew a picture in 2007 which is very alarming indeed. He asked 'In a world that is in chaos politically, socially and environmentally, how can the human race sustain another 100 years?' The open question was posted on the Internet, as quoted by The Guardian, and "Watching the World" in Awake magazine (June 2007). A month after the posting he explained: "I don't know the answer. That is why I asked the question, to get people to think about it, and to be aware of the dangers we now face." This came from a man who is not religious and believes that the universe is governed by the laws of science and that even if God exists, He may not intervene to break the laws which He has decreed. This is a very grim picture. If God doesn't intervene and the situation is left for us humans to cope with, then Stephen Hawking doesn't see it surviving for another 100 years.

The responsibility to affect change falls heavily on the shoulders of like-minded spiritualists, scientists and parapsychologists to avert the disaster Stephen Hawking is dreading. He further gives an interesting observation on the chaotic situation by saying "Although September 11 was horrible, it didn't threaten the survival of the human race, like nuclear weapons do." [217]. Here, he was hinting at the international war-game apparently being planned between 'state' and 'non-state' actors. Unfortunately, some of the 'state actors' are trigger happy and eager to use their arsenals. Meanwhile, most of the 'non-state actors' are trying their best to get hold of these lethal weapons. Muslim fundamentalists are considered to be on top of the list of those 'non-state actors'. Some believe they would have no problem using them. The world, in the truest sense, has become a dangerous place to live in.

REFERENCES

[I],   (History of religions - Wikipedia, the free encyclopedia)
[2]   (Ref, whatistheology.net/) 'philosophy'
[3]   (en.wikipedia.org/wiki/Philosophy_of_religion), and 'spirituality'
[4]   (What Is Spirituality | The History Of Spirituality)
[5]   (Spirituality: A new dimension, page 31)
[6]   (Organized religion - Wikipedia, the free encyclopedia)
[7]   (Spirituality - Definition and More from the Free Merriam-Webster)
[8]   (Definition of Spirituality - Xavier University of Louisiana)
[9]   (Spirituality; A new dimension. Page 12)
[10] (Ancient Egyptian concept of the soul - Wikipedia, the free)
[11] (Psuche)
[12] (Mana - Wikipedia, the free encyclopedia)
[13] (Main Page | Huna.hu)
[14} (Fravashi - Wikipedia, the free encyclopedia)
[15] (Nephesh - Wikipedia, the free encyclopedia)
[16] (soul: The Soul in Christianity | Infoplease.com)
[17[(Nafs - Wikipedia, the free encyclopedia)
[18] (Taoism - What is Te - Taoism Initiation Page)
[19] ("The Yoga Sutras of Maharishi Patanjali - a translation and commentary by Yogacharya Shivaji Mizner")
[20] (Ref, Lao Tzu: Father of Taoism).
[21] (Ref, The Axial Age)
[22] (The Hebrew Name for God - Eloah - Hebrew for Christians)
[23] (Yahweh - Wikipedia, the free encyclopedia).
[24] (Nine miracles of Moses - Quran-Islam.org - True Islam)
[25] (Kingdom of Israel (united monarchy) - Wikipedia, the free).
[26] (Solomon's Temple - Wikipedia, the free encyclopedia)
[27] (Ezra - Wikipedia, the free encyclopedia)
[28] (Nehemiah—The Man Behind the Wall – Biblical Archaeology Society).
[29] (Books of Chronicles - Wikipedia, the free encyclopedia).
[30] (Ben Sira - Wikipedia, the free encyclopedia).
[31] (Jewish Factions at the Time of Jesus).
[32] (Ref, Essenes).
[33] (Sadducees - Wikipedia, the free encyclopedia).

[34] (Pharisee (Jewish history) -- Encyclopedia Britannica).
[35] (Mishnah - Wikipedia, the free encyclopedia)
[36] (Gemara - Wikipedia, the free encyclopedia)
[37] (Talmud - Wikipedia, the free encyclopedia)
[38] (Siege of Jerusalem (70) - Wikipedia, the free encyclopedia)
[39] (Karaite Judaism - Wikipedia, the free encyclopedia).
[40] (Kalonymos family - Wikipedia, the free encyclopedia)
[41] (Shekhinah - Wikipedia, the free encyclopedia).
[42] (Abulafia's Life and Work - Kabbalah – Netplaces) (Kabbalah
       -Wikipedia, the free encyclopedia).
[43] (Isaac Ben Solomon Luria - Jewish Virtual LibraryIsaac Luria).
[44] (Rabbi Judah Loew - "The Maharal of Prague").
[45] (The Ten Sefirot of the Kabbalah - University of Calgary)
[46] (Sabbatai Zevi - Wikipedia, the free encyclopedia)
[47] (The Cult of Mary - John Provost)
[48] (Rabbi Yisrael Baal Shem Tov - Jewish Virtual Library)
[49] (Baruch Spinoza - Wikipedia, the free encyclopedia).
[50] (Jacob Frank - Wikipedia, the free encyclopedia)
[51] (Martin Buber - Wikipedia, the free encyclopedia)
[52] (Extraordinary Evidence About Jesus in the Dead Sea Scrolls)
[53] (Flight into Egypt - Wikipedia, the free encyclopedia)
[54] (What Did Jesus Really Say? - The Dead Sea Scrolls and the
       Gospel)
[55] (Pontius Pilate - Wikipedia, the free encyclopedia).
[56] (The Gospel According to Paul - Sigler Ministries)
[57] ("Gospel of Barnabas)
[58] (325 Council of Nicaea - Islam Tomorrow)
[59] (St. Augustine of Hippo > By Individual Philosopher >
       Philosophy).
[60] (School of Saint Victor - Wikipedia, the free encyclopedia).
[61] (Catholic Doctrine on the Holy Trinity).
[62] (Søren Kierkegaard - Wikipedia, the free encyclopedia),
[63] (St. Benedict - founder of comon sense living),
[64] (Augustine of Hippo - Wikipedia, the free encyclopedia).
[65] (The Gate to the City of Knowledge - Google Group)
[66] (Spirituality: A new dimension, page 180)
[67] (Qiyas)
[68] (Fiqh - Wikipedia, the free encyclopedia).

[69] (The Sufi Movement)

[70] (Asceticism - Wikipedia, the free encyclopedia)

[71] (Irfan - Wikipedia, the free encyclopedia)

[72] (Wajad - Wikipedia, the free encyclopedia)

[73] (Bayazid Bastami - Wikipedia, the free encyclopedia)

[74] (Mansur Al-Hallaj - Wikipedia, the free encyclopedia)

[75] (Ibn Arabi - Wikipedia, the free encyclopedia)

[76] (Werner Heisenberg - Biographical – Nobelprize.org)

[77] (Kitty Ferguson - Wikipedia, the free encyclopedia)

[78] (Indeterminism - Wikipedia, the free encyclopedia).

[79] (Stephen Hawking Quotes (Author of A Brief History of Time).

[80] (Uncertainty principle - Wikipedia, the free encyclopedia)

[81] (The Secret Science Behind Miracles by Max Freedom Long
      – Whale)

[82] (Appendix from From the New Physics to Hinduism –
      Karma2Grace.org)

[83] (PakistanForum : Message: Re.Quantum Physics and God, Part
      III)

[84] (quantum entanglement - The Worlds of David Darling)

[85] (Wholeness and the Implicate Order)

[86] (The Probability of the Impossible, by Dr. Thelma Moss
      – essentialsaltes)

[87] (God and the New Physics - Google Books Result)

[88] (Spirituality: A new dimension, page103-104)

[89] (Spirituality: A new dimension, page 141)

[90] (Eightfold Way (physics) - Wikipedia, the free encyclopedia).[91]
      (Poincaré recurrence theorem - Wikipedia, the free encyclopedia)

[92] (John Archibald Wheeler - Wikipedia, the free encyclopedia)

[93] (Werner Heisenberg | Shift Frequency)

[94] (Creation Big Bang Theology)

[95] (islamic concept of creation of universe, big bang and science).

[96] (Black Holes and Baby Universes and Other Essays (1993)

[97] ("Kahuna: Keeper of the Secret" by S. D. Smith).

[98A]   (Quran 14: 24-25) [98B] (Ref, Quran 112;1-4)

[99] (Quran 3:97)

[100] (Ref, Quran 3:117)

[101] (Ref Quran 3:30)

[102] (Ref Quran XX-10)

[103] (The Quranic Sufism - Page 90 - Google Books Result)
[104] (God as 'I','He', and 'We' - Yahoo! Groups)
[105a] a,..(The experience and doctrine of love in Ibn 'Arabî).[105b].
   ((Bihar al- anwar, xxvi, 247).
[106] (Quran, 6:100)
[107] (Ref, Quran, XVII-79)
[108] (Four Valleys (Chahar Vádí)
[109] (Ref, Quran, 50:16)
[110] (Ref, Quran, 37:76)
[111] (Ref, Quran, 37:80)
[112] (Miraj - Wikipedia, the free encyclopedia).
[113] (ask Jamil Qalandar)
[114] (Ref, Quran, 2:115)
[115] (Ref, Quran XXV-45)
[116] (Ref, Quran, XLVIII-10)
[117] (Ref, Quran, XLI-54)
[118] (Ref, Quran, XXXIII-72)
[119] (The Quranic Sufism - Page 69 - Google Books Result)
[120] (The Triumphal Sun: A Study of the Works of Jalaloddin Rumi-
   page 166)
[121] (Bihar al- anwar,-xv, 3 ff.) (Twenty First Hadith: On Shukr-xv, 3 ff.)
[122] (Four Valleys (Chahar Vádí)
[123] (Forty Hadith of Nawawi - Shakeel Mahate)
[124] (4:78)
[125] (Stephen Hawking and the Theory of Everything | Brain Pickings).
[126] (dictionary of Islam, page 608)
[127] (unedited - Islamic Philosophy Online).
[128] (Rumi Quotes (Author of Essential Rumi) – Goodreads)
[129] (Tadhkira Ghauthya - Page 154 - Google Books Result).
[130] (Abu Yazid al-Bistami – Naqshbandi.org)
[131] (sheiknazimforum : Message: How God Manifests in Man and
   the)
[132] (I am the Truth" - what did Mansur Really meant?)
[133] (Ref, Quran, LXVII-23)
[134] (Ref, Quran SXXVIII-20).
[135] (Ref, Quran, XXII-17)
[136] (Ref, Quran, 45:7).
[137] (Spirituality: A new dimension, page 43-44)

[138] (Sirat Al-Mustaqim or Siratulmustaqim)

[139] ('Spirituality-a new dimension' Page 46)

[140] (Boulas: A kindled word. - Hazrat Inayat Khan Study Database?)

[141] (I know that I know nothing - Wikipedia, the free encyclopedia).

[142] (Ref Quran, XXIV-52)

[143] (Ref, Quran, XLI-53)

[144] (Ref, Quran XII-108)

[145] (Ref, Quran 51:20-21)

[146A] (Ref, Quran 38:26) [146B] (Ref, Quran, 38:20)

[147] (Ref, Quran, 39:9)

[148] (Ref, Quran, 12:53)

[149] (Ref, Quran, LXXIV-27?)

[150] (Ref, Quran, LXXV-3? Ask JQ)

[151] (Ref, Quran 13:99 (18)

[152] (Ref, Quran, LXXXIX-12? Ask JQ)

[153] (Ahmad in Musnad, al Bukhari, Eng. trans. vol.6, p. 501, hadith no. 545)

[154] (Mirat ul Arifeen)

[155] (41:53).

[156] (Level of Nafs - Adapted from Ibrahim Hakki Erzurumi (ks) | Halveti)

[157] (Ref, Quran, 2:207)

[158] (Ref, Quran, 3:185)

[159] (Ref, Quran 2:281)

[160] (Ref, Quran, 2:286)

[161] (Ref, Quran, 3:117)

[162] (Ref, Quran, 5:105)

[163] (Ref, Quran, LXVII-23)

[164] (Ref, Quran XXVIII-20)

[165] (Ref, Quran, 45:7)

[166] (38:26)

[167] (Ref, Quran, LXXXII-14)

[168] (Ref, Quran, LXXXII-7)

[169] (THE WISDOM OF MUHAMMAD (FASM-MUHAMMADIYVAH),)

[170] (I try not to whine... much.: August 2011)

[171] (Stations of Realization of God | Seema Arif's Blog)

[172] (PakistanForum : Message: RE: The concepts of Nafs and Ruh!)

[173] (Ref, Quran, XXLIX-14)
[174] (Ref, Quran, II-260)
[175] (Ref, Quran, V-55)
[176] (Ref, Quran, LXIII-3)
[177] (Ref, Quran, 47:16)
[178] (Ref, Quran, XIII-28)
[179] (Back - Khwaja Enayetpuri)
[180] (Ref, Quran, LVII-16)
[181] (Rumi Quotes (Author of Essential Rumi) – Goodreads)
[182] (Mansur Al-Hallaj – Wikiquote)
[183] (Jerrahi Midwest » Level of Nafs - Adapted from Ibrahim Hakki Erzurumi)
[184] (Dictionary of Islam-page 605)
[185] (Ref, Quran, XCVII-4)
[186] (Ref Quran, LXXXII-14)
[187] (Ref, Quran, LXXXII-7)
[188] (Ref, Quran XVII-87)
[189] (Dictionary of Islam, page 605)
[190] (Ref Ibid)
[191] (ibid)
[192] (Ibid)
[193] (Ibid)
[194] (Ibid)
[195] (Ibid)
[196] (41:6)
[197] (Ref, Quran XL-15)
[198] (Ref, Quran LVIII-23)
[199] (Level of Nafs - Adapted from Ibrahim Hakki Erzurumi (ks) | Halveti)
[200] (SUFISM: ITS ORIGINS - AHYA Call and Guidance Center)
[201] (15:29)
[202] (39:6)
[203] (Dictionary of Islam, page 605)
[204] (Ibid page 604)
[205] (Ref, Quran Al Qadr,4)
[206] (I died a mineral, and became a plant)
[207] (Ref, Quran, Shura, 52)
[208] (Ref, Qurn Suratul Mu'min XI-15)

[209] (Ref, Quran, Suratul Maryam, 17)

[210] (History of Islam, page 605)

[211] (Ref Quran Al-Anmbia, Tahrrim)

[212] (Ref, Quran Sajda, Alhajr, Saad)

[213] (Quoted in "Leaping the Abyss" (April 2002) by Gregory Benford, in Reason Magazine)

[214] (Level of Nafs - Adapted from Ibrahim Hakki Erzurumi (ks)

[215] (Life and our physical bodies originated from CLAY (soil, dust and)

[216] (The Fire in the Equations: Science Religion & Search For God- page 39)

[217] (Interview "Colonies in space may be only hope, says Hawking" by Roger Highfield in Daily Telegraph (16 October 2001)

THE END

Printed in the United States
By Bookmasters